Academic Writing for Graduate Students

Academic Writing for Graduate Students

ESSENTIAL TASKS AND SKILLS

SECOND EDITION

John M. Swales and Christine B. Feak

 MICHIGAN SERIES IN ENGLISH FOR
ACADEMIC & PROFESSIONAL PURPOSES

The University of Michigan Press

Ann Arbor

Published in the United States of America by
The University of Michigan Press
Manufactured in the United States of America
♾ Printed on acid-free paper

2013   2012   2011   10   9   8

A CIP catalog record for this book is available from the British Library.

Library of Congress Cataloging-in-Publication Data

Swales, John.
    Academic writing for graduate students : essential tasks and skills /
John M. Swales and Christine B. Feak. — 2nd ed.
        p.   cm. — (Michigan series in English for academic & professional
purposes)
    Includes bibliographical references and index.
    ISBN 0-472-08856-4 (paper : acid-free paper)
    1. English language—Rhetoric.   2. English language—Textbooks for
foreign speakers.   3. Academic writing—Problems, exercises, etc.   I. Feak,
Christine B.   II. Title.   III. Series.

PE1408.S7836   2004
808'.0428—dc22   2004042505

ISBN 978-0-472-08856-0 (paper : acid-free paper)

Acknowledgments

Grateful acknowledgment is given to the following authors, publishers, and journals for permission to reprint previously published materials.

AIAA for "High Angle-of-Attack Calculations of the Subsonic Vortex Flow in Slender Bodies," by D. Almosnino, *AIAA Journal* 23, no. 8, 1995. Copyright © 1985. Reprinted with permission.

AIChE for "Optimal design of reverse osmosis module networks," by Fazilet Maskan, Dianne E. Wiley, Lloyd P. M. Johnston, and David J. Clements, *American Institute of Chemical Engineers Journal* 46:946–54, Copyright © 2000.

Benny Bechor for "Navigation."

Larry Bridwell and ICSA Labs for data for table 6 from "1992 IEEE and ICSA Labs Computer Virus Prevalence Study." Copyright © 2001.

Prudencia Ceron-Mireles for her description of preeclampsia.

Elsevier for the table reprinted from "Hospitalized children's descriptions of their experiences with postsurgical pain relieving methods" by T. Pölkki, A. M. Pietilä, and K. Vehviläinen-Julkunen, from *International Journal of Nursing Studies,* 40:1, pp. 33–44, copyright © 2003, with permission from Elsevier; for "Wetland Plants: Biology & Ecology" by J. K. Cronk and M. S. Fennessey, from *Ecological Engineering,* Vol. 19, pp. 351–52, copyright © 2003, with permission from Elsevier; for "Brief Report: Types of bullying among Italian school children" by A. C. Baldry and D. P. Farrington, from *Journal of Adolescence,* Vol. 22, pp. 423–26, copyright © 1999, with permission from Elsevier; for "Keeping up one's appearance: Its importance and the choice of type of hair-grooming establishment" by R. K. Schwer and R. Daneshvary, from *Journal of Economic Psychology,* Vol. 21, pp. 207–22, © 2000, with permission from Elsevier; for "Measuring road rage: Development of the propensity for angry drving scale" by J. P. DePasquale, E. S. Geller, S. W. Clarke, and L. C. Littleton, from *Journal of Safety Research,* Vol. 32, pp. 1–16, copyright © 2001, with permission from Elsevier; for "Selling Cities: Promoting new images for meetings tourism" by A. Bradley, T. Hall, and M. Harrison. From *Cities,* Vol. 19, pp. 61–70, copyright © 2002, with permission from Elsevier; for "Review of *Academic Writing for Graduate Students*" by D. Belcher. *English for Specific Purposes,* Vol. 14, No. 2, pp. 175–79, copyright © 1995, with permission from Elsevier.

ICSA Labs for data for table 5, "Source of Computer Virus Infections," © ICSA Labs. Reprinted with permission.

Indiana University Press for adapted excerpts from *Conversational Joking,* by Neal R. Norrick, copyright © 1993.

Yasufumi Iseki for "Reducing Air Pollution in Urban Areas: The Role of Urban Planners."

Jiyoung Lee for "Comparison of the Actual CO_2 Levels with the Model Predictions."

Abdul Malik for his textual outline.

Pierre Martin for his textual outline.

Diane Martindale for "Sweating the Small Stuff," *Scientific American,* February 2001:52–53. Copyright © 2001 Diane Martindale. Reprinted with permission.

William S. Martinus and Allen Kurta for "Eastern Pipistrelle in Ottawa Co., MI." *Michigan Birds and Natural History* 8, 133–35, © 2001. Reprinted with permission.

Mei-Lan for her interview.

Oxford University Press for material adapted from *The birds of Egypt,* edited by Steven Goodman, Peter Meininger, et al., copyright © 1989.

Physical Review for "Nuclear-Structure Correction to the Lamb Shift," by Krzysztof Pachucki, Dietrich Liebfried, and Ted W. Hänsch, *Physical Review A,* 48, pp. 1, July 1993. Copyright © 1993.

Horace H. Rackham School of Graduate Studies, University of Michigan, for data for table 14, "Years to Doctorate for Doctoral Programs at University of Michigan, Ann Arbor, for Academic Years 1996–2001."

Riley Publications, Inc., for "University-Community Agency Collaboration: Human Service Agency Workers' Views" by Mojisola F. Tiamiyu, *Journal of Multicultural Nursing and Health* 6, 29–36, © 2000. Reprinted with permission.

Hiroe Saruya for her description of nationalism.

Taylor & Francis Ltd for figure adapted from "The effects of phase control materials on hand skin temperature within gloves of soccer goalkeepers," by A. J. Purvis and N. T. Cable, *Ergonomics,* Vol. 43, No. 10, p. 1484, copyright © 2000; and for figure adapted from "Exercise and Cold" by T. D. Noakes, *Ergonomics,* Vol. 43, No. 10, p. 1473, copyright © 2000. *http://www.tandf. co.uk/journals/tf/00140139.html.* Reprinted with permission.

John Wiley & Sons Limited for "Procrastinators lack a broad action perspective" from *European Journal of Personality* by S. Dewitte and W. Lens. Copyright © 2000, John Wiley & Sons Limited. Reproduced with permission.

David Wilson for "The Englishisation of academe: a Finnish perspective," copyright © 2002. Jyväskylä: University Printing House. Reprinted with permission.

Jun Yang for "Binding Assay and Down Regulation Study."

Every effort has been made to contact the copyright holders for permission to reprint borrowed material. We regret any oversights that may have occurred and will rectify them in future printings of this book.

Contents

Introduction to the Second Edition

The Changing Scene

The first edition of *Academic Writing for Graduate Students* (henceforth *AWG*) was published in 1994. In the ensuing decade, a number of important developments have taken place in graduate education. E-mail and the Internet have become much more widely used, especially in distance education. The American practice of requiring graduate students to take courses as part of advanced research degrees has been adopted by more and more countries. Coauthorship of papers written by graduate students and their professors is on the increase. Doctoral students are attending and presenting at more conferences and are doing so at earlier stages in their Ph.D. programs. Those with overall responsibility for graduate education, such as graduate schools, are offering more workshops for graduate students, many of them concerned with strengthening communication skills in some way. Finally, the traditional distinction between native and non-native speakers of English is becoming less and less clear-cut. In the research world, in particular, there are today increasing numbers of "expert users" of English who are not traditional native speakers of that language.

When *AWG* was originally published, the number of courses in academic writing for graduate students was both rather small and largely restricted to entering international graduate students. Today, we believe, the number and range of these courses have both increased, although perhaps few research universities can offer the *five* levels of writing courses for graduate students that currently exist at the University of Michigan. As part and parcel of these developments, research in *English for Academic Purposes* (EAP) has also grown, particularly through dissertation studies on various aspects of academic discourse.

Approach and Organization

A second edition of an EAP textbook usually indicates that the first one has enjoyed some success. And this has also been the case with *AWG*. As a result, we have retained the basic approach of the first edition.

- This book has evolved out of both research and teaching experience.

- It is as much concerned with developing academic *writers* as it is with improving academic *texts*.

- It is targeted primarily, but not exclusively, at those whose first language is other than English.

- The general approach is analytical and rhetorical: users are asked to apply their analytical skills to the discourses of their chosen disciplines and to explore how effective academic writing is achieved.

- The tasks and activities are richly varied, ranging from small-scale language points to issues of how graduate students can best "position" themselves as junior researchers.

- The book is fairly fast paced, opening with a basic orientation and closing with writing an article for publication.

- With the help of the accompanying *Commentary,* students and scholars should be able to use this volume profitably on their own.

We have also retained the original organization. Initially, we thought we would reorganize the units, combine some, and perhaps add new ones. However, after reading through surveys from heavy users of the book, we realized that this may do more harm than good. The surveys revealed that any changes we made to the overall organization of the units would please some, but alienate others. Thus, we decided to keep the eight-unit organization.

- The first three units are essentially preparatory; they prepare the way for the more genre-specific activities in later units.

- Unit One presents an overview of the considerations involved in successful academic writing, with a deliberate stress on early exposure to the concept of positioning.

- Units Two and Three deal with two overarching patterns in English expository prose: the movement from general to specific and the movement from problem to solution.

- Unit Four acts as a crucial link between the earlier and later units, since it deals with how to handle the discussion of data.

- Units Five and Six deal with writing summaries and critiques, respectively.

- Finally, Units Seven and Eight deal with constructing a real research paper, that is, one that makes an original contribution to knowledge.

Innovations

However, within this retained basic approach and structure, there have also been a number of important changes. Certain older sets of data and older texts have either been updated or replaced. Data from the first edition that was simplified, adapted, or reconfigured has been replaced with authentic data, with the exception of a couple of our favorites, such as the test-retest data in Unit Four. The title of a table or figure with data that is not authentic is followed by a ‡. The range of disciplines covered has increased with textual examples from areas such as nursing, marketing, and art history. We have retained the citation formats used in these examples for authenticity. On the other hand, the amount of material dealing with discourse analysis/applied linguistics has been reduced; indeed, our own "miniproject" that featured so strongly in Units Seven and Eight has been relegated to Appendix Four. Both of these changes have principally come about because of comments made by reviewers, instructors, and other commentators. Among other changes, the work on definitions has been considerably expanded in Unit Two, and Unit Six now includes work on book reviews. Throughout, new findings from discourse analysis have been incorporated, perhaps especially in the final two units.

AWG has been designed as a *first* course in graduate-level writing and is most suited to the first two years of graduate education. (It has also been successfully used with advanced undergraduates.) For the later years, the University of Michigan Press published in 2000 our *English in Today's Research World: A Writing Guide* (*ETRW*). This deals with more advanced topics such as conference presentations and posters, aspects of writing dissertations or theses, and various types of academic correspondence, including fellowship applications and letters of recommendation. Because of this second volume, this edition of *AWG* no longer closes with a preliminary look at conference abstracts.

The Teaching Context

We have designed this textbook to be used for graduate students who come from a broad range of disciplines. After all, this has been our primary experience as writing instructors at Michigan's English Language Institute. Even at our large research university, the logistic problems of organizing and staffing courses along disciplinary lines mean that such courses remain the exception rather than the rule. Although it is often believed that disciplinary courses are "better" or "more efficient," it is our experience, especially with students in their second year or beyond, that a multidisciplinary class has several advantages over a "monodisciplinary" one. The former turns attention away from whether the information or content in a text is "correct" toward questions of rhetoric and language. In this way it encourages rhetorical consciousness-raising. It also leads to interesting group discussion among members who come from very different parts of the university. This kind of class can also create a special—and more tolerant and lighthearted—community among its members, since students are much less likely to be competing with others from their own departments.

Irrespective of whether the teaching context is multidisciplinary or not, *AWG* is a text that instructors should use selectively. Often, there is more material than can really be handled in a timely and efficient manner. Further, instructors should be encouraged to substitute activities and, more particularly, texts more suited to their own particular circumstances. In effect, we look upon our fellow instructors more as distant partners and collaborators in an educational enterprise rather than as people expected to obediently follow the course we have set out. In the same light, we have not tried to impose our own beliefs (which are by no means identical in every case) about how *AWG* should actually be taught. We have nothing to say about such matters as error analysis, NNS peer feedback, the role of revising, or product-process approaches to teaching academic writing. So, rather than a traditional teacher's manual, *AWG* is supported by a slim companion volume carefully entitled *Commentary*. This consists of synopses of what each unit attempts to achieve, further discussion of certain points, occasional teaching hints, and sample responses to the more controlled tasks. The *Commentary* should therefore also be useful for students and scholars using *AWG* in self-study situations.

Thanks to Others

Finally, we turn to those who have helped us prepare this second edition. We would like to acknowledge the insights of all those who took the trouble to write and publish reviews of the first edition and to complete the penetrating anonymous surveys forwarded to us by the University of Michigan Press. Then there are the hundreds of graduate students who have taken our writing courses over the last decade and who have taught us much about what works and what doesn't. Feedback from our fellow writing instructors at Michigan (and at other places such as Ohio State University and University of Arizona) has also been an important input, and here we would particularly like to single out Sandra Rothschild, who over the years has offered many useful suggestions for revision; Alan Hirvela, who has opened our eyes to creative ways of using *AWG* and the *Commentary;* and Susan Reinhart, who took the trouble to read through and comment on a prefinal draft. We are also very grateful to Carson Maynard, who was an invaluable research assistant in the rushed final weeks of getting this manuscript ready for the Press.

A particularly significant player in the emergence of this volume has been Kelly Sippell, the dynamic ESL editor at the University of Michigan Press, who not only provided enthusiastic encouragement but also kept the pressure on when it mattered most. Chris would like to thank Glen, Karl, and Angie. They again willingly endured the uncertainty of her schedule and unselfishly picked up the slack so that this book could be completed. John is very grateful to Vi Benner for once again accepting with such grace the distractions arising from his coauthoring yet another book-length manuscript.

CBF & JMS
Ann Arbor
June 2003

Unit One

An Approach to Academic Writing

Graduate students face a variety of writing tasks as they work toward their chosen degrees. Naturally, these tasks will vary from one degree program to another. They are, however, similar in two respects. First, the tasks become progressively more complex and demanding the farther you go in the program. Second (with few exceptions), they need to be written "academically." In the first six units of this textbook, we focus on the writing tasks that may be required in the earlier stages of a graduate career. In the last two units we look a little farther ahead.

We begin by providing an overview of some important characteristics of academic writing. Academic writing is a product of many considerations: **audience, purpose, organization, style, flow,** and **presentation** (fig. 1).

AUDIENCE

PURPOSE

ORGANIZATION

STYLE

FLOW

PRESENTATION

Fig. 1. Considerations in academic writing

Audience

Even before you write, you need to consider your audience. The audience for most graduate students will be an instructor, who is presumably quite knowledgeable about the assigned writing topic. To be successful in your writing task, you need to have an understanding of your audience's expectations and prior knowledge, because these will affect the content of your writing.

TASK ONE

Read the first few paragraphs of the following two texts. For whom were they written? What aspects of each text helped you decide the audience? In what kind of publication would you expect to find these texts? Sentence numbers have been added here (and in subsequent texts) for ease of reference.

A. ❶ People have been pulling freshwater out of the oceans for centuries using technologies that involve evaporation, which leaves the salts and other unwanted constituents behind. ❷ Salty source water is heated to speed evaporation, and the evaporated water is then trapped and distilled. ❸ This process works well but requires large quantities of heat energy, and costs have been far too high for nearly all but the wealthiest nations, such as Kuwait and Saudi Arabia. (❹ One exception is the island of Curacao in the Netherlands Antilles, which has provided continuous municipal supplies using desalination since 1928.) ❺ To make the process more affordable, modern distillation plans recycle heat from the evaporation step.

　　❻ A potentially cheaper technology called membrane desalination may expand the role of desalination worldwide, which today accounts for less than 0.2 percent of the water withdrawn from natural sources. ❼ Membrane desalination relies on reverse osmosis—a process in which a thin, semipermeable membrane is placed between a volume of saltwater and a volume of freshwater. ❽ The water on the salty side is highly pressurized to drive water molecules, but not salt and other impurities, to the pure side. ❾ In essence, this process pushes freshwater out of saltwater. (Martindale 2001)

B. ❶ Reverse osmosis (RO) membrane systems are often used for seawater and brackish water desalination. ❷ The systems are typically installed as a network of modules that must be designed to meet the technical, environmental, and economic requirements of the separation process. ❸ The complete optimization of an RO network includes the optimal design of both the individual module structure and the network configuration. ❹ For a given application, the choice and design of a particular module geometry depends on a number of factors, including ease and cost of module manufacture, energy efficiency, fouling tendency, required recovery, and capital cost of auxiliary equipment. ❺ With suitable transport equations to predict the physical performance of the membrane module, it should be possible to obtain an optimal module structure for any given application. (Maskan et al. 2000)

As you were thinking about the audiences of these two published texts, you most likely noticed differences in the amount of technical vocabulary as well as in the amount of background information given. You probably also noted the different points at which the authors introduced the term *reverse osmosis*. These differences reflect some of the assumptions that the author has made about the typical reader's familiarity with the subject. In the first text the author assumes the reader is probably not familiar with reverse osmosis and thus provides a fair amount of background information along with a clear definition of the process.

TASK TWO

In each of the texts in Task One, can you identify sentences that define *reverse osmosis?* Consider how these definitions differ. Now write a short definition of a term in your field for two different audiences: one will be graduate students in a totally unrelated field, while the other consists of fellow students in your own graduate program. Exchange your definitions with a partner and discuss how your definitions differ.

Purpose and Strategy

Audience, purpose, and strategy are typically interconnected. If the audience knows less than the writer, the writer's purpose is often instructional (as in a textbook). If the audience knows more than the writer, the writer's purpose is usually to *display* familiarity, expertise, and intelligence. The latter is a common situation for the graduate student writer.

The interesting question now arises as to what strategy (or strategies) a graduate student can use to make a successful display. Consider the case of an Asian student who in the United States calls himself "Gene." Gene is enrolled in a master's program in public health. He has nearly finished his first writing assignment, which focuses on one aspect of health care costs in the United States. This is a short assignment rather than a major research paper. The deadline is approaching, and there is no more time for further data analysis. He wants to make a good impression with his concluding paragraph. He believes (rightly) that final impressions are important.

Gene (quite appropriately) begins his last paragraph by reminding his audience (i.e., his instructor) of what he has done in the paper. He begins as follows:

> Conclusion
>
> The aim of this paper has been to examine the health care costs of non-profit and for profit hospitals in the United States. In particular I have examined the effects of decreasing copayments under each system.

So far, so good. His first attempt at completing his paper is as follows:

> As the tables show, in non-profit hospitals, costs increased by 4.8%, while in for profit hospitals, increases averaged 24.7%. As I have explained, the probable cause of this difference is that physicians in for-profit hospitals ordered many more tests when the copayment was reduced.

What do you think of this?

Gene does not like the conclusion. "Wrong strategy," he says. "This is just repeating what I have already written; it makes it seem that I have run out of ideas. There is nothing new here; my paper dies at the end." Gene tries again. "This time," he says to himself, "I will take my results, summarize them, and then try to connect them to some wider issue. That's a better strategy." Here is his second version.

> As the tables show, in non-profit hospitals the effect was relatively minor, whereas in for-profit contexts cost increases were considerable. In the latter case, the reduced copayments apparently gave rise to a noticeable increase in the number of tests ordered by physicians. These findings support other studies which show that cost containment may prove very difficult in a "free market" medical economy.

Gene likes this version; however, he is also worried. He knows—but he has not said so anywhere yet—that there is a serious problem with the data he has been using. Luckily, this is not Gene's thesis research; this is data that he has found for this assignment. The comparison between the two types of hospitals may not be valid.

He now writes:

> The findings should be considered somewhat provisional at this stage. This is because the patients in the two systems have not been equated for such variables as patient income, age, and level of satisfaction with the health care provider.

Gene is now asking himself the question: Is it actually better to admit that there are problems with the data or not to mention this at all? Which strategy is better? Will I appear more or less intelligent by discussing the problem? And if I do discuss it, should I put it right at the end or at the beginning of my conclusions? In effect, how should I *position* myself as a junior graduate student?

TASK THREE

What advice would you give Gene? Write down your suggestions in note form. Then edit or rewrite his final paragraph to reflect your advice.

Organization

Information is presented to readers in a structured format. Even short pieces of writing have regular, predictable patterns of organization. You can take advantage of these patterns, so that readers can still follow, even if you make errors.

Although our goal in this text is not to work on letter writing, we'd like to begin our discussion of organization by looking at two letters, which may in fact resemble letters you have recently received. Each letter has a clear, predictable pattern of organization. The first is a good-news letter.

Dear Ms. Wong:

Thank you for your interest in our university.	**Acknowledgment**
On behalf of the Dean of the Graduate School, I congratulate you on being accepted to the program in Aerospace Engineering to begin study at the master level.	**Good News**
This letter is your official authorization to register for Fall 20XX. As a reflection of the importance the Graduate School places on the ability of its students to communicate effectively, the Graduate School requires all new students whose native language is not English to have their English evaluated. Specific details for this procedure are given in the enclosed information packet.	**Administrative Details**
We look forward to welcoming you to Midwestern University and wish you success in your academic career.	**Welcoming Close**

Sincerely,

TASK FOUR

Read the bad-news letter and label the four parts.

preparation for bad news   bad news   close
acknowledgment

	Parts
Dear Mr. Lee:	
Thank you for your interest in the graduate program in Industrial and Operations Engineering. We have now finished our rigorous review process for Fall 20XX applications. We received an unusually high number of applications for the Fall term and we unfortunately had to limit the number we could accept. While your background is impressive, I regret to inform you that your application to the program has not been accepted. Given your excellent qualifications, I trust you will be able to pursue your academic interests elsewhere and wish you luck in your further endeavors.	
Sincerely,	

As you have noticed, the acceptance letter is organized differently than the rejection letter. The news in the letters does not come at the same place. Why do you suppose this is?

The writer of the good-news letter wants the correspondence to continue, while the writer of the bad-news letter wants the correspondence to end. Can you think of any other difference in purpose?

Academic writing also employs a variety of organizational patterns. You are already familiar with external organization features, such as chapters, sections, and paragraphs. As you work your way through this book, you will become familiar with the various approaches to internal organization as well. One very common strategy in academic writing is to organize Information in terms of problem-solution (Hoey 1983). This pattern usually has four parts.

1. Description of a situation

2. Identification of a problem

3. Description of a solution

4. Evaluation of the solution

TASK FIVE

Draw boxes around and label the four parts of this problem-solution text. The first part has been done for you. After marking up the text, answer the questions that follow.

1. *Description of a situation*

❶ For over 20 years now biologists have been alarmed that certain populations of amphibians* have been declining. ❷ These declines have occurred both in areas populated by humans as well as areas seemingly undisturbed by people. ❸ However, offering clear proof of the declining numbers of amphibians has been difficult because in most cases there is no reliable data on past population sizes with which to compare recent numbers. ❹ Moreover, it is not entirely clear whether the declines are actually part of a natural fluctuation in populations arising from droughts or a scarcity of food. ❺ To address this problem biologists are changing the way that they observe amphibian populations. ❻ One

*Frogs, toads, and salamanders.

good documentation method involves counting species over the course of several years and under a variety of climatic conditions. ❼ This method should yield reliable data that will help researchers understand the extent to which amphibian populations are in danger and begin to determine what can be done to stem the decline in populations.

How serious does the problem seem to be? How does the author evaluate the solution? What do you think of the solution? What is one major problem being worked on in your field of study?

TASK SIX

Here is another passage with the same structure. Read it and answer the questions that follow.

❶ India has the second largest population in the world. ❷ In 2001 it was 1027 million, which constituted nearly 17% of the world's people (Census of India, 2001). ❸ Growth of population in urban areas is about twice as fast as that of the total country. ❹ The city of Delhi, for example, has been experiencing rapid population growth because of its administrative importance in the country and better than average opportunities for education and health care. ❺ Within the next two decades its population is expected to be around 27 million.

❻ One of the major challenges facing Delhi today is the lack of affordable housing. ❼ Because of this housing shortage, numerous unauthorized housing settlements have emerged and are scattered around the city. ❽ Despite the low level of amenities and facilities in these thriving, unauthorized colonies, they are the only option for those who cannot afford either public or privately developed housing.

❾ Although many solutions have been considered to solve this problem, some urban planners have argued that government policies should be implemented to regularize and expand these unsanctioned settlements. ❿ Along with this effort, the government could co-ordinate efforts to upgrade these areas and provide basic services such as water supply, sewerage, and electricity. ⓫ If the settlements are better regulated and offer basic services, the housing shortage may begin to be alleviated. (Sivam 2003)

1. For what type of audience was this written?

2. What assumptions does the author make about the audience's knowledge background?

3. What is the author's purpose?

4. How is the problem introduced?

5. What does *this effort* in sentence 10 refer to?

6. What does the author think of the solution?

7. If the writer had thought that the solution would not work, what might he have written for the last sentence? In such a case would this last sentence be enough to complete the text? If not, what would need to be added?

In addition to the problem-solution structure, some other ways of organizing information include the following.

- Comparison-contrast (see pages 75, 174)

- Cause-effect (focusing on one cause and multiple effects as in an earthquake or describing multiple causes and one effect as in global warming)

- Classification (categorizing as suggested by the following example: "Earthquake effects on underground structures can be grouped into two categories: (1) ground shaking and (2) ground failure such as liquefaction, fault displacement, and slope instability." Note the cause-effect aspect of this as well.)

Research paper introductions in your field may also follow an established organizational pattern, which we will address in Unit Eight.

Style

Academic writers need to be sure that their communications are written in the appropriate style. The style of a particular piece must not only be consistent but must also be appropriate both for the message being conveyed and for the audience. A formal research report written in informal English may be considered too simplistic, even if the actual ideas and/or data are complex.

One difficulty in using the appropriate style is knowing what is considered academic and what is not. The grammar-check program on your computer is likely not of much help in this matter since it was intended to mainly find spelling and basic grammar errors and not to offer stylistic advice for *academic* writers. Moreover, what little stylistic advice is offered may not be right for what you are writing. For example, contrary to what your grammar checker might suggest, if you are describing a procedure or process, you can and probably even should use passive voice in some cases.

Deciding what is academic or not is further complicated by the fact that academic style differs in terms of what is acceptable from one area of study to another. Exceptionally, contractions (e.g., *don't*) may be used in philosophy but are not widely used in most other fields. And, as noted in a study by Yu-Ying Chang and John (1999), informal elements such as beginning sentences with *but,* using imperatives (as in the common expression *consider the case of . . .*), and the use of *I* are creeping into academic writing, causing even more confusion when trying to determine what is "academic."

Finally, academic style is not used in all academic settings. Research based on the Michigan Corpus of Spoken Academic English (MICASE) shows that academic and research speech, in linguistic terms, is much more like casual conversation than written academic English. It is not uncommon to hear U.S. lecturers use words and phrases like *stuff, things, bunch,* or *a whole lot of,* which would not be appropriate for an academic writing task. They may also use elaborate metaphors and other vivid expressions to enliven their speaking style. (For some examples of spoken academic English, check MICASE at http://www.hti.umich.edu/m/micase/.)

TASK SEVEN

Find and make a copy of one or two articles in your field that you think are well written. The articles do not necessarily have to be written by native speakers of English. Bring your the article(s) to class so that you may compare some of our general suggestions about academic writing style with writing conventions in your field.

Language Focus: The Vocabulary Shift

Although there are increasing challenges in describing academic writing style, we do our best here to offer you some advice. One distinctive feature of academic writing style is choosing the more formal alternative when selecting a verb, noun, or other part of speech.

Verbs

English often has two (or more) choices to express an action or occurrence. The choice is often between a phrasal verb (verb + particle) or prepositional verb (verb + preposition) and a single verb, the latter with Latinate origins. Often in lectures and other instances of everyday spoken English, the verb + preposition is used; however, for written academic style, there is a tendency for academic writers to use a single verb wherever possible. This is one of the most dramatic stylistic shifts from informal to formal style. Here is an example.

> According to some biologists, *coming up with* clear proof of the decreasing numbers of frogs has been difficult. (less formal style) →

> According to some biologists, *offering* clear proof of the decreasing numbers of frogs has been difficult. (academic style)

TASK EIGHT

Choose a verb from the list that reduces the informality of the sentence. Note that you may need to add tense to the verb from the list. Write down any other single verbs that you think could also work in the sentences.

review	maintain	develop	cause	eliminate
reach	determine	investigate	decrease	constitute

1. The six leading causes of death in the U.S.—coronary heart disease, stroke, lung cancer, colon cancer, diabetes, and chronic obstructive pulmonary disease—are mainly *brought on* by overeating, a lack of exercise, and cigarette smoking.

_____

2. Scientists are *looking into* innovative ways to combat AIDS.

   _____

3. The purpose of this paper is to try to *figure out* what is lacking in our current understanding of corrosion and corrosion protection in concrete.

   _____

4. Researchers have recently *come up with* hybrid vehicles that use a fuel-cell engine and a battery-assisted power train.

   _____

5. Rice and aquatic products *make up* a major part of the diet of the people in the Mekong Delta, Vietnam.

   _____

6. The use of touch-screen voting systems could *get rid of* many problems associated with traditional paper-based ballots.

   _____

7. Worldwide consumption of pesticides has *gone up to* 2.6 million metric tons.

   _____

8. Although labor unions in the U.S. have been able to *keep up* their membership numbers over the last two decades, they have been losing their political strength.

   _____

9. The number of mature female green turtles that return to their primary nesting beach has *gone down* from 1,280 ten years ago to 145 today.

   _____

10. The U.S. Defense Threat Reduction Agency *looks over* nearly 25,000 export license applications to make sure that no equipment or materials are sent to places where they could be used to make advanced weapons.

   _____

TASK NINE

Reduce the informality of each sentence by substituting a single verb for the one in italics. In each case try to find two or three possibilities and be prepared to discuss them.

1. Researchers have *come up with* a number of models to describe the effect of certain beverages on dental enamel erosion.

   _____

2. AIDS researchers have *run into* a variety of unexpected problems in their efforts to develop a vaccine.

   _____

3. Recent studies on car scrapping have *brought up* the important question as to whether CO_2 emissions can be significantly reduced.

   _____

4. Problems with this policy *showed up* soon after its implementation.

   _____

5. In the past five years many studies have *looked at* the effect of different grassland management practices.

   _____

Nouns and Other Parts of Speech: Choosing the More Formal Alternative

English has a very rich vocabulary derived from many languages. Because of this, there may be more than one way to express an idea. You should strive to choose words that are less informal in nature and also precise. In lectures, you will likely hear less formal speech; however, in writing you should use a more formal form if one exists and seems to be more precise than its less formal alternative.

TASK TEN

Which of the italicized words would be more suitable for an academic paper? Can you think of additional alternatives?

1. Crash test dummies are *really important for/an integral part of* automotive crash tests.

2. In Hong Kong there is one cell phone for *just about/nearly* every two people.

3. There has been *a lot of/considerable* interest in how background sounds such as music affect an individual's ability to concentrate.

4. We *got/obtained* encouraging results using structural bamboo rather than timber.

5. Consumer interest in electronic billing and payment is *getting bigger and bigger/increasing.*

Of course, when you are offered the choice between two alternatives, the more academic choice is fairly clear. The more difficult task is making good language choices on your own. We've helped you a bit in this next part of the task by italicizing the phrases that you should change. You may need to make other changes so that the sentence is still grammatical.

6. The competition faced by U.S. growers from imports of Mexican fresh vegetables has *gotten more intense.*

_____

7. Many urban areas *do not have enough* land to build new public schools.

_____

8. Allergic reactions to local dental anesthesia *do not happen very often.*

_____

9. The doors on these ferries were *made bigger to make it easier to load and unload* vehicles.

_____

Language Focus: Formal Grammar Style

The following are some nonvocabulary-related recommendations for maintaining a formal academic writing style

1. Generally avoid contractions (but keep in mind that in some fields it may be OK to use them).

Export figures won't improve until the economy is stronger.	→	Export figures will not improve until the economy is stronger.

2. Use the more appropriate formal negative forms.

not . . . any	→	*no*
The analysis didn't yield any new results.	→	The analysis yielded *no* new results.
not . . . much	→	*little*
The government didn't allocate much funding for the program.	→	The government allocated *little* funding for the program.
not . . . many	→	*few*
This problem doesn't have many viable solutions.	→	This problem has *few* viable solutions

3. Limit the use of "run-on" expressions, such as *and so forth* and *etc.*

These semiconductors can be used in robots, CD players, etc.	→	These semiconductors can be used in robots, CD players, and other electronic devices.

4. Avoid addressing the reader as *you* (except, of course, if you are writing a textbook or other instructional materials).

You can see the results in Table 1.	→	The results can be seen in Table 1.

| You can classify individuals as Morning Types (MTs), Evening Types (ETs), or Neither Type (NTs). | → | Individuals can be classified as Morning Types (MTs), Evening Types (ETs), or Neither Type (NTs). |

5. Be careful about using direct questions. In some fields they are common, while in others they are not.

| What can be done to lower costs? | → | It is necessary to consider how costs may be lowered. |

or

We now need to consider how costs may be lowered.

6. Place adverbs within the verb.

In academic writing adverbs are often placed midposition rather than in the initial or final positions. In informal English adverbs often occur at the beginning or end of sentences.

| Actually, very little is known about the general nature and prevalence of scientific dishonesty. | → | Very little is actually known about the general nature and prevalence of scientific dishonesty. |

| This model was developed by Krugman (1979) originally. | → | This model was originally developed by Krugman (1979). |

7. Consider whether you should split infinitives.

The prescriptive view of grammar condemns the use of split infinitives (placing an adverbial modifier between *to* and the infinitive as in *to sharply rise*). Although we would agree that split infinitives are not so common in academic writing, they are sometimes used, particularly in order to avoid awkwardness or ambiguity. We would recommend that you find out your reader's preference for splitting (or not splitting) infinitives and decide what to do. (Both Chris and John use split infinitives in their writing.)

Here are some examples of split infinitives that we found in published papers. Can you guess why the authors chose to use them?

We need *to adequately meet* the needs of those enrolled in the program.

Neural networks have the ability *to correctly classify* new patterns.

The size of the container could be modified *to downwardly adjust* the portion size and amount of consumption.

8. Aim for an efficient use of words.

Use as many words as you need to express your points; try to use no more than you really need.

It may be difficult to make a decision about the method that we should use. → Choosing the proper method may be difficult.

There are some inorganic materials that can be used by bioengineers in the process of tissue engineering that have been shown to be very promising. → Some inorganic materials used in tissue engineering have shown great promise.

In summary, in one way or another most of our recommendations are designed to help you maintain a scholarly and objective tone in your writing. One question that you may still have is whether you should use *I* or *we* in your writing. Check in several journals to determine what is done in your field. The use of *I* or *we* does not necessarily make a piece of writing informal. The vocabulary shift and some of the other features we have mentioned are more important for maintaining a consistent academic style. In fact, you may remember that Gene wrote, "I have examined . . ."

TASK ELEVEN

Working with a partner, look through one of the articles you chose for Task Seven. Can you find examples where the authors seem to follow some of our suggestions?

TASK TWELVE

Reduce the informality of each sentence.

1. You can use this model to analyze the effects of several parameter changes.

2. OK, what are the reasons that coffee prices have fallen? There're a lot of possibilities.

3. You can see the difference between these two approaches to designing underground subway stations clearly.

4. Recent research has shown that the arms are used commonly for protection during a fall to the ground.

5. So far there hasn't been any comprehensive study looking into the role of smiling in getting the initial trust of individuals.

6. There are some studies that have concluded that bamboo could be used by builders more widely than it is now as a construction material.

7. These special tax laws have been enacted in six states: Illinois, Iowa, Ohio, etc.

8. There isn't very much research on the use of oil palm shell as coarse aggregate in the production of concrete.

TASK THIRTEEN

Now that you have become more familiar with some of the conventions of academic writing, write a one-paragraph problem-solution text about a problem in a country that you are familiar with. Try to choose a problem unique to that country. Refer, if you like, to the text in Task Six. Your audience is a group of American peers and professors interested in your selected country. Follow the style guidelines on pages 18–24 as you write.

Flow

Another important consideration for successful communication is flow—moving from one statement in a text to the next. Naturally, establishing a clear connection of ideas is important to help your reader follow the text. We have already tried to demonstrate good flow of ideas in the amphibian passage in Task Five.

TASK FOURTEEN

Consider the following passages. Underline the parts in passage B that differ from passage A. Why does B have better "flow" than A?

A. Lasers have found widespread application in medicine. Lasers play an important role in the treatment of eye disease and the prevention of blindness. The eye is ideally suited for laser surgery. Most of the eye tissue is transparent. The frequency and focus of the laser beam can be adjusted according to the absorption of the tissue. The beam "cuts" inside the eye with minimal damage to the surrounding tissue—even the tissue between the laser and the incision. Lasers are effective in treating some causes of blindness. Other treatments are not. The interaction between laser light and eye tissue is not fully understood.

B. Lasers have found widespread application in medicine. For example, they play an important role in the treatment of eye disease and the prevention of blindness. The eye is ideally suited for laser surgery because most of the eye tissue is transparent. Because of this transparency, the frequency and focus of the laser beam can be adjusted according to the absorption of the tissue so that the beam "cuts" inside the eye with minimal damage to the surrounding tissue—even the tissue between the laser and the incision. Lasers are also more effective than other methods in treating some causes of blindness. However, the interaction between laser light and eye tissue is not fully understood.

Language Focus: Linking Words and Phrases

As demonstrated in Task Fourteen, linking words and phrases can help a writer maintain flow and establish clear relationships between ideas. Table 1 lists some of the more common linking words and phrases, arranged according to their function and grammatical use.

Sentence connectors raise a small, but important, issue—namely, punctuation. Many general style guides and style guides for your specific area of study are available (online and in book form) that can provide detailed explanations of punctuation use. Therefore, we will limit our discussion to a few key points regarding semicolons (;), colons (:), dashes (—), and commas (,).

Table 1   Linking Words and Phrases

	Subordinators (introduce a dependent clause that must be joined to a complete sentence)	Sentence Connectors (introduce a complete sentence)	Phrase Linkers (introduce a noun phrase)
Addition		furthermore in addition moreover	In addition to
Adversativity	although even though	however nevertheless	despite in spite of
Cause and Effect	because since	therefore as a result consequently hence thus*	because of due to as a result of
Clarification		in other words that is (i.e.)	
Contrast	while whereas	in contrast however on the other hand conversely	unlike
Illustration		for example for instance	
Intensification		on the contrary as a matter of fact in fact	

*Note that *thus* may also be used in nonfinite clauses of result, as in this example: "The accounting scandal deepened, thus leading to the firing of many high-ranking officials." See Unit Three for further discussion of this point.

Semicolons join two completely independent sentences and work much like a full stop.

> Air traffic delays due to high traffic volume have increased considerably over the last decade; these delays have become a major public policy issue.

Semicolons can be used with sentence connectors. In the following example, note the use of the comma after the connector.

> Increasing the size of airports is one solution to traffic congestion; however, this is a long-term solution whose benefits may not be seen for many years into the future.

Because semicolons are a "stronger" type of punctuation (they mark a stronger break in the flow of ideas) than commas, they can be used to chunk longer sequences into parts.

> In recent years GNP growth rates have varied considerably for the countries in this study (China, 6%; U.S., 3%; Japan, 1%).

> Several researchers have examined whether capital income should be taxed in the steady state (Moriyama, 2003; Correia, 1996; Chamley 1986).

In addition, semicolons can be used to separate rather long items in a list.

> Some of the solutions to the air traffic delay problem include increasing the size of airports that routinely experience major flight delays; overhauling the air traffic control system so that more flights can be safely handled; and increasing landing fees (which are currently based on the weight of an aircraft) during peak periods.

Although commas could be used in the preceding example, the length of the elements suggests that semicolons would work better; note the use of the semicolon before *and* toward the end of the sentence.

Similar considerations apply to sentences that use a colon to introduce a list.

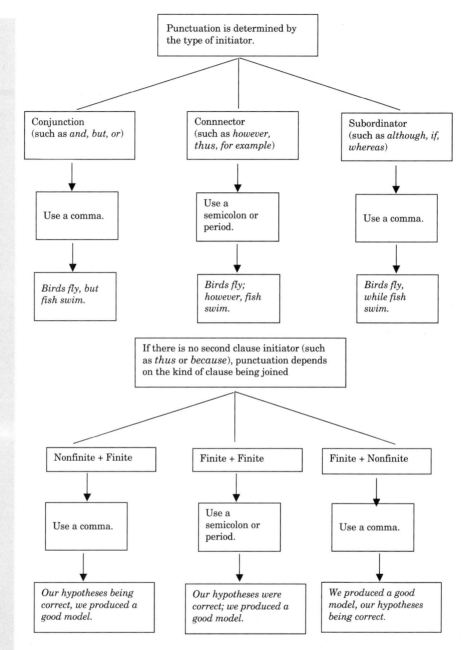

Fig. 2. Punctuation

There are four main causes of airport congestion: bad weather, excessive volume, runway closures, and equipment outages.

There are four main causes of airport congestion: bad weather, such as a snowstorm, may ground planes; too many planes may be scheduled to arrive or depart within a short period; runways may be closed; and equipment may be out of service.

Sometimes a dash is used to introduce a list as well. Often dashes are used to intrude into a sentence with some additional information.

Commas are used in a variety of situations. It's best to check a style manual for the many uses. For our purposes here, however, we will say only that commas are used with many of the subordinators.

Although weather is a major cause of airport delays, excess traffic volume is also a major factor.

TASK FIFTEEN

Edit the following passage by adding semicolons or commas where necessary.

❶ Although most major companies provide their employees e-mail accounts as well as Internet access many of these companies are concerned about potential abuse and monitor their employees' use of these media. ❷ In fact more than 75% of all major corporations report that they monitor their employees' use of e-mail and Internet access either by spot-checking or constant surveillance. ❸ Businesses have many reasons for monitoring e-mail and Internet use for example they may be concerned about protecting sensitive company information or they may be worried about lawsuits arising from sexual harassment because of mass mailing of offensive jokes. ❹ In addition there may be concerns about productivity. ❺ Recent studies have shown that nearly 86% of employees use e-mail and cruise the Web for personal reasons thus leading many companies to ban unproductive e-mail, such as jokes, and to restrict Web access.

TASK SIXTEEN

Supply linking words or phrases that enhance the flow of one of the following passages. Look carefully at the punctuation to help you make an appropriate choice.

A. ❶ It has long been documented that individuals in an organization may voluntarily carry out tasks that are not part of their regular job duties. ❷ _____ , individuals may go above and beyond the call of duty to help coworkers, prevent problems or volunteer to stay late when not expected to do so. ❸ This behavior is intended to help others in the organization or the organization itself and is often referred to as organizational citizenship behavior (OCB). ❹ _____ it is recognized that OCB is important for an organization to effectively function, there is debate among researchers as to how OCB can be encouraged and rewarded. ❺ This debate is further complicated when considering the role of OCB in multinational corporations pursuing global diversity. ❻ Most OCB research has focused on Western cultures; _____ , it is not clear whether these research findings can be extended to other cultures, _____ suggesting a need to investigate OCB as it exists in other cultures, particularly those described as "collectivist."

B. **1** Shape Memory Alloys (SMA) are a group of metallic materials that can return to some previously defined shape or size when subjected to the appropriate temperature. **2** When some SMA are cold they can be deformed at a low temperature; _____ _____ , when the material is heated above this temperature it undergoes a change in crystal structure, _____ _____ causing it to return to its original shape. **3** Some materials exhibit shape memory only when heated, _____ others can undergo a shape change both when heated and when cooled.

4 _____ many alloys are known to have the ability to "remember" their shape, only some may actually find widespread commercial use. **5** Of particular interest are those that can recover substantial amounts of strain or that generate significant force upon changing shape. **6** _____ _____ , one common nickel and titanium SMA, Nitinol, has this ability and is being used in surgical implants, clamps, miniature valves and switches, and other devices.

Language Focus: this + Summary Word

Another way to maintain flow is to use *this / these* + a noun to join ideas together. Consider the following sentences.

> ESL lecturers know that students need to understand the differences between formal and informal language. However, this understanding cannot usually be acquired quickly.

What does *this understanding* refer to?
  Consider the following sentences.

In recent years, the number of students applying to Ph.D. programs has increased steadily, while the number of places available has remained constant. This situation has resulted in intense competition for admission.

What does *this situation* refer to? What is the effect of using *this* instead of *that?*

The phrases in italics contain a summary noun or word that refers back to the idea in the previous sentence. These phrases summarize what has already been said and pick up where the previous sentence has left off. You may have noticed in your academic reading that *this* is not always followed by a noun, that is, *this* is "unsupported." Keep in mind, however, that if there is a possibility your reader will not understand what *this* is referring to, your best strategy is to follow *this* with a noun so that your meaning is clear.

TASK SEVENTEEN

Choose a noun to complete the following.

1. According to a recent survey, 26% of all American adults, down from 38% 30 years ago, now smoke. This _____ can be partly attributed to the mounting evidence linking smoking and fatal diseases, such as cancer.

   a. decline   c. improvement   e. drop
   b. reduction   d. decrease

   Can you think of any other nouns that could complete the sentence?

2. Early in September each year, the population of Ann Arbor, Michigan, suddenly increases by about 20,000 as students arrive for the new academic year. This _____ changes the character of the town in a number of ways.

   a. influx   c. invasion   e. jump
   b. increase   d. rise

   Can you think of any other nouns that could complete the sentence?

3. Nowadays, laptop computers are lighter, more powerful, and easier to use than they were five years ago. These _____ have led to an increase in the sales of these machines.

a. changes   c. advances
b. developments   d. improvements

TASK EIGHTEEN

Choose a summary word from the list to complete each sentence. Can you think of other possible summary words in addition to those on the list?

process   situation   finding   estimation
problem   difficulty   disruption   view

1. The traditional economic and consumer behavior models assume a rational, thoughtful consumer who gathers information about a good and then carefully makes a purchase. This _____ has recently been challenged, particularly because of the growing number of consumer choices.

2. Our pilot study has shown that wind turbines used to generate electricity can pose a threat to flying birds. This _____ suggests a need for further research on improving the safety of these mechanisms.

3. In soccer, goalkeepers routinely wear gloves that may restrict heat loss from the hands and cause discomfort. In order to alleviate this _____ , special materials, called phase control materials (PCMs), have been incorporated into gloves to reduce the amount of heat inside the glove, thus maintaining a comfortable temperature.

4. Normal average human skin temperature is 37°C. At any lower environmental temperature, heat will be lost from the skin to the environment as the body attempts to heat up the air in direct contact with the body. This _____ is known as conduction.

5. Until adjustment of the body clock has occurred, individuals suffering from "jet lag" feel tired during the new daytime, yet are unable to sleep properly during the new night. For athletes in particular this _____ of sleep can affect mood and powers of concentration and might result in poorer training performances and competition results (Reilly et al. 1997b).

6. Until recently, the support needs of frail older people in Sweden have been met primarily by the state, with there being little expectation that the family would provide care. This _____ _____ is now changing as increasing emphasis is being placed on the role of the family.

TASK NINETEEN

Now try to find summary words that can complete these sentences.

1. Irrigation in sub-Saharan Africa is in most cases performed using a rope and bucket to raise and distribute water from a shallow open well. While this _____ has the advantage of being inexpensive, its low capacity and labor-intensive nature is decidedly a disadvantage.

2. Motor vehicle deaths in the U.S. declined from nearly 60,000 in 1966 to just over 40,000 last year, even though Americans drive millions more miles now and millions more vehicles are on the road. The death rate, which was 7.6 deaths per 100 million miles in 1950, declined from 5.5 in 1966 to 1.6 last year. This _____ can be attributed to the manufacture of safer vehicles, with features such as airbags and antilock brakes.

3. Haigney concludes from his study that driving performance decreases when drivers use their cell phones. This _____ is consistent with recent reviews of the literature on driving distractions.

4. Although it seems that the construction of new roads and widening of existing roads should reduce traffic congestion, recent research has shown that these activities actually lead to increases in traffic. This _____ is known as the "induced traffic" effect.

5. In 1900 average life expectancy at birth was 47 years for individuals born in developed countries. In 1950 life expectancy was nearly 68. For newborns today life expectancy is about 77 years. This _____, however, does not mean that humans are undergoing some physiological change. Rather, it is a result of advances in medicine and technology.

Summary words may be expanded into phrases to add clarity. However, long and complicated summary phrases may be unnecessary. Consider the following opening sentences and options a–e. Which of the options would you choose as the third sentence?

> In the past, flood impact assessments have focused primarily on the economic losses resulting from a flood. Now, however, emphasis is also being placed on potential environmental benefits.

a. *This* will result in a more complete picture of the gains and losses from a flood.

b. *This expansion* will result in a more complete picture of the gains and losses from a flood.

c. *This expansion of focus* will result in a more complete picture of the gains and losses from a flood.

d. *This expansion in assessment focus* will result in a more complete picture of the gains and losses from a flood.

e. *This expansion in assessment focus with regard to flooding* will result in a more complete picture of the gains and losses from a flood.

Finally, we need to say something about the use of *it* or *this* to refer back to something in the previous text.

TASK TWENTY

Consider sentence 1 and the sets of sentences that follow. Which of the sentences in each set make better sense as a follow-up? Why?

1. The amount of rain the Midwest received in spring was much heavier than usual.

   a. In fact, it was the second heaviest on record.
   b. In fact, this was the second heaviest on record.

   c. In fact, it was even heavier than the amount of rain recorded in 1999.
   d. In fact, this was heavier than the amount of rain recorded in 1999.

e. It has led to huge losses in the millions of dollars.

f. This has led to huge losses in the millions of dollars.

g. This may be connected to increasing destruction of wetlands.

h. It may be connected to increasing destruction of wetlands

For the first two sets you may have rightly chosen sentences *a* and *c*, for the last two sets sentences *f* and *g*. *It* in *a* and *c* clearly refers to the subject (the amount of rain in the Midwest), which is appropriate for the first two sets. In the second set, *this* refers to the entire idea of the first sentence (the amount of rain in the Midwest was heavier than usual in spring).

Now take a look at the following short text on traffic and consider which sentence best concludes.

2. Researchers have found that it is easier to start a traffic jam than to stop one. A small, but temporary, increase in the number of cars entering a highway can cause a bottleneck; however, after the number of cars decreases, traffic jams generally continue.

   a. It has been verified through the use of sensor data from Germany and the Netherlands.

   b. This has been verified through the use of sensor data from Germany and the Netherlands.

   c. This phenomenon has been verified through the use of sensor data from Germany and the Netherlands.

   d. This traffic phenomenon has been verified through the use of sensor data from Germany and the Netherlands.

TASK TWENTY-ONE

Revise the following draft, taking into account the suggestions for revision that appear at the end. Be sure to consider whether the suggestions are reasonable or not.

❶ Turkey is located in a region that is shaken by severe earthquakes. ❷ They occurred almost every year. ❸ Central Anatolian Fault Zone is one of the most active fault zones in the world, and it lies along the northern part of the country, going from south east to northwest. ❹ The reason of that most of these severe earthquakes causes a lot of damage and death of many people is not only the nature of the fault zone, but also that there are many cities and highways settled on it. ❺ Because of the ignorance of this big giant in the regional planning of the country. ❻ There is no way that big cities can't be affected from severe shakings in each year. ❼ The most serious damage occurred in August 1999. ❽ It affected a big area as wide as two kilometer and caused approximately 20,000 people death and millions dollars physical damage in three cities. ❾ In recent years, some early warning systems have been developed to be aware of the upcoming shakings. ❿ Although these can make warnings as short as 10 second before the shakings, if there is a well-planned rescue organization, it may help to decrease, at least, the death rates in the earthquakes.

Instructor's Comments

You have a good topic here. Nice first draft. Your problem-solution organization is clear. Here are a few suggestions for making your text even better.

1. *The connection of your points in sentences 1–3 could be improved. I see what you're saying, but you could say it more efficiently. The point in sentence 2 could be woven into another sentence using 2 or 3 words. This would also eliminate the past tense in sentence 2, which should not be used because you are making a statement of fact.*

2. *Think about clarifying for your reader that the earthquakes are caused by the Central Anatolian Fault Zone.*

3. *In sentence 4 keep your focus on the earthquakes. Beginning the sentence with "the reason that the earthquakes cause a lot of damage" suggests that you have already stated that the earthquakes cause a lot of damage. Of course, readers should know that earthquakes cause serious damage, but I think you should say this. Consider beginning this sentence by saying that the earthquakes cause a lot of damage and then continue with your explanation.*

4. *Sentence 5 is not a complete sentence. "Because" introduces a dependent clause that can't stand alone. Can you think of a way to connect this sentence to the following one? Or make some other change?*

5. *Also in 5, "ignorance" doesn't work. I see what you want to say, but you need to change this. While ignore means to not pay attention to, the*

noun form _ignorance_ often makes us think of the state of being uneducated or unaware because of a lack of education. You could try to use the verb form and then your meaning will be clear.

6. Do you really need sentence 6? I'm not sure it adds much to the discussion.

7. Sentence 7 provides a good, concrete example of the destructiveness of earthquakes in the region. What do you think about giving the example earlier when you first say that the earthquakes are destructive?

8. In sentence 8 the referent for the pronoun _it_ is not 100% clear. What is "_it_"?

9. Again in sentence 8, "a big area" is rather vague. Can you be more precise?

10. Sentence 9 describes a way to possibly minimize the destructiveness of earthquakes. Can you think of a smoother transition into the solution here? Something "_like one way to . . ._" or "_one possible method of . . ._"? A phrase to introduce the solution can be helpful to the reader.

11. Can you find another word for "_make_" in sentence 10? I understand what you are saying, but we usually don't use _make_ with _warning_. Also in this sentence, your use of _it_ is not clear. What is _it_ referring to?

12. Make any other changes you think are necessary.

Presentation

Most instructors tolerate small errors in language in papers written by nonnative speakers—for example, mistakes in article or preposition usage. However, errors that could have been avoided by careful proofreading are generally considered less acceptable. These include the use of an incorrect homophone (a word that sounds exactly like another, such as *too* / *to* / *two*); basic grammar errors (e.g., in subject-verb agreement); and misspelled words, including those that are not identified in a computer spell-check routine.

In addition, your presented work is more likely to receive a positive response if you perform the following tasks.

1. Consider the overall format of your written work.

Does your paper look as if it has been carefully prepared?
Are there clear paragraphs?
Is the line spacing appropriate?
Have you used standard fonts and font sizes?

2. Proofread for careless grammar mistakes.

Do subjects and verbs agree?
Have the appropriate verb tenses been used?
Have the articles *a, an,* and *the* been used when necessary?
Is *the* used too much?

3. Check for misspelled words, even if you have spell-checked your work.

Has the correct homophone been used?
Did the spell-checker miss anything?

TASK TWENTY-TWO

There are numerous small mistakes in grammar in the following passage. Can you identify and correct them? (Because some of the errors are in article usage, you might wish to refer to Appendix One.)

The discovery of fossil fuels have had a big effect on development of cities. The use of the automobile has become most important element supporting the modern society. And, since a few decade ago, the finiteness of natural resources is a source of heated controversy. The cities and its development will certainly be affected.

Greater focus on accessible public transportations is one change in current urban planning discussions. It widely believes that there will be an effort to redesign cities in order promote the use of public transportation.

TASK TWENTY-THREE

The following short passage has been spell-checked. Although all the words are spelled correctly as far as the spell-check program is concerned, seven usage and spelling errors remain. Can you identify and correct them?

> Their is considerable doubt weather this solution will be affective. The
>
> initial reaction too the report has not been complementary. In fact
>
> many observers belief that collapse of the system is eminent.

Positioning

Now that you are familiar with the most important characteristics of academic writing, you are ready to "position" or establish yourselves as junior members of your chosen fields (see Fig. 3).

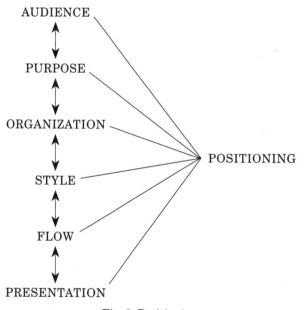

Fig. 3. Positioning

TASK TWENTY-FOUR

Mark these writing characteristics as **H** (helpful for positioning) or **U** (unhelpful for positioning). In some cases there is room for disagreement.

1. Choosing any writing style that you like ———

2. Expressing enthusiasm and commitment ———

3. Writing in a formal academic style ———

4. Making broad generalizations ———

5. Being cautious about generalizations ———

6. Using references to support your points ———

7. Writing mainly from experience and personal knowledge ———

8. Reevaluating the work of authorities in the field ———

9. Showing an awareness of the "hot" issues in your field ———

Can you explain your choices?

Unit Two

Writing General-Specific Texts

Each remaining unit in this book deals with a particular kind of writing task. We have chosen to begin with a type of text sometimes called general-specific (GS) because its structure involves general-to-specific movement. There are three reasons to begin with GS texts. They are quite common in graduate student writing, they are comparatively simple, and they are often used as introductions for longer pieces of writing. You may need to produce a GS text for

a. an answer to an examination question,

b. an opening paragraph of an assignment, or

c. a background (or scene-setting) paragraph to an analysis or discussion.[1]

GS texts usually begin with *one* of the following:

a. a short or extended definition,

b. a contrastive or comparative definition,

c. a generalization or purpose statement, or

d. a statement of fact.

As their name implies, GS texts move from broad statements to narrower ones. However, they often widen out again in the final sentence. The shape is similar to that of a glass or cup (see fig. 4).

---

[1]Both *b* and *c* may also take the form of a descriptive summary. See Unit Five.

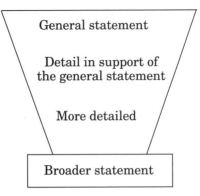

Fig. 4. Shape of G-S texts

TASK ONE

Here is a slightly shortened version of a published GS text. Read the text and answer the questions that follow.

Selling Cities: Promoting New Images for Meetings Tourism

1 Meetings tourism, which we define as travel associated with attendance at corporate or association meetings, conferences, conventions or congresses or public or trade exhibitions, has emerged as a significant subsection of the tourist industry both in terms of volume of travel and expenditure generated. **2** "Meetings" demonstrate enormous variety, ranging from small business meetings of a few participants to large conventions of, for example, professional associations which might attract in excess of 20,000 delegates. **3** The range of locations within which these meetings take place is also broad, including such sites as hotels, universities, sports venues, and specially built convention centers.

4 The meetings tourism market has been vigorously pursued by many former industrial cities in Europe and the U.S. as part of their strategies of post-industrial urban regeneration (Law, 1987, p 85). **5** This market offers a number of obvious attractions to such cities, not least the rapidity of its growth during the 1970s and 1980s, the very period during which many cities were suffering contractions in their industrial base. **6** Figures for the U.S.A. suggest the business conference industry almost doubled during the 1980s. **7** The growth is particularly marked for international conferences, which bring the greatest financial returns for host cities (Labasse and Law, p 47).

8 In many European cities the economic contributions of business tourism outweigh those from leisure tourism by two to three times (Van den Berg et al, 1994, p 161) making it both a seemingly appropriate and rewarding sector for former manufacturing cities to pursue. (Adapted from Bradley, Hall, and Harrison 2002)

1. The "shape" of this passage is something like this. Complete the diagram.

    1) _____

        a. *Size of meetings* _____

        b. _____

    2) _____

        a. *Growth in the meetings tourism market in the U.S.*

        b. *Growth in international conferences* _____

        c. _____

2. The authors of this passage have decided it is too short. Here are two additional statements. Where would you place them?

    a. Meetings tourism has grown, and seems destined to continue to grow, at rates above those of most European national economies.

    b. Meetings tourists, at small as well as large meetings, are higher spenders on average per day than leisure tourists, bringing in on average nearly $360 per day more (Law, 2002).

3. In sentence 1, why do you think the authors used the expression "which we define as . . ."?

The GS meetings tourism passage in Task One could have been part of an answer to an essay question on an in-class exam, perhaps in an economics or urban planning course. The exam question could have been:

A medium-sized city in your home state or country is considering constructing a conference facility that can accommodate up to 15,000 conference-goers and exhibitors. Choose a medium-sized city. Describe the city and then discuss whether you think a conference facility would benefit the local economy.

Alternatively, the passage on meetings tourism could also have been the *opening* paragraph to a longer assignment—perhaps one asking the student to analyze some data on the impact of meetings tourism on the economy of the city where his or her university is located. Or it could have been an assignment focusing on the advantages or disadvantages of this kind of economic activity.

As in many GS texts, the meetings tourism passage began with a general statement, which also just happened to include a definition. General statements of fact or tendency can often be useful starting points.

General Statements

General statements can include general statements of fact as well as broad statements made about a topic that are usually, but not necessarily always, true. Here are a few examples.

Individuals in organizations exhibit a wide range of behaviors, from the minimalist who does the least possible to maintain membership to those who go beyond expectations, engaging in extra-role behavior to promote the effective operation of the organization or to benefit others.

In the last decade, tremendous strides have been made in the science and technology of organic light-emitting diodes (OLEDs)[1,2].

Over the years interest in the economic benefits of meetings tourism has been growing.

After making a general statement, some support or explanation for the statement should be offered, which in turn helps move the passage from general to specific. Support can take the form of specific detail or perhaps a reference to earlier work, as in the second example above. Whether you begin a GS text with a general statement or a definition is a matter of personal preference. However, sometimes one may be a strategically better choice than the other.

Suppose, for instance, the topic assigned is "The English Language." Now, if we were to write on this topic as philologists, we might still open the text with a definition.

> English is a language that belongs to the West Germanic subgroup of the Indo-European language family. It began its history as a distinct tongue in England around 500 A.D.

However, in most other circumstances, it is more likely that we would start with a generalization.

> In comparison to many of the world's better-known languages, English is relatively new. Indeed, the English of 600 years ago can be understood only by specialists.

> Although Chinese has the greatest number of speakers, English is the most widely distributed language in the world today. This position derives from the fact that English is widely taught as a second language in schools and widely used in international communication.

TASK TWO

Below you will find three pairs of sentences, each consisting of a definition and a generalization. When would it be better to begin a text with the first sentence in each pair rather than the second?

1. a. Russian is the first language of about 150 million inhabitants of the former Soviet Union.

   b. Russian is a language belonging to the East Slavic subgroup of the Indo-European language family.

2. a. AIDS has emerged as a devastating infectious disease for which there is presently no cure.

   b. AIDS is a disease caused by a virus that attacks the immune system.

3. a. A catalyst is a substance which increases the rate of a chemical reaction.

   b. Catalyst technology has progressed quickly as researchers better understand the complex interactions of molecules.

Definitions

Definitions are a common way of getting started; they are "hooks" from which GS paragraphs can be hung. Such paragraphs typically open with full-sentence definitions. Textbooks, in contrast, often introduce the definitional information as a minor part of the sentence, as in the following example.

> The majority of corporate profits, or *earnings after all the operating expenses have been deducted,* are subject to tax by the government.

Textbook definitional information is used to clarify terms that may be unfamiliar to the reader. However, this is not your task, since your audience is already familiar with the terms and expects you to write a text that *demonstrates* your understanding of complex concepts.

In the next part of this unit, we will highlight certain aspects of the structure of these key definitional sentences. Then we will consider more extended definitions, contrastive definitions (e.g., organic versus inorganic chemistry), and comparative definitions (i.e., discussions of the advantages and disadvantages of competing definitions).

Writing a Definition

The term *definition* comes from the Latin word *definio,* which means "to limit or bound; to interpret ideas or words in terms of each other; to understand one thing by another." A definition sets the boundaries for a word's meaning. As you are aware, one term can have different meanings depending on the context. The dictionary definition of *cold,* for example, usually has something to do with low temperature or a deficiency of heat. But cold is a relative term whose meaning changes with context. In the following text, how does the author define *particularly cold* for the reader?

Only when environmental conditions are particularly cold, for example (1) during winter conditions at latitudes above about 50° in either hemisphere, or (2) when cold is associated with windy and especially wet conditions, or (3) when the athlete exercises in cold water for prolonged periods, does the risk arise that the athlete will lose heat faster than he or she can produce it. (Noakes 2000)

Words and phrases may also have different meanings depending on the field of study. For example, *tone* has several definitions. In music a *tone* can be a sound of distinct pitch, quality, and duration; while in linguistics *tone* can refer to the rise or fall of the voice on a particular syllable (as in Chinese). In interior design *tone* may be a color or shade of color. And finally *tone* in physiology may be used to describe the normal state of elastic tension or partial contraction in resting muscles.

TASK THREE

Write down some terms in your own field with meanings different from those in everyday life. Now define one or two of those terms as we did for *tone* in linguistics and physiology.

Within some fields of study, usually in the less hard sciences and the humanities, the definition of a term may not be agreed upon by members of the discipline. There may be multiple or competing definitions. We will return to the issue of multiple definitions later (see page 73). First, we need to lay some groundwork.

Some Common Ways to Define in Academic Writing

Definitions may simply be short, parenthetical additions to a sentence or perhaps a larger part of a paper. The extent of the definition depends on the purpose of the paper, the level of familiarity your audience has with the subject, and the extent to which there is an agreed upon definition of the concept. Some common ways to define include the following.

1. *Short definitions or "glosses"* that give information about a term in a word or phrase and are placed within either parentheses or

commas in a sentence; phrasal definitions signaled by such devices as *e.g., or,* or *i.e.,* or phrases such as *known as, defined as,* and *called.*

2. *Sentence definitions,* which are brief and somewhat similar to a dictionary definition.

3. *Extended definitions,* which are longer and more detailed than definitions found in dictionaries.

❖❖ Language Focus: The Language of Defining and Naming

a. The verb *name* itself is rare and seems restricted to a focus on the name itself.

This new species was *named Ascochyta mycoparasitica.*

b. The verb *denote* is quite common but seems largely restricted to matters of notation.

Any rotational velocity is usually *denoted* by f.

Any vector in this paper will be *denoted* by a bold letter.

c. The verb *call* is quite common, but using it in full sentences can be tricky. One danger in written papers is that it can give the impression of stating the obvious, as in

A book containing lists of word definitions is *called* a dictionary.

While this kind of definitional explanation may be fine for a tutor or instructor, it does not work so well when writing for experts. Only use *call* for introducing new information. Notice the general-to-specific order of information in the following examples.

This new method is *called* activity-based costing, or simply ABC.

Fig. 15 shows two simple mirrors, bending around the light. The configuration may be *called* a two-dimensional corner reflector.

d. The phrase *known as* is not very common in definitional sentences.

Another principle source of heat is the natural increase in temperature as the depth increases. This is *known as* the geothermal gradient.

e. The phrase *define as* is widely used and often represents a safe option, especially in more elaborate explanations and for terms or concepts that can be defined in more than one way.

Shadow work may be *defined as* those subsistence activities engaged in by the homeless which are outside of the regular employment system, but not necessarily outside of the market system altogether (Ilich 1981).

For the purposes of this study, fast food is *defined as* food sold by a franchised restaurant chain offering both dining and take-out facilities with no "table" service (e.g., McDonald's).

One important product attribute is perceived product sophistication, which I *define as* the degree to which a product exhibits the latest technological advances.

In the preceding examples, what expressions suggest to you that other definitions may be possible?

f. Finally, the verb *refer* is widely used in academic writing but tends, as far as definitions are concerned, to be used for terminological explanations. In the following examples, only the first two sentences refer (!) to terminology.

The natural gas contained in coal formations is generally referred to as coal bed methane.

Individuals may go above and beyond the call of duty to help coworkers, prevent problems, or volunteer to stay late when not expected to do so. This behavior is intended to help others in the organization or the organization itself and is often referred to as organizational citizenship behavior (OCB).

Reductionism primarily refers to inappropriate simplification.

TASK FOUR

Identify and underline the definitional elements in the following.

1. In addition to the examination of historical records, a study of the geologic record of past seismic activities, called paleo-seismology, can be used to evaluate the occurrence and size of earthquakes in the region. Geomorphic (surface landform) and trench studies may reveal the number of past seismic events, slip per event, and timing of the events at a specific fault.

2. It should be noted that cell phones are not necessarily the same as car phones, i.e., devices intended for permanent installation in the vehicle and which may have separate handset/dial units.

3. The uncertainty associated with the energy obtained from other types of nonutility generators (NUGs), i.e., thermal and hydro, is relatively small compared to that associated with wind.

4. Average raw scores on IQ tests have been rising for years (Flynn, 1984, 1987, 1999), by an estimated three IQ points per decade (Neisser 1998). This rise, known as the Flynn effect, has received much attention, though its exact nature was recently questioned.

5. Phytoremediation is the direct use of living green plants for *in situ,* or in place, risk reduction for contaminated soil, sediments, and groundwater.

6. Procrastination refers to deliberately putting off one's intended actions.

7. Tax evasion is defined as intentionally paying fewer taxes than the law requires, as a deliberate act of noncompliance.

8. Software watermarking is a process in which identifying information is embedded into a file, enabling authors to control the distribution of and verify ownership of their digital information. The purpose of software watermarking is to protect the intellectual property that belongs to the author.

9. Road pricing is a transportation control measure that requires motorists to pay directly for using a particular roadway or driving in a particular area. Economists have long advocated road pricing as an efficient and fair way to pay roadway costs and encourage more efficient transportation. Road pricing has three general objectives: revenue generation, a reduction in pollution, and congestion management. One simple road pricing instrument is area licensing, which requires a motorist to purchase a permit to take a vehicle into a designated urban area during peak traffic hours.

10. Collecting, defined as the process of actively, selectively, and passionately acquiring and possessing things removed from ordinary use and perceived as part of a set of nonidentical objects or experiences (Belk 1995), is an acquisitive, possessive, and materialistic pursuit.

TASK FIVE

Skim one or two journal articles in your area of study, looking for definitions. Highlight any definitions you find, and try to categorize them as one of the types described above. In which section of the article did you find the definitions? Why? Bring your findings to class.

Formal Sentence Definitions

Sentence definitions can take different forms. They may be signaled by a single verb phrase or may be expressed using a class term and restrictive clause. As we showed you earlier, some verb phrases that can be used to define include *refer to as, is/are known as,* and *is/are defined as.*

> Dental erosion *is defined as* a progressive loss of hard dental tissues by a chemical process without bacterial action.

> This variant of the efficiency wage hypothesis *is known as* the shirking model.

> Dalle de verre, commonly referred to as faceted glass, is a thick, modern cast glass, which is used in concrete-set windows.

TASK SIX

You might have noticed that each of the preceding examples is written in the passive voice. Why do you think this is the case? Can any of these be rewritten in the active? Discuss your answers with a partner.

Elements of Formal Sentence Definitions

Let us now look at formal sentence definitions. A sentence definition is often a useful starting point for a GS paragraph. In a formal sentence definition, such as the examples that follow, the term being defined is first assigned to a class or group to which it belongs and then distinguished from other terms in the class. The class word is a superordinate—a category word one level of generality above the term. Some common superordinates, or class words, are *technique, method, process, device,* and *system* (Pearson 1998).

> Annealing is a metalworking process in which a material is subjected to elevated temperatures for a period of time to cause structural or electrical changes in its properties.

To what class does annealing belong? How is it different from other members of the class, such as hammering or welding?

> A sole proprietorship is a business which is owned and operated by one individual for personal profit.

To what class does the sole proprietorship belong? How is it different from other members of the class? How would you define a partnership?

> A star is a celestial body that shines by itself and whose source of energy is nuclear fusion occurring in its core.

To what class does a star belong? Can you think of other celestial bodies? How is a star different from these?

> Kava is a Pacific shrub *(Piper methysticum)* whose dried rhizome and roots can be ground, grated, and steeped in water to produce a non-alcoholic drink.

To what class does kava belong? Do you know of other members of the class?

Notice that each of these definitions is completed by some form of restrictive clause and has the structure shown here.

Term	Class	Distinguishing Detail
(A) _____ is	(a) _____	Wh-word[2] _____ .
A solar cell is a	device that/which	converts the energy of sunlight into electric energy.

---

[2]Although the *Chicago Manual of Style* and other style manuals recommend using *that* instead of *which* in restrictive relative clauses, research shows that *which* continues to be used in definition statements. Therefore, we have used both *which* and *that* in the sample definitions presented in this unit.

Language Focus: The Grammar of Definitions

Notice the use of the indefinite articles *a* and *an* in the first part of the preceding definitions. (For a more complete discussion of articles, see Appendix One.)

> A sole proprietorship is a business . . .
> Annealing is a metalworking process . . .
> A star is a celestial body . . .
> Road pricing is a transportation control measure . . .

In most definitions, the indefinite article (or no article in the case of uncountable nouns) is used before both the term and the class. The indefinite article before the class indicates that you are classifying a term. The indefinite article before the term conveys the meaning that any representative of this term will fit the assigned class.

You may ask why *the* is not used in a formal sentence definition. Take a look at the following sentences.

a. A disinfectant is *an* agent capable of destroying disease-causing microorganisms.

b. A disinfectant is *the* agent capable of destroying disease-causing microorganisms.

Sentence *a* classifies the term; it does not refer to a particular representative. Sentence *b*, however, identifies or describes the term. Further, in sentence *b* it is implied that there has been some previous mention of other agents that are not capable of destroying disease-causing microorganisms and suggests to us that there is only one such agent with this capability.[3]

TASK SEVEN

Insert the article *a* or *an* where necessary in the following definitions.

1. Helium is gas with atomic number of 2.

2. El Niño is disruption of ocean-atmosphere system in tropical Pacific having important consequences for weather worldwide.

[3]There is one main exception to the absence of *the* in formal definitions; this occurs in *explanations* of fields, as in "Phonetics is *the* study of speech sounds."

3. White dwarf is star that is unusually faint given its extreme temperature.

4. Rice is cereal grain that usually requires subtropical climate and abundance of moisture for growth.

5. Transduction is technique in which genes are inserted into host cell by means of viral infection.

6. In seismology, liquefaction is phenomenon in which soil behaves much like liquid during earthquake.

7. Disability is physical or mental impairment that substantially limits one or more major life activities such as seeing, hearing, speaking, walking, breathing, performing manual tasks, learning, caring for oneself, and working.

8. Hydrothermal vent is crack in ocean floor that discharges hot (350–400°C), chemically enriched fluids and provides habitat for many creatures that are not found anywhere else in ocean.

Now let us turn to the grammar of the second part of a sentence definition. The distinguishing information in the restrictive relative clause can be introduced by either a full or a reduced relative clause. There are two common ways of reducing a restrictive relative. One involves a *simple deletion,* while the other involves *a change in word form or an entire word.* Although there have been claims that reduced relatives are uncommon in academic English, this is not the case. Reduced relatives are often preferred because they are shorter and "snappier."

Deletions

You may reduce the restrictive relative if

1. The relative clause consists only of the relative pronoun, the verb *to be*, and one or more prepositional phrases.

    A wharf is a structure *that is along* a waterfront providing a place for ships to load and unload passengers or cargo. →

    A wharf is a structure along a waterfront providing a place for ships to load and unload passengers and cargo.

    In dentistry, enamel is a hard, white inorganic material *that is* on the crown of a tooth. →

    In dentistry, enamel is a hard, white inorganic material on the crown of a tooth.

    (Note how the opening phrase "In dentistry" restricts the scope of the definition.)

2. The relative clause consists of a passive verb plus some *additional* information.

    A theater is a building *that has been* specifically designed for dramatic performances. →

    A theater is a building specifically designed for dramatic performances.

    A collagen is a white, inelastic protein *that is* formed and maintained by fibroblasts. →

    A collagen is a white, inelastic protein formed and maintained by fibroblasts.

3. The relative clause contains the relative pronoun, an adjective ending in *-ble,* and *additional* information.

A robot is a multiprogrammable device *which is* capable of performing the work of a human. →

A robot is a multiprogrammable device capable of performing the work of a human.

Change in Word or Word Form

You may reduce the relative if

1. The relative clause contains the verb *have.* In this case the relative pronoun and *have* can both be dropped and replaced by *with.*

A parliament is a national governing body *which has* the highest level of legislative power within a state. →

A parliament is a national governing body *with* the highest level of legislative power within a state.

2. The relative clause contains an active state verb (a verb that expresses a state or unchanging condition). The relative pronoun is dropped and the verb changed to the *-ing* form. Exceptions to this are *to be* and *have.*

Pollution is a form of contamination *that often* results from human activity. →

Pollution is a form of contamination often *resulting* from human activity.

A moon is a natural satellite *which orbits* around a planet. →

A moon is a natural satellite *orbiting* around a planet.

Russian is a language *that belongs* to the East Slavic subgroup of the Indo-European language family.→

Russian is a language *belonging* to the East Slavic subgroup of the Indo-European language family.

It is also important to note that a relative clause containing a modal auxiliary cannot be reduced. Look at the following example. What would be the effect on the meaning of the definition if the modal *may* were omitted?

> In human resource management, a shock is a sudden and unexpected event that may cause employees to think about how that event will affect their jobs.

TASK EIGHT

Edit the following by reducing the relative clauses *where possible.*

1. Aluminum is a lightweight metal that is often used for high-tension power transmission.

2. Heat is a form of energy which can be transmitted through solid and liquid media by conduction.

3. A brake is a device that is capable of slowing the motion of a mechanism.

4. A dome is generally a hemispherical roof which is on top of a circular, square, or other-shaped space.

5. Snow is a form of precipitation which results from the sublimation of water vapor into solid crystals at temperatures below 0°C.

6. An antigen is a substance which causes the formation of antibodies, the body's natural response to foreign substances.

7. A piccolo is a small flute that is pitched an octave higher than a standard flute.

8. Membrane permeation is a separation process that involves the selective transport of gas molecules through a permeable polymeric film.

9. A catalyst is a substance that can speed up the rate of a chemical reaction without changing its own structure.

10. A black hole is a celestial body which has approximately the same mass as the sun and a gravitational radius of about 3 km.

Now notice also that in a full relative clause, the relative pronoun can be preceded by a preposition. The relative pronoun *which* must be used in this type of restrictive relative clause. This construction is common in formal academic writing. These clauses cannot be reduced.

A foundation is a base *on which* a structure can be built.

TASK NINE

Complete the following definitions by inserting an appropriate preposition.

1. A thermometer is an instrument _____ which temperature can be measured.

2. Photosynthesis is a process _____ which sunlight is used to manufacture carbohydrates from water and carbon dioxide.

3. A credit bureau is an organization _____ which businesses can apply for financial information on potential customers.

4. An anhydride is a compound ＿＿＿＿＿＿ which the elements of water have been removed.

5. An eclipse is a celestial event ＿＿＿＿＿＿ which one body, such as a star, is covered by another, such as a planet.

6. An axis is an imaginary line ＿＿＿＿＿＿ which a body is said to rotate.

7. Large-diameter tunnels are linear underground structures ＿＿＿＿＿＿ which the length is much larger than the cross-sectional dimension.

8. Demographers are concerned with changes in population size and the degree ＿＿＿＿＿＿ which fertility (i.e., births), mortality (i.e., deaths), and migration (i.e., movement into and out of an area) contribute to these changes.

9. The ease ＿＿＿＿＿＿ which a fraudulent business operation can set up shop on the Internet is unfortunately high.

10. "Hotelling" is a new type of office design ＿＿＿＿＿＿ which employees who mostly work at home or in the field are not given permanent offices but, rather, shared, temporary space as needed.

Whereby is commonly used in formal writing instead of *by which, by means of which,* and *through which.*

> Collective bargaining is a process *whereby* employers agree to discuss work-related issues with employee representatives.

Care in Constructing Formal Definitions

In this section we make a few final comments on how information should be presented in a one-sentence definition. First, care should be taken to find the precise word or phrase for the class.

A microscope is an object . . .

is less precise than

A microscope is an *instrument* . . .

A vowel is a sound . . .

is less precise than

A vowel is a *speech sound* . . .

TASK TEN

Choose a word or phrase that assigns at least half of the following terms or phrases to a precise class. Use your dictionary if necessary.

Term	*Class*
1. a consonant	_____
2. an ellipse	_____
3. mitosis	_____
4. neon	_____
5. a composite	_____
6. a semiconductor	_____
7. thermal toughening	_____
8. oxidation	_____
9. cancer	_____
10. privatization	_____
11. intervention	_____
12. (one of your own)	_____

Now consider the formal sentence definitions in the following set 1 and their less academic counterparts in set 2.

1. a. A solar cell is a device that converts the energy of sunlight into electric energy.

   b. In tissue engineering, a scaffold is a structure onto which cells can be seeded and grown.

2. a. A solar cell is something that changes sunlight into electricity.

   b. In tissue engineering, a scaffold is something that cells can be seeded and grown on.

The sentences in set 2 are perfectly acceptable in spoken English or e-mail. However, they would not be the most effective means of establishing yourself in your academic field. In sentences 2a and 2b, for instance, *something* is both too broad and informal, and the verb consists of a verb + preposition combination (which in Unit One we suggested you avoid in academic writing). In sentence 2b, the placement of the preposition at the end of the sentence may be considered "wrong" by those who believe that an academic English sentence should never end with a preposition. In reality, however, it is quite natural and in some cases perhaps even desirable to place a preposition at the end of a sentence. Look at the following two sets of sentences. Which sentence in each set do you prefer? Why?

It is not clear what these new devices will eventually be used for.

It is not clear how these new devices will eventually be used.

This is precisely the question that we are interested in.

This is precisely the question in which we are interested.

Here are two final pieces of advice about writing formal definitions. If possible, avoid using any form of your term in the definition. Using the term itself in the definition can result in a circular definition and is likely to be noted as such by your audience.

> Erosion is a process during which the surface of the earth *erodes.* →

> Erosion is a process during which the surface of the earth is degraded by the effects of the atmosphere, weather, and human activity.

> The four-wheel Antilock Braking System (ABS) is a braking system that helps provide straight, more controlled stops, while helping the driver maintain steering control under most road and weather conditions. →

> The four-wheel Antilock Braking System (ABS) helps provide straight, more controlled stops during braking, while helping the driver maintain steering control under most road and weather conditions.

Finally, avoid using *when* and *where* in definitions. These are less appropriate for a formal definition.

> Pollution is when the environment becomes contaminated as a result of human activity. →

> Pollution is a form of environmental contamination resulting from human activity.

> A fault is where there is a fracture in the earth's crust and the rock on one side of the fracture moves in relation to the rock on the other side. →

> A fault is a fracture in the Earth's crust in which the rock on one side of the fracture moves in relation to the rock on the other side.

TASK ELEVEN

Now write a one-sentence definition for two of the following terms (or one from Task Ten) and for at least one term from your own field. Make sure you provide enough specific detail to distinguish your term from other members in its class.

a bridge	a computer virus	a laser
a conductor	a carcinogen	a mentor
a piano	a landfill	a residence hall or dormitory

Exchange and discuss your definitions with a partner.

Extended Definitions

So far we have dealt only with sentence definitions. In some cases, one sentence may be enough before continuing with your GS passage (as with the text on meetings tourism at the beginning of this unit). However, in others, it may be relevant and important to expand your definition. In this way you can demonstrate your knowledge of a concept more fully. An extended definition usually begins with a *general,* one-sentence definition and then becomes more *specific* as additional details are provided. There may be a need to focus on such aspects as components, types, applications, history, or examples.

TASK TWELVE

With a partner, read through the following extended definitions. Discuss the kind of information that has been included. Does the definition mainly discuss components, applications, history, examples, or something else?

1. A microscope is an optical instrument with which the apparent size of an object can be enhanced. A simple microscope consists of a double convex lens and a magnifying glass. A compound microscope, on the other hand, will contain more than one of each of these lenses, which are situated at the ends of a cylinder.

2. Pollution is a form of environmental contamination resulting from human activity. Some common forms of pollution are wastes from the burning of fossil fuels and sewage running into rivers. Even

litter and excessive noise or light can be considered forms of pollution because of the impact they can have on the environment.

3. Perspective is a technique in art that is used to represent three-dimensional objects and depth relationships on a flat surface. Modern linear perspective (which involves making objects seem smaller the more distant they are from the observer) was probably first used in the 1400s by the artist Masaccio and the architects Filippo Brunelleschi and Leon Battista Alberti in Florence, Italy. Before this time, artists paid little attention to realistic perspective. In recent decades, many modern artists have returned to the practices of early artists and have abandoned realistic perspective.

4. An acrylic plastic is a polymer which can take a high polish, is clear and transparent, and can be shaped while hot. Because of these and other characteristics, acrylic plastic is used in situations where glass is not suitable or desirable, for instance, in certain types of windshields.

An extended definition may also include information regarding operating principles or causes and effects. A description of operating principles is also known as a *process analysis*. A process analysis has some unique characteristics, which will be discussed in greater detail in Unit Three. Extended definitions may also include information about many other features, such as rarity and cost. You can even go beyond the type of specific detail just described and display your breadth of understanding by discussing problems, exceptions, and future predictions.

Lateralization is a developmental process during which the two sides of the brain become specialized for different functions. As a child develops, the two sides of the brain become asymmetric in that each side controls different abilities. Language, for instance, is controlled by the left side of the brain, and certain types of pattern recognition by the right. However, there is some disagreement as to when this specialization is complete. Some researchers believe the process is not complete until puberty, while others maintain that the brain is lateralized by age five.

A CD is an optical storage medium onto which information has been recorded digitally. In CD recording of sound, sound waves are converted into digital numbers and inscribed on the disc. The digital data on the disc is read by a laser beam, thus eliminating any form of mechanical friction that could distort sound quality. Despite the excellent sound quality offered by CDs, some believe that they will eventually be replaced by other optical disc formats such as DVDs.

(Before CDs became a part of everyday life, the writer would likely have first given the full name of the term *compact disc* before introducing and using the acronym *CD*. This is no longer necessary, however, for this particular term.)

TASK THIRTEEN

Now read the following extended definition and answer the questions that follow.

> ❶ Navigation is a process by which means of transport can be guided to their destination when the route has few or no landmarks. ❷ Some of the earliest navigators were sailors, who steered their ships first by the stars, then with a compass, and later with more complicated instruments that measured the position of the sun. ❸ We are reminded of this by the fact that the word *navigation* comes from the Latin word for "ship." ❹ However, the history and importance of navigation changed radically in the 20th century with the development of aircraft and missiles, which fly in three dimensions. ❺ Today, both ships and aircraft rely heavily on computerized navigational systems, known as Global Positioning System (GPS), that can provide a continuous, immediate, and accurate report of position. ❻ In fact, the capabilities of GPS render the older positioning technologies impractical and obsolete. (Based on a text by Benny Bechor, student)

1. What type of information is included in each of the sentences in the definition?

2. How is the passage organized?

3. What tenses are used for which sentences? Why?

4. Sentence 3 begins with *we*. Is this appropriate?

5. The term *navigation* is also used in connection with the Internet. How and under what circumstances could this connection be included in the discussion?

Notice how the paragraph moves from a very general statement at the beginning to specific details, then "widens out" again in the final sentence to describe the current status of navigation. As we noted at the beginning of this unit, this pattern is quite common in paragraphs of this type.

TASK FOURTEEN

Here are the sentences of a GS passage on an unusual but interesting topic. Work with a partner to put them back in the correct order. Write *1* next to the first sentence, *2* next to the second, and so on.

Palindromes

_____ a. The term itself comes from the Ancient Greek word *palindromos* meaning "running back again."

_____ b. Another good and more recent example is "draw pupils lip upward."

_____ c. Now, however, computers have allowed word puzzlers to construct palindromes that are thousands of words long, but these are simply lists of unrelated words that do not have meaning when taken together.

_____ d. A palindrome is a word or phrase that results in the same sequence of letters no matter whether it is read from left to right or from right to left.

_____ e. One of the classic long palindromes is "A man, a plan, a canal, Panama."

_____ f. Before we had computers, long palindromes used to be very hard to construct, and some word puzzlers spent immense amounts of time trying to produce good examples.

_____ g. Some common English words are palindromes, such as *pop, dad, noon,* and *race car.*

TASK FIFTEEN

This task presents a draft of a definition along with some instructor comments. Revise the text after reading the comments. Rewrite the entire passage to reflect all of your revisions.

1 Automotive airbag is occupant restraint system. **2** It provides protection for occupant of vehicle in crash. **3** Although airbags may seem to be somewhat recent innovation, rapidly inflating air cushions designed to prevent crash injuries existed for quite some time. **4** Before being used in the automobiles. **5** In fact researchers filed very first patents for inflatable safety cushion to be used in airplanes during World War II.

6 A recent study by the National Highway Traffic Safety Administration concluded that airbags save nearly 1,000 lives annually. **7** In the future even more lives will be saved as new airbag technologies are developed. **8** Currently, for example, research is being done on as many as six different types of airbags that will offer protection in a wider range of accidents beyond front-end and side-impact collisions.

9 Automotive airbag technology developed between 1940 and 1960 was quite similar to that of airbags currently in use. **10** Those early airbag systems were very difficult to implement and costly. **11** The main concern for design engineers at the time centered on storage. **12** And the efficient release of compressed air. **13** The housing of the system had to be large enough for a gas canister. **14** The canister had to keep the gas at high pressure for a long period of time. **15** The bag itself had to have a special design. **16** It would deploy reliably and inflate within 40 milliseconds. **17** The solution to these problems came in the early 1970s with the development of small inflators. **18** Inflators used hot nitrogen instead of air to deploy the bag. **19** It allowed the widespread installation of airbags in vehicles beginning in the 1980s.

Instructor's Comments

Your draft looks pretty good. Tenses are just fine, but there still are a few things you need to work on.

1. Consider beginning with a formal sentence definition, as we discussed in class.

2. *Take a look at the organization of the text. It seems to me that your text would flow better if you used situation-problem-solution-evaluation in your definition.*

3. *Some of your sentences are incomplete and/or should be joined with another sentence to improve the flow of ideas. See specifically sentences 3 and 4, 9 and 10, 15 and 16, 17 and 18.*

4. *Add some connectors to improve the flow. You need a connector in sentence 10. Sentences 13, 14, and 15 also need connectors.*

5. *Your use of articles is generally good except for the first paragraph. Check each noun, and remember to consider whether the noun is countable or not as you make your choices about articles (a, an, the, ∅).*

6. *Sentence 19 would be clearer if you used this + summary word instead of it.*

7. *In sentence 18 consider adding some description of nitrogen as a harmless gas. Use a short definition within the sentence.*

8. *In sentences 6 and 8 consider placing the adverb in midposition.*

TASK SIXTEEN

Choose one of the following.

1. Write an extended definition of an important term or concept in your field of study. Try not to use any resources if you can, but if you need to refer to a source, provide the name of the source for your instructor and make sure that you use your own words.

2. Write an extended definition for a key innovation or discovery in your field. For example, this could be a process, an approach to doing something, or a device. Include the following information: a sentence definition of the innovation, when the innovation came about, the importance of the innovation, the problem that the innovation addressed, and some discussion of how the innovation changed your field.

Competing Definitions

As we said earlier, sometimes a definition of a term or concept is not fixed. There may be a lack of agreement as to a precise definition, or perhaps there are competing perspectives. While uncommon in the hard sciences, this is something that students in other fields may encounter. If competing definitions exist for a term that you will be using, a good strategy when writing is to acknowledge some of the different definitions, but then make clear to your reader the definitions you will adopt. Notice how the authors of the following examples express the lack of agreement surrounding a term.

> For two decades, and particularly during the 1990s, authors and practitioners concerned with vulnerability as related to food security and famine have engaged in a lengthy attempt to define vulnerability and develop methods to measure it. Nonetheless, just what the term means and how it informs assessment methods remain unclear.

> Preeclampsia has been defined as a pregnant condition characterized by arterial hypertension, proteinuria, and edema during the second half of pregnancy. Although this definition seems simple and includes the main clinical signs, actually, there is a wide diversity in the use of this term in clinical and epidemiological studies, leading to difficulties in comparing research outcomes. (Prudencia Ceron-Mireles, minor editing)

> For centuries scholars have attempted to define, explain, and theorize nationalism. Despite their efforts, it seems there is little agreement on the definition of this concept among researchers. (Hiroe Saruya, minor editing)

Here are some skeletal phrases that you could use to present the definition that you have chosen.

> While debate exists regarding a precise definition of . . . , the stance adopted in this paper is that . . .

> For the purposes of this paper, . . . refers to/is defined as/is considered to be . . .

Here we define . . . as . . .

In this paper I have adopted [author's] definition of . . .

This paper follows [author's] definition of . . .

TASK SEVENTEEN

Take a look at this discussion of road rage and answer the questions that follow.

❶ The term "road rage" was first coined in 1988 (Fumento, 1998) and is defined in the Oxford English Dictionary as "violent anger caused by the stress and frustration of driving in heavy traffic." ❷ Some researchers suggest that this definition is not entirely accurate. ❸ For example, road rage has been described as a cultural habit of retaliation that occurs as a result of frustration and can occur independent of heavy traffic (James & Nahl, 1998). ❹ Some have even gone so far as to label road rage a mental disorder (Schmid, 1997). ❺ Classifying this cultural phenomenon as a mental disorder may be a stretch, but there is substantial evidence that some drivers become very angry when confronted by an adverse driving event. ❻ Elevated levels of anger may prompt aggressive and other risk-taking behavior, behavior that can increase accident risk, and risk of other negative behavior such as physical assault between drivers or argument with passengers (Deffenbacher, Oetting, & Lynch, 1994). (DePasquale et al. 2001).

1. How many and what kinds of different definitions of road rage do the authors include? Why?

2. How is the text organized? Does it seem to be a GS text?

3. What verb tenses and aspects are used? Why?

4. In sentence 5 what is *this cultural phenomenon?*

5. In which sentences do the authors seem to be cautious about their claims? Which words or phrases suggested that the authors were hedging (i.e., being careful)?

6. What do the authors mean when they say, *Classifying this cultural phenomenon as a mental disorder may be a stretch?*

7. What is the purpose of the second sentence (i.e., *Some researchers suggest that this definition is not entirely accurate.*)?

8. What do you think the authors are going to write about next? Their data? Their method? Their hypothesis? Something else?

Contrastive Definitions

So far, we have concentrated on developing a text starting from the definition of a single term. Often, however, you may be asked to display your knowledge about two (or more) related terms. Consider, for example, the following pairs.

a. An optical and an electron microscope

b. Concrete and cement

c. An acrylic and a polyester

d. Annealing and welding

e. A CD and a DVD

f. A good-news and a bad-news letter

g. A star and a planet

h. Formal and informal English

If you were asked in an in-class examination to explain the differences between the members of each pair, how many could you do?

Read this *draft* of a contrastive definition. The draft focuses on patents and copyrights, the differences of which may not be clear to nonlawyers.

❶ A patent, in law, is a right that grants an inventor sole rights to the production, use, or sale of an invention or process for a limited period of time. ❷ The inventor is guaranteed the possibility to earn profit for a reasonable period, after which the public is guaranteed eventual free use. ❸ On the other hand, a copyright is a form of protection which grants an originator of artistic work exclusive use of the artistic creation for a specific period of time. ❹ Copyrights are issued to authors, playwrights, composers, artists, and publishers, who then have control over publication, sale, and production of their creations for a period of time.

This is a good start, but the two terms have been presented rather independently. The passage does not reveal the writer's understanding that there is one major characteristic linking patents and copyrights, namely, that they both have a legal basis. The writer has also not made clear the distinction between the two. One way to do this would be to say

> The former deals with . . . , while the latter is concerned with . . .

TASK EIGHTEEN

Discuss with a partner how you could rewrite the patent/copyright passage using *the former* and *the latter*. The missing information could be placed at either the beginning or the end of the passage. Which strategy would result in the most effective presentation? Can you suggest other changes that might improve the passage?

Now look at the following two suggestions from our students. How do they differ? Do you prefer one over the other?

A. **❶** Patents and copyrights are forms of legal protection concerned with the rights of an individual who has created something. **❷** The former grants an inventor sole rights to the production, use, or sale of an invention or process for a limited period of time, while the latter grants an originator of artistic work exclusive use of the artistic creation for a specific period of time. **❸** Patents guarantee an inventor the possibility of earning profit for a reasonable period, while the public is guaranteed eventual free use. **❹** Copyrights, however, are issued to authors, playwrights, composers, artists, and publishers, who then have control over publication, sale, and production of their creations.

B. **❶** Patents and copyrights are forms of legal protection that grant inventors or artists exclusive rights to their creations for a limited period of time. **❷** Patent and copyright owners are guaranteed the possibility to earn a profit and have control over their creations, while the public is guaranteed eventual free use. **❸** However, the former deals only with the creator of an invention or process, while the latter is concerned with authors, playwrights, composers, artists, and publishers.

Did you notice how the second contrastive definition naturally makes use of contrastive connectors (see page 27 for other contrastive connectors)?

TASK NINETEEN

Read through the following discussion of procrastination, which views the term from a variety of perspectives and answer the questions that follow. Does it seem like a competing or a contrastive definition, or is it another kind?

1 Procrastination refers to deliberately putting off one's intended actions. **2** This means that procrastinators intend to perform an action at a certain moment, but do not engage in it at the moment that it was planned. **3** Instead, they postpone it, or even never do it at all. **4** This phenomenon is defined at the behavioral level (not doing what was intended) as well as at the cognitive level (postponing decisions) and does not refer to the possible causes of the dilatory behavior. **5** There may be several reasons for putting off one's intentions, some of which we are not interested in, such as illness, technical problems, and so on. **6** Moreover, sometimes procrastination might even be functional (for instance postponing a decision because crucial information is lacking, Ferrari, 1994). **7** Two types of procrastinator have been described: the optimistic procrastinator and the pessimistic procrastinator. **8** Optimistic procrastinators put off their intentions but do not worry about doing so (Milgram et al., 1992). **9** They are confident that they will succeed in the end, regardless of their engagement in the intended action now or later. **10** Moreover, they overestimate their progress and their chances to succeed and underestimate the time needed to achieve their goal (Lay, 1987, 1988). **11** In contrast, pessimistic procrastinators do worry about their dilatory behavior (Milgram et al., 1992). **12** They are aware of the fact that they get behind schedule. **13** Nevertheless, they still procrastinate because they do not know how to deal with the task (Lay, 1987, 1988). **14** They feel incompetent and are afraid that their involvement in the task will prove their incompetence. ⓯ Therefore, they procrastinate to avoid unpleasant experiences. (Dewitte and Lens 2000)

1. What elements in the passage make the passage seem "academic"?

2. Why do the authors include the general discussion of procrastination in sentences 1–6?

3. What is the purpose of sentence 7? Is this sentence helpful to a reader? Why?

4. Underline the sentence connectors in the text. What kinds of connector did the author use (see p. 27)? How do these affect the flow of ideas?

5. In sentence 4 there is a summary phrase. What does *this phenomenon* refer to?

6. Why do you suppose the authors used *sometimes* and *might* in sentence 6?

7. If, during the revision process, you thought that the passage would be improved by breaking it into two paragraphs, where would you put the paragraph break?

8. The authors have chosen to place the references to previous work in parentheses. What would be the effect of clearly making the reference part of the sentences, as in the following example?

   They are aware of the fact that they get behind schedule. Nevertheless, Lay (1987, 1988) states that they still procrastinate because they do not know how to deal with the task.

   How do writers refer to previous work in your field? Do they use numbers, parentheses, something else? If you do not know, check a journal in your field.

9. What might the authors of this text discuss next?

10. What question (or questions) might this passage be a part of an answer to?

11. What field do you think the passage is from?

TASK TWENTY

We offer two choices here. Write an extended definition of a term for which there are competing definitions. Or write a contrastive definition for a term in your field. If you can't think of a term, use the information given in either Table 2 or Table 3, or write a contrastive definition for one of the pairs listed at the beginning of this section (on p. 75).

Table 2   Speech Sounds

Vowels	Consonants
Common in all languages	Common in all languages
Produced by allowing unobstructed flow of air through the mouth	Produced by obstructing the flow of air through the mouth
No points of articulation or contact-position of tongue	Many points of articulation—lips, tongue and teeth, tongue and palate, etc.
Lip rounding important	Lip rounding rarely important
Voiced	Voiced or voiceless
Can easily be produced alone and even constitute an entire word, e.g., *eye*	Many are difficult to produce without an accompanying vowel
Can carry pitch and loudness	Cannot carry pitch and loudness

Table 3   Nuclear Reactions

Fission	Fusion
Releases energy stored in nucleus of an atom	Releases energy stored in nucleus of an atom
Occurs with heavy nuclei	Occurs with light nuclei
Neutrons bombard nuclei of atoms, splitting the nuclei apart	Energy released even greater than that released in fission
Splitting releases energy	Two nuclei combine at high temperatures
Can occur in a nuclear reactor to generate electricity	One nuclei is formed along with a neutron, releasing energy
Could also occur spontaneously	Occurs in the sun and stars
Does not require extreme temperatures	Requires temperatures of 1,000,000°C
Fuel is usually uranium, which is expensive and difficult to extract	Fuel is hydrogen, an abundant element

Comparative Definitions

Comparative definitions typically occur in introductory sections
of papers. They can be used to display your knowledge of the
complexities surrounding key terms in your field of study. There are
basically two approaches to this type of task. One is to present a
historical account of how a concept has changed over time. The other
is to present an overview of how various experts today view a concept
differently. Good comparative definitions often contain elements of
each approach.

TASK TWENTY-ONE

Read the following comparative definition and answer the questions
that follow. This passage is more complex than any we have presented
so far. Use a dictionary to check the meanings of words you do not
know.

Competing in Defining Humor

❶ Generally speaking, humor is a quality in an event or expression of
ideas which often evokes a physical response of laughter in a person.
❷ It is an evasive quality that over the centuries has been the subject
of numerous theories attempting to describe its origins. ❸ There are
essentially three main theories of humor, each of which has a number
of variants: the superiority theory, the incongruity theory, and the relief
theory. ❹ The superiority theory, which dates back to Aristotle,
through Thomas Hobbes (1651) and Albert Rapp (1951), describes all
humor as derisive. ❺ In other words, people laugh at the misfortunes
of others or themselves. ❻ Humor is, therefore, a form of ridicule that
involves the process of judging or degrading something or someone
thought to be inferior.

   ❼ The incongruity theory, on the other hand, maintains that humor
originates from disharmony or inappropriateness. ❽ Koestler (1964),
for example, argues that humor involves coexisting incompatible
events. ❾ In other words, when two opposite or opposing ideas or
events exist at the same time, humor may emerge. ❿ Finally, the relief
theory rejects the notion that either superiority or incongruity are the
bases for humor. ⓫ Rather, proponents of this theory believe that
humor is a form of release from psychological tension. ⓬ Humor

provides relief from anxiety, hostility, aggression, and sexual tension. ⓭ Humor gratifies repressed feelings that operate on an unconscious level. ⓮ Early psychologists, such as Freud, Dewey, and Kline, were strong proponents of this theory.

⓯ More modern theories of humor are essentially variations of one of these three traditional ones. ⓰ For instance, Duncan (1985), in his superiority theory, states that humor is linked to social status. ⓱ Deckers and Buttram (1990) expand incongruity theory to include elements of schema theory. ⓲ In their view, distinctions between and within schemata* are necessary for an understanding of humor. ⓳ While each of these theories can explain some aspect of humor, none can successfully be applied to all instances of humor.

1. In which sentences are the different theories introduced?

2. What verb tense is used to introduce the definitions of the various researchers? Why do you suppose this is?

3. Underline the sentence connectors in the passage. Why were they used?

4. What do you think might follow this discussion of humor theories—a presentation of the author's own definition of humor, an analysis of one event using the different theories, something else?

5. Do you think that the whole passage is a GS text, that part of it is, or that none of it is?

6. Does the passage mention a modern version of relief theory?

7. Do you think that the author of this passage (Chris) has positioned herself as neutral, or do you think she has a preference? If you think she has a preference, what do you think it is? Why do you think so?

---

*Schemata are the types of background knowledge that a person brings to a context. For instance, you may have schemata for going to a restaurant or for going to a birthday party.

We will return to the writing of comparative summaries in Unit Five.

TASK TWENTY-TWO

Write a general-specific paragraph on your own first language or on a topic from your field of study. Begin with either a definition or a generalization.

Unit Three

Problem, Process, and Solution

In Unit Two we explored one common kind of underlying structure to academic writing, that of general-to-specific movement. This structure will prove useful in later units, when producing data commentaries (Unit Four) or writing introductions to research papers (Unit Eight). In this unit, we explore and practice a second underlying structure in academic writing, that of problem-to-solution movement. This structure will again prove useful later on, when writing critiques (Unit Six) and once more in introductions. In addition, we have built into the problem-solution structure some discussion of process descriptions. In many cases, it makes sense to see describing the parts of a process as the *steps required* to provide a solution to some problem. Alternatively, a problem may be described in terms of a process, for example, how an airbag deploys or how a tsunami (tidal wave) forms.

As we have seen, general-specific passages tend to be descriptive and expository. In contrast, problem-solution texts tend to be more argumentative and evaluative. In the former, then, graduate students will most likely position themselves as being informed and organized; in the latter as questioning and perceptive.

The Structure of Problem-Solution Texts

We begin this unit with a passage on a topic that is likely of interest to you and others who want or perhaps need to publish in English. This passage is organized as a problem-solution text.

TASK ONE

The following passage is about the role of English today in research and scholarship. Before you read the passage, circle the answer of your choice to question 1. Briefly discuss your estimate with a partner.

1. What is the current percentage of research papers published in English—as opposed to other languages?

   30%   40%   50%   60%   70%   80%   90%

Now read on.

The Role of English in Research and Scholarship

❶ There are many claims that a clear majority of the world's research papers are now published in English. ❷ For example, in 1983 Eugene Garfield, President of the Institute for Scientific Information (ISI),[1] claimed that 80% of the world's scientific papers are written in English (Garfield 1983). ❸ Comparable estimates have more recently been produced for engineering, medicine, and nonclinical psychology.

❹ It is not clear, however, whether such high percentages for English provide an accurate picture of languages chosen for publication by researchers around the world. ❺ The major difficulty is bias in the databases from which these high percentages are typically derived. ❻ The databases are those established by the major abstracting and indexing services, such as the ISI indexes and Medline, which are predominantly located in the United States. ❼ As a result, these services have tended to preselect papers that *(a)* are written in English and *(b)* originate in the Northern Hemisphere. ❽ For these two reasons, it is probable that research in languages other than English is somewhat underrepresented.[2] ❾ Indeed, Najjar (1988) showed that no Arabic language science journal was consistently covered by the *Science Citation Index* in the mid-1980s.

❿ We can hypothesize from the previous discussion that the role of English in research may be considerably inflated. ⓫ In fact, several early small-scale studies bear this out: Throgmartin (1980) produced English percentages in the 40% range for social sciences, and Velho and Krige (1984) showed a clear preference for publication in Portuguese among Brazilian agricultural researchers. ⓬ A complete bibliography on schistosomiasis, a tropical disease, by Warren and

---

1. The Institute for Scientific Information (ISI) publishes the *Science Citation Index* (SCI), the *Social Science Citation Index* (SSCI), and the *Arts and Humanities Citation Index* (AHCI).
2. The ISI itself has concluded that it may underrepresent useful research from the lesser developing countries by a factor of two (Moravcsik 1985).

Newhill (1978) revealed an English language percentage of only 45%. ⓲ These studies would seem to indicate that a more accurate percentage for English would be around 50% rather than around 80%.

⓴ However, so far no major international study exists to corroborate such a conclusion. ⓯ Until such a study is undertaken—perhaps by UNESCO—the true global picture of language use in research publication will remain open to doubt and disagreement. ⓰ Until such time, nonnative speakers of English will remain uncertain about how effective their publications are in their own languages.

2. The passage consists of four short paragraphs, which deal in turn with the four parts of the standard problem-solution text (see Table 4).

    Are sentences 1, 4, 10, and 14 the key sentences in **the** passage? If not, which other sentences might you suggest? Would you suggest sentence 13, for example?

Table 4   Parts of a Problem-Solution Text

Situation	Background information about claims for research English
Problem	Reasons for doubting the accuracy of the figures
Solution	Alternative data leading to more accurate figures
Evaluation	Assessment of the merits of the proposed answer

3. In the opening words of the paragraph, it is not clear at this time that *however* is a signal that a problem will be introduced. The text then goes on to explain the problem in some detail. The author (John) wants to convince the reader that the problem is indeed a problem. How does he accomplish this?

4. How successful do you think the type of explanation employed in this text would be for other kinds of problems?

5. Where do you think the author (John) is more convinced? Is it in the statement of the problem in paragraph 2, or in the statement of the solution in paragraph 3? Why do you think this?

6. List (using name and year) the citations used by the author. Do you have any criticisms?

7. Do you have any evidence to contribute about the languages of publication in your own field? What about the languages of research publication in your home country?

✼ *Language Focus: Midposition Adverbs*

In the section on style in Unit One (p. 22), we noted that adverbs tend to occur within the verb in formal academic writing. In this Language Focus, we develop this point a little further. First, look at some of these occurrences from sentences in the text in Task One.

❶ . . . are now published . . .

❸ . . . have more recently been produced . . .

❽ . . . is somewhat underrepresented . . .

If *today* had been used in sentence 1, it would have occurred immediately after the verb.

. . . are published today in English.

In sentence 3 we have a three-part verb in the present perfect passive: *have been produced.* Notice that the adverb phrase occurs after *have.* Read through the text again and find the other four instances of midposition adverbs.

TASK TWO

Find a single adverb to replace the phrase in italics and then place the adverb in midposition.

1. The provisions of the law must be applied *with care.*

   _____

2. Part II of this paper describes *in only a couple of paragraphs* the laws of the U.S. that pertain to agricultural biotechnology.

   _____

3. Myopia, which is referred to as shortsightedness *most of the time,* is a common cause of visual disability throughout the world.

   _____

4. This study revealed that American and Japanese thresholds for sweetness and saltiness did not differ *a lot.*

   _____

5. *As a rule,* pulsed semiconductor lasers do not use the broad gain bandwidth to full advantage in the generation of subpicosecond pulses.

_____

6. Environmental managers are faced with having to determine the extent of environmental contamination and identifying habitats at risk *all the time.*

_____

7. The water supply lines must be inspected *now and then* to prevent blockages.

_____

8. Although many elaborations of this model have been developed over the years, *to a considerable extent* all of them have followed the traditional specification in presupposing that an individual will choose to make a tax report.

_____

TASK THREE

Part of your answer to question 6 in Task One was very probably that the citations looked "old," the most recent being 1988. This is not particularly surprising, since the passage was written in the early 1990s. But now consider this passage and answer the questions that follow.

The Role of English in Research and Scholarship: An Update

❶ The problem of accurately assessing the role of English in contemporary research was identified in the 1994 text as residing in the pro-Western and pro-Anglophone bias in the major databases. ❷ The "solution" offered was then to look at small-scale empirical studies that suggested that the role of English had been exaggerated. ❸ These studies apparently indicated that "a more accurate percentage for English would be around 50% rather than 80%." ❹ The earlier text, however, had failed to recognize that over the last thirty years many leading European (and Japanese) journals have switched from publishing in German, French, Dutch, Swedish, Japanese, etc., to new editorial policies that increasingly require submissions written in English. ❺ As long ago as 1978, Lippert listed 33 German journals from the health and life sciences which by 1977 had changed their titles and editorial policies from German to English. ❻ More recently, comparable accounts have been produced for German chemistry (Wood 2001), Swedish medical research (Gunnarsson 1998), and French geology (Dressen 2002). ❼ This new data, plus studies showing the increasing anglicization of doctoral dissertations in many countries, now suggests that the figure of 80% may be more accurate than previously believed. ❽ However, there is also evidence that the dominance of English may be causing a counterreaction, especially in situations where local concerns and interests encourage publication in local languages. ❾ Rey-Rocha & Martin-Sempere (1999), for example, have shown this to be the case for earth scientists in Spain. ❿ As ever, further research is necessary.

1. Which sentences indicate the beginnings of the situation-problem-solution-evaluation sections?

2. If you were to divide this ten-sentence paragraph, where would you divide it? Would you opt for two paragraphs or three?

3. Can you produce a version of an opening sentence from your own discipline using the following skeletal phrase?

   The problem of . . . was identified as residing in . . .

4. Why is "solution" in sentence 2 in quotation marks?

5. Underline all the time expressions in this passage. What conclusions can you draw?

6. Do you think this second text makes a stronger argument than the first one? What kinds of studies would, in your opinion, actually resolve the debate?

7. Do you have information to share about the language policies of journals in your own country?

Procedures and Processes

The "Role of English" texts are typical *research question* examples of a problem-solution text. In essence, they use the problem-solution structure to *review* the current state of knowledge. The review approach, in each case, allows the author to raise a question about the current state of knowledge and to offer a possible or part answer. However, "classic" problem-solution texts are usually more *technical* in nature and may describe procedures and processes. We see this in the passage in Task Four.

TASK FOUR

Read the following passage written by Chris and answer the questions that follow. The passage is a problem-solution text about an area in Chile that has a desert climate—the Atacama Desert.

Clouds and Fog as a Source of Water in Chile

❶ Many of Chile's poor, northern coastal villages have suffered in recent years from water shortages, despite the abundance of cloud cover and fog in the region. **❷** When the cold air from the Pacific Ocean's Humboldt Current mixes with the warm coastal air, a thick, wet fog, called *camanchaca* by the Andes Indians, forms along with clouds. **❸** However, rather than developing into rain, the clouds and fog are quickly evaporated by the hot sun. **❹** This absence of rainfall has imposed severe hardship on communities. **❺** They cannot grow crops and must carefully ration their water, which has to be delivered by truck.

❻ One interesting solution to this problem is now being tested in the village of Chungungo, a village of 300. **❼** Using conventional technology, researchers have redevised a centuries-old method to capture the water droplets of the fog. **❽** In this method, triangular-weave polypropylene nets are attached to wooden support posts on El Tofo mountain to serve as water collectors. **❾** Each of these nets can collect approximately 40 gallons of water each day. **❿** When the fog develops, droplets of water are trapped in the nets and join to form larger drops that then fall into a trough. **⓫** From the troughs the water drains through filters into a series of underground tanks. **⓬** The water is then piped to a 25,000-gallon storage tank, where it is chemically treated to kill disease-causing organisms. **⓭** Finally, the water flows to individual households, just as in traditional water systems. **⓮** This collection system can supply as much as 2,500 gallons per day, enough for the entire community to drink, wash, and water small gardens.

⓯ The water is not only clean but far less expensive than water delivered to the area. ⓰ Moreover, it is collected at no apparent cost to the environment. ⓱ It is likely that this system could be successfully implemented in other areas around the world with similar environmental conditions and economic constraints. ⓲ Researchers are also investigating how this new water collection system could be adapted for noncoastal regions as well.

1. As it happens, this passage and the passage in Task One each contain almost the same number of sentences, but this passage has three paragraphs rather than four. Why?

2. This passage contains a process description in paragraph 2. Make a sketch of the process.

3. What is the predominant verb tense used in sentences 6 through 14? Why is this?

4. Underline the instances of passive voice in paragraph 2.

5. In sentence 6 we have "is now being tested." Why is the progressive used here?

6. Underline the adverbs in paragraph 2. How many of them are midposition adverbs?

7. Identify the phrases consisting of *this* + summary word in the text. Where do they occur in the second paragraph? Does this placement tell us anything?

8. How is the solution introduced?

9. As you may have noticed, the passage is a bit short on details. Put a check next to those details you think would be important to help the writer create a text that displays expertise and familiarity with the topic.

___ the dimensions of the nets
___ the trough material
___ the storage tank materials and dimensions
___ the brand name of the netting
___ where the netting can be purchased
___ the duration of the fog season
___ the method of connecting the mesh to the posts

___ a description of the post material

___ the time of day the fog comes in

___ the time needed to construct the system

10. This passage could be extended to provide information on maintenance of the fog collection system. This would include a discussion of the importance of regular inspection, cleaning, and repair of the nets, troughs, and tanks. Where would you place this information?

11. Where might you add the following information about cost?

The cost of operating and maintaining the system, which averages nearly $12,000 annually, is quite low compared to other means of providing water to the village.

✤ Language Focus: Verbs and Agents in the Solution

In most technical solutions, it is necessary to describe a process or a method. In the previous passage, the explanation of how the water is collected provides this necessary information. In addition, when you are describing the method you used to carry out some research, you will essentially be writing a process description. We have looked at adverbs in process descriptions; it is now time to turn to verbs.

Passive Voice

The passive voice often plays an important role in process descriptions. We can see why in the following simple illustration. Look at these brief notes about how to prepare a flu vaccine.

Flu virus strains—three most common identified

Three strains—grown separately and harvested

Harvested virus—purified and inactivated

Inactivated virus strains—blended with a carrier fluid and dispensed into vials

We could turn these notes into a set of instructions to be followed in the lab.

Identify the three most common strains of flu virus.

Grow each of the strains separately and harvest.

Purify the harvested virus.

Inactivate the purified virus.

Blend the inactivated virus strains together with a carrier fluid and dispense into vials.

These activities are listed so that somebody could perhaps complete the task of preparing a flu vaccine. Imperative forms are therefore used to indicate these necessary steps. The imperatives form a set of instructions.

However, if we are interested not in providing guidance for actually doing a particular task but in explaining *how something is done*—as in a process—we would more likely write:

First, the three most common strains of flu virus are identified. These strains are then separately grown and harvested. The harvested virus is purified and inactivated. Finally, the inactive virus strains are blended together with a carrier fluid and dispensed into vials.

Notice that each sentence now refers to a particular stage in the process:

the identification stage,

the preparation stage, and

the dispensing stage.

Now, what would be the effect if the process were described using the active? As you can see from the following passage, the focus on the stages is lost and the emphasis shifts to the agent (the person doing the steps, i.e., the technician). Since the same person is involved, the process itself is backgrounded.

The technician identifies the virus strains in the lab. The technician separately grows and harvests the virus. The technician purifies and inactivates the virus. The technician blends the inactive virus strains together with a carrier fluid and dispenses them into vials.

Of course, there may be some occasions when *different* agents are an important part of *different* steps in the process.

> Technician A identifies the virus strains in the lab. Technician B separately grows and harvests the virus. Technician C purifies and inactivates the virus. Technician D blends the inactive virus strains together with a carrier fluid and dispenses the mixture into vials.

But this now looks more like a job specification or duty roster than a process description. If information about the *agent* is important—which is uncommon—it would be better to describe the process in the following way.

> First, the three most common strains of flu virus are identified by technician A. These strains are then separately grown and harvested by technician B. The harvested virus is purified and inactivated by technician C. Finally, the inactive virus strains are blended together with a carrier fluid and dispensed into vials by technician D.

According to research studies, using *by* + a *human agent* is fairly uncommon in formal academic writing, except when describing the history of the field, as in the following examples.

> The theory of transformational grammar was first developed *by Noam Chomsky.*

> The Bayesian method has been used *by statisticians* for many years to aid decision making on the basis of limited information.

In fact, we are more likely to find *by* + *process* or *by* + a *nonhuman agent.*

> The chances of finding oil are often estimated *by seismic survey.*

> This enzyme is used *by the cancer cells* to replicate.

> The increased mobility provided *by this new joint* allows wearers of the finger prosthesis to hold a cup, to pick up a piece of paper, and in some cases to write again.

Do the three *by*-phrases in this next short passage introduce a process or a nonhuman agent?

> The rate at which heat will be lost *by conduction* from the body will be determined *by the magnitude of the temperature gradient*—the steeper the gradient, the greater the heat loss—and the rapidity with which the cooler air in contact with the skin is replaced *by colder air.*

The *by + process* statements just given provide no details. Such *by*-phrases are typical in published journal articles, especially in the Methods section (see Unit Seven) of articles in the sciences. However, sometimes further information is useful. For instance, when you are writing a paper for a class, it might be to your advantage to make the *by*-phrases more informative.

TASK FIVE

Expand three of the following statements, making them more informative by replacing the noun phrase with one or more verb phrases. Here is an example.

Teaching can be improved by in-service training. →

Teaching can be improved by asking teachers to attend a range of short courses throughout much of their careers.

1. Bacteria found in meat can be killed by radiation.

2. Possible harmful effects of drugs can be reduced by tests.

3. One class of rocks is formed by sedimentation.

4. Information on political preferences can be obtained by polling.

5. Cultures are partly preserved by ceremony and ritual.

6. Sequences of events at archaeological sites can be established by stratification.

7. Changes in land use can be detected by remote sensing.

8. The spread of infectious diseases can be controlled by vaccinations.

Flow of Ideas in a Process Description

In Unit One we introduced the concept of flow, focusing mainly on sentence connectors and summary words. Good flow of ideas can also be achieved by combining or linking verb phrases. In the "Clouds and Fog" passage in Task Two, there were no occasions where two or more passives were linked together in the same sentence. Often, however, this may be desirable, as in our example of the flu vaccine.

> These strains *are* then separately *grown* and *harvested.* The harvested virus *is purified* and *inactivated.* Finally, the inactive virus strains *are blended* together with a carrier fluid and *dispensed* into vials.

Some care needs to be taken when putting verbs together in this way, because this can sometimes lead to an unfortunate ambiguity. How are the following ambiguous, and what can you do about it?

1. The liquid is collected and kept for 24 hours.

2. The sample is collected and stored in a sterile container.

3. In consumer research, individuals are selected and interviewed by telephone.

TASK SIX

Consider the following passages discussing treatment for water birds after an oil spill. Underline the parts in passage B that differ from passage A, including the linked passives. Why does B have better "flow" than A?

A. ❶ Once a bird has been brought to a rehabilitation center, basic procedures are followed. ❷ The bird is sedated, if necessary. ❸ The bird is examined to detect broken bones, cuts, or other injuries. ❹ Oil is flushed from its eyes and intestines. ❺ Heavily oiled birds are then wiped with absorbent cloths to remove patches of oil. ❻ Stomach-coating medicines may be administered orally to prevent additional absorption of oil inside the bird's stomach.

❼ The bird is warmed. ❽ It is placed in a quiet area. ❾ Curtains are hung around the area to limit the bird's contact with people.

B. ❶ Once a bird has been brought to a rehabilitation center, basic procedures are followed. ❷ First, the bird is sedated, if necessary, and examined to detect broken bones, cuts, or other injuries. ❸ Next, oil is flushed from its eyes and intestines. ❹ Heavily oiled birds are then wiped with absorbent cloths to remove patches of oil. ❺ Stomach-coating medicines may be administered orally to prevent additional absorption of oil inside the bird's stomach. ❻ The bird is then warmed and placed in a quiet area. ❼ Finally, curtains are often hung around the area to limit the bird's contact with people. (EPA, http://www.epa.gov/oilspill/rescue.htm)

In addition to the linked passives, good flow is also achieved in passage B through the use of several time adverbials that help establish the sequence of events—*once, first, next, then,* and *finally.* (See also the time adverbials in the passage in Task Three.)

Participles

You may also have noticed, through our flu virus examples, that flow can be maintained by taking the *-ed* participle in the passive construction and using it as an adjective.

First, the three most common strains of flu virus are identified. These strains are then separately grown and *harvested*. The *harvested* virus is purified and *inactivated*. Finally, the now *inactivated* virus strains are blended together with a carrier fluid and dispensed into vials.

By changing *harvest* and *inactivate* into their adjectival forms, the writer establishes a strong connection between the sentences and indicates a newly acquired characteristic of the virus. As a result of the steps in the process, the virus can be described as *harvested, inactivated,* or even *purified.*

TASK SEVEN

Can you improve the flow of ideas for the following process descriptions by adding a time adverbial, linking passives, or using an -*ed* participle? There may be several possibilities. To help you, we have stated the process being partially described.

Example

Phytoremediation—using plants to remove metal from the soil

The plants are selected. The plants are planted at a particular site based on the type of metals present and other site conditions. The plants are allowed to grow for some time. The plants are harvested. They are either incinerated or composted to recycle the metals. →

The plants *are selected* and *planted* at a particular site based on the type of metals present and other site conditions. *After* the plants have been allowed to grow for some time, *they are harvested* and either incinerated or composted to recycle the metals.

1. Oil spill cleanup

   The oil is skimmed from the surface using a boom. The oil is pumped into a tank for recycling.

2. Wine making

   The grapes are harvested. The grapes are crushed to release the pulp and seeds. The grapes are fermented for three weeks.

3. Tempering glass

   The glass is cut to size. It is inspected to determine if it has any imperfections. The glass is heated to over 600°C. The glass is cooled in a step known as quenching.

4. Coronary bypass surgery

A vessel is taken from the leg. The vessel is grafted to the aorta and the coronary artery beyond the narrowed area. The vessel allows blood to flow to the heart muscle.

5. Geyser eruption

Water from rain or melted snow percolates into the ground through cracks. The water is heated by the underlying rocks to temperatures well above the boiling point. The water does not boil. It becomes superheated. It also becomes pressurized. The water bursts out of the ground in an explosive steam eruption.

Active Voice in Process Descriptions

So far we have emphasized the use of the passive voice in process descriptions. Part of the reason for this is that we have until now concentrated on processes that involve human action. There are, however, many natural processes that take place outside of direct human intervention. In such cases, active voice is often used, or there may be a mix between active and passive, depending on the process.

TASK EIGHT

Read through this problem-solution text and then discuss the questions that follow. Note the frequent use of active voice in the process.

❶ Coral reef ecosystems are well known for their beauty and diversity. ❷ Found throughout tropical and subtropical regions of the world, they are often thought to be the marine equivalent of terrestrial rainforests. ❸ During the last several decades, however, coral reefs have been undergoing alarming changes as a result of environmental stresses, the most serious of which is whitening or bleaching. ❹ Although the mechanism of bleaching is not fully understood, this phenomenon is linked to the breakdown of the symbiotic relationship between the coral and an algae known as zooxanthellae. ❺ The algae, which give the coral its color, live inside the coral and perform photosynthesis, sharing the food that they produce. ❻ When the coral is stressed as a result of increases in temperature or the amount of light, the zooxanthellae carry out too much photosynthesis and in response the coral expels the algae. ❼ The loss of the algae exposes the white calcium carbonate skeletons, thus leaving the coral unable to grow or reproduce. ❽ Coral can survive for brief periods of time without the zooxanthellae, but if the reef environment does not return to normal, the coral dies.

❾ Coral reefs require from 30 to 100 years to recover from bleaching, if they recover at all. ❿ Researchers are now investigating whether this recovery time can be accelerated. ⓫ One approach currently under study involves transplanting healthy coral into a bleached reef. ⓬ However, thus far, the process has seen limited success.

1. Identify the situation, problem, solution, and evaluation. Which of these sections receives the greatest treatment? Why?

2. What linking words and phrases are used to indicate cause and effect?

3. In sentence 10 the author wrote, *are now investigating*. Why was the progressive used?

4. Also in sentence 10 we see a passive construction—*can be accelerated*. Why was this used rather than the active?

5. In sentence 2 the author wrote, *they are often thought to be the marine equivalent of terrestrial rainforests*. How would the meaning change if the author had omitted the phrase in the passive voice (i.e., *they are often thought to be*) and opted for *they are the marine equivalent of*?

If a process description employs verbs that indicate a change of state, such as *expand, rise, cool,* and *form,* active voice will also be used. Here are some examples.

The Sun *rises* in the east and sets in the west.

Most metals *expand* and *contract* with variations in temperature.

The beam *fractures* when the load upon it becomes too great.

Tropical storms *can form* only in areas of high humidity and temperature. First, the warm sea *heats* the air above its surface. The warm, moist air then *rises* above the sea, creating a center of low pressure.

Now notice that scholars often use active verbs of this kind to make generalizations about human society.

When demand *increases,* prices are likely to *rise.*

Can you think of some other examples?

TASK NINE

Researchers have been trying to develop artificial muscles for medical purposes and have recently come up with a way to re-create muscle action using a type of artificial silk. Below is a set of instructions for the preparation of the material, followed by information on the way in which the material simulates actual muscle. Write a problem-solution text that uses the information below as part of the solution. Use your imagination to create a situation and problem that could be solved through the use of an artificial muscle. Be sure to include all the required parts of a problem-solution text and to present the process in an appropriate manner, using passive voice and sequential connectors. Show cause-and-effect relationships where appropriate.

1. Cook the Orlon. Orlon is a form of artificial silk.

2. Boil the Orlon until it turns into a liquid rubbery substance.

3. Pour the solution onto Plexiglas to form a thin film.

4. Vacuum away excess water from the film. Allow the film to dry.

5. Cut the dried film into two-centimeter-wide strips. Bake it in a 90° oven. The material is ready for use after it has been baked.

6. Prepared Orlon has a structure similar to that of human muscle fiber and is naturally negatively charged with electricity.

7. If you apply acid to the material, you introduce a positive charge and you cause the ions to attract. This attraction contracts the material like a muscle.

8. If you apply a base material, you introduce a negative charge, the ions repel, and the muscle expands.

Causes and Effects

In order to help your reader understand a problem and/or a solution, you may need to use expressions to highlight causes and effects. For example, the last example sentence given (*When demand increases, prices are likely to rise.*) is a cause-and-effect statement. Such statements can take many forms. Here are a few.

An increase in demand *is likely to cause* a rise in prices.

Increases in demand *usually lead to* price increases.

Demand increases; *as a result,* prices tend to rise.

Increases in price *are often caused by* increases in demand.

In the first three longer texts we examined in this unit, the authors described some causal relationships. Can you identify them here?

1. The databases are those established by the major abstracting and indexing services, such as the ISI indexes and Medline, which are predominantly located in the United States. As a result, these services have tended to preselect papers that *(a)* are written in English and *(b)* originate in the Northern Hemisphere. For these two reasons, it is probable that research in languages other than English is somewhat underrepresented.

2. However, there is also evidence that the dominance of English has been causing a counterreaction.

3. When the cold air from the Pacific Ocean's Humboldt Current mixes with the warm coastal air, a thick, wet fog, called *camanchaca* by the Andes Indians, forms along with clouds.

Alternatively the authors could have written:

1. These services have tended to preselect papers that *(a)* are written in English and *(b)* originate in the Northern Hemisphere, *thus causing* research in languages other than English to be somewhat underrepresented.

2. However, as NNS researchers recognize the increasing domination of English, they are having second thoughts, *thus creating* a counterreaction.

3. The cold air from the Pacific Ocean's Humboldt Current mixes with the warm coastal air, *resulting in* the formation of clouds and a thick, wet fog, called *camanchaca* by the Andes Indians.

Such -*ing* clauses of result can be particularly useful in writing a problem-solution text.

Language Focus: -ing *Clauses of Result*

As an alternative to using sentence connectors such as *therefore* and *as a result*, causal relationships can also be expressed by-*ing* clauses of result.

A. The magma flows into the pores of the rocks; as a result, the rocks rupture. →

The magma flows into the pores of the rocks, *thus causing* them to rupture.

B. A current is sent through the material. As a result, the electrons are polarized. →

A current is sent through the material, *polarizing* the electrons.

Sometimes writers also use a preliminary subordinate clause to set the scene for the process.

C. When the ABS controller senses that a wheel is about to lock up, it automatically changes the pressure in the brake lines of the car. As a result, maximum brake performance is achieved.

When the ABS controller senses that a wheel is about to lock up, it automatically changes the pressure in the car's brake lines to prevent the lockup, *(thus) resulting* in maximum brake performance.

Subordinate clause (optional)	When the ABS controller senses that a wheel is about to lock up,
Main clause	it automatically changes the pressure in the brake lines of the car to prevent the lockup,
(thus/thereby) -ing *clause*	(thus) resulting in maximum brake performance.

This structure is particularly useful in problem-solution texts, because it can be used to express the next step in the process, a resulting problem, or a resulting solution. Here is a simple example.

Process: Prices rise, thus leading to a drop in demand.

Problem: Prices rise, thus increasing the chance of hyperinflation.

Solution: Prices rise, thus increasing earnings that can then be reinvested in the enterprise.

TASK TEN

Read the following sentences containing *-ing* clauses of result. Would you expect to find these sentences in the problem, process, or solution part of a text? Discuss your decision with a partner. There is certainly room for disagreement on some of them.

1. The databases tend to preselect papers published in English, thus underrepresenting research published in other languages.

   _____

2. The warm moist air rises above the surface of the sea, creating an area of low pressure.

   _____

3. The cold air from the Pacific Ocean mixes with the warm coastal air, forming fog and clouds.

   _____

4. The system can collect as much as 2,500 gallons per day, thus providing a cheap and environmentally friendly supply for a small community.

   _____

5. The laser light forms an EM field, thereby slowing the vibration of the atoms.

   _____

6. When manufacturing output drops, demand for business loans falls, leaving the banks with a strong lending capacity.

   _____

7. In fact, sustainable development would require industry to reduce both pollution and resource use, thus creating excellent opportunities for stimulating technical innovation.

   _____

8. The two predictor variables together (family demands and caregiving demands) explained 62% of the variance in mothers' well-being, thus supporting the need for an appropriate intervention.

   _____

TASK ELEVEN

Combine the ideas presented in each of the following statements, using an *-ing* clause of result. Work together in groups.

1. Sustainable development would require industry to reduce pollution output and resource use; as a result, technical innovation will be stimulated.

2. The researcher supposedly manipulated the data. As a result, an apparent effect was created where none existed.

3. The computer viruses infect executable files; as a consequence, the host computer is damaged when the executable is run.

4. The plants extract the nickel and zinc; hence, the soil is left uncontaminated.

5. Rainfall levels plummeted. A slow, but steady, loss of grasses occurred. As a result, the region was transformed into a desert.

6. Countries sign treaties on the use of "free resources" such as air and ocean fish. Serious ownership questions arise; therefore, it is difficult to enforce any agreement.

TASK TWELVE

Read through the following text, which has been broken into three parts. Choose the item that best completes the sentences. Each of the choices is grammatically correct; however, not all will work equally well. Before making your choices, consider the flow of the *entire* passage, not just the individual items.

Since the onset of air travel in the early 1900s aircraft collisions with birds and other wildlife have been an ongoing threat to human safety. These collisions, known as wildlife strikes, have destroyed nearly 400 aircraft _____

a. ; as a result, 420 have been killed.

b. , resulting in 420 deaths.

c. . These collisions have resulted in 420 deaths.

Over the last 40 years the number of wildlife strikes has been increasing. In the last decade alone 34,370 strikes were reported, which represents a threefold increase over the period from 1980 to 1990. Several factors have contributed to this growing threat. First, most airlines are replacing older 3- or 4-engined aircraft with quieter, more efficient aircraft with two engines _____

a. ; thus, aircraft have less engine redundancy and a greater likelihood of engine failure in a collision with wildlife.

b. , resulting in less engine redundancy and a greater likelihood of engine failure in a collision with wildlife.

c. , which has resulted in less engine redundancy and a greater likelihood of engine failure in a collision with wildlife.

Second, wildlife management programs have contributed to growth in the populations of many species of wildlife that are often involved in strikes. For example, the once-endangered Canadian goose population has grown by over 10% each year for the last 30 years. Canadian geese and other birds, such as gulls, have expanded into urban and suburban areas, including airports. Third, the number of commercial and noncommercial flights has more than doubled over the last two decades _____

a. ; therefore, the parallel increases in wildlife populations and air traffic contribute to a higher probability of a wildlife strike.

b. . This concurrent increase in wildlife populations and air traffic contributes to a higher probability of a wildlife strike.

c. , contributing to a higher probability of a wildlife strike.

There is a close parallel between process descriptions and descriptions of methods in research papers (see Unit Seven). If there is a difference, it is that process descriptions deal with standard procedures, while methods descriptions are typically new modifications or developments of earlier methods.

TASK THIRTEEN

In the article(s) from your field of study that you chose for Unit One, Task Seven, can you identify a methods section? Does it describe a series of procedural steps that the authors followed? If so, is the description mainly written in the active or passive? Is it written in present tense? How is the flow of information maintained? In particular, are there time adverbials at or near the beginning of some sentences?

TASK FOURTEEN

Write a process description of your own choice. If possible, choose a topic that you can later incorporate into a full problem-solution text.

❖ *Language Focus: Indirect Questions*

In one important sense, this unit has been about formulating questions (problems) and evaluating the answers to those questions (evaluations). For example, if we look back at two sentences in the text in Task One, we can see two examples of this.

> ❹ It is not clear, however, whether such high per-centages for English provide an accurate picture of languages chosen for publication by researchers around the world.

> ⓖ Until such time, nonnative speakers of English will remain uncertain about how effective their publications are in their own languages.

You probably noticed that in both cases the writer has opted to use an *indirect* question rather than a *direct* question.

As you know, indirect questions follow the standard word order (the subject followed by the verb). They do not require that the subject and the verb be inverted, as in a direct question. Indirect questions also end with a period rather than a question mark. Here is a simple example.

> *Direct question:*   What time is it?
>
> *Indirect question:*   He asked what time it is/was.

The main difficulty in using indirect questions involves remembering that the *subject and verb should not be inverted* in an indirect question. Both research and experience suggest that *not inverting* is learned relatively late. Presumably, the use of a "question word" may automatically trigger the inversion. As a result, even native speakers may *incorrectly* produce

> It is unclear what will be the price of oil next year.

or

> It is unclear what will the price of oil be next year.

rather than *correctly* produce

It is unclear what the price of oil will be next year.

TASK FIFTEEN

The verb *to be* is missing from the following statements. Insert it in the correct position for each. As you do so, note the typical language of indirect questions.

1. The question remains whether it possible to develop a reliable earthquake warning system.

2. Current studies provide little information on how this policy being implemented in rural areas.

3. We need to know what precautions being taken to prevent the spread of the disease.

4. There is some question as to whether the current crisis can eventually overcome.

5. It has not been determined how these policies likely to affect small businesses.

6. It might also be of interest to investigate to what extent persistence a major factor in graduate student success.

7. Another issue raised by this study is whether and to what extent poverty and climate linked.

8. The process uses the CPU power it needs, depending on what it doing and depending on what other processes running.

9. The research investigated whether time money and found that $V = (\{W[(100-t)/100]\}/C$, where V is the value of an hour, W is a person's hourly wage, t is the tax rate, and C is the local cost of living.

10. It is unclear what the optimal level of government debt.

Indirect questions have a number of functions in academic writing; for example, they can be used in explaining purpose.

A questionnaire was distributed in order to determine whether . . .

However, perhaps their most important use has been illustrated in Task Fifteen. They are often used to "problematize" issues, cases, phenomena, statements, and so on. For this reason, they are particularly common in problem-solution texts, first as one way of introducing the problem, and second as one way of offering a (critical) evaluation of the solution. In Task Sixteen you will have an opportunity to use indirect questions.

Although we have stressed indirect questions as a way of introducing or discussing problems, we do not want to imply that this is the only way. In some cases, direct questions may be possible.

> However, is the data reliable?

Keep in mind, however, that you should limit your use of these in academic writing, as we stated in Unit One.

Another common way to introduce a problem is to use an adversative sentence connector, such as *however* or *nevertheless* (see p. 27). Here are some examples. Notice how each of these is somewhat negative.

> However, this system/process/idea has its problems.
>
> Nevertheless, few solutions have been found to . . .
>
> Despite this, little progress has been made in . . .
>
> Nevertheless, the problem remains as to how . . .
>
> However, there remains the issue of reliability.
>
> Even so, this model has some serious limitations.
>
> Even so, researchers still have to find a way to . . .

TASK SIXTEEN

One of us (John) interviewed a student writing up her first research paper for her master's in social work. Mei-Lan said she was interested in finding out more about the Chinese elderly living in the United States. She said that she had chosen this topic because many people believed that Chinese communities traditionally had always looked after their elderly and, further, that such old people would not easily accept help from outsiders. She wondered whether this was still true in the United States. She also observed that the available research had mainly been conducted in the larger Chinese communities in the major cities on the east and west coasts. She therefore decided to study small communities in the Midwest. John then asked her about her methods.

JS: How did you find your subjects?

ML: I used friends and friends of friends in the local Chinese community to introduce me.

JS: How did you collect your data?

ML: I used face-to-face interviews. I wanted one-on-one situations since I was afraid that if family members had been there, my interviewees might not have been truthful about their feelings and experiences.

JS: Did you have to get permission from the review board?

ML: Yes, because I was dealing with human subjects.

JS: Did you have any problems with this?

ML: No, not at all. Interview methods are usually quickly approved.

JS: How many people did you interview?

ML: I only managed to interview about ten. Not much time, and not all of my contacts worked out. I also got some refusals. So this was just a small-scale pilot study. There were not enough subjects for any statistical analysis.

JS: How long did the interviews last, and did you use a fixed list of questions?

ML: About an hour. I had some questions but did not always use them all. I guess my data could be said to be based on what sociologists call "semi-structured" interviews.

JS: Did you use English?

ML: The interviewees used whatever language they were most comfortable with—Mandarin, Taiwanese, or English. I think this was a strong point in my method.

Now write up Mei-Lan's investigative procedure. Maintain a formal style. You may decide not to include all the information contained in the preceding conversation or not to handle it in the order given.

Introducing the Solution

Looking back at the texts we have examined, we see the following solutions introduced.

One interesting solution to this problem is now being tested in the village of Chungungo, a village of 300.

One approach currently under study involves transplanting healthy coral into a bleached reef.

Here are some additional skeletal sentences based on sentences we found in published articles.

Solutions to this problem are now widely discussed. One remedy is to . . .

One method to address this difficulty is to . . .

There are two possible ways of handling this problem. The first . . . The second . . .

Several options are available to address this obstacle. However, the best one seems to be . . .

A radically different design/model is needed to overcome this limitation.

Recently, researchers have made significant progress in overcoming this difficulty by . . .

TASK SEVENTEEN

Write your own problem-solution text that includes both a process description and a definition, or write a *review* of the current state of knowledge in your field, raising a question about the current state of knowledge and offering a possible or part answer. Refer to the "Role of English" texts on pages 84 and 87 for some guidance.

Unit Four

Data Commentary

In many writing assignments, there comes a place where graduate students need to discuss data. In many disciplines the data is displayed in a table, graph, figure, or some other kind of nonverbal illustration. The data may come from a source or it may be the outcome of your own work, that is, your *results*. (For more on writing up your results, see Unit Seven.) This data may be incorporated in the main text or in some cases attached as an appendix. We have called these writing subtasks *data commentaries*.

Strength of Claim

Like many other aspects of graduate student writing, data commentaries are exercises in positioning yourself. There are, as a result, both dangers and opportunities. One danger is to simply repeat in words what the data has expressed in nonverbal form—in other words, to offer description rather than commentary. An opposite danger is to read too much into the data and draw unjustified conclusions. The art of the matter is to find the right strength of claim for the data and then order your statements in some appropriate way (such as from the more significant to the less significant). In most cases, this means moving in a general-specific direction (see Unit Two).

TASK ONE

Working with a partner, put the following sentence variations in order from 1 (strongest claim) to 6 (weakest claim). Some disagreement is reasonable. Can you think of other verbs or verb phrases that could complete the sentence? How would you evaluate the strength of claim for your alternatives?

Unsound policies of the International Monetary Fund (IMF) _____ the financial crisis.

_____ a. contributed to

_____ b. caused

_____ c. may have contributed to

_____ d. were probably a major cause of

_____ e. were one of the causes of

_____ f. might have been a small factor in

As you can see, each of the options "fits" in that each makes sense; however, only one may actually be the "right" choice for a particular context.

It is not easy to predict precisely what you might need to do in a data commentary, but here are some of the more common purposes.

- Highlight the results.

- Assess standard theory, common beliefs, or general practice in light of the given data.

- Compare and evaluate different data sets.

- Assess the reliability of the data in terms of the methodology that produced it.

- Discuss the implications of the data.

Typically, of course, a data commentary will include at least three of these elements.

TASK TWO

Look over Table 5, read the data commentary that follows, and then answer the questions.

Table 5   Source of Computer Virus Infections

Source of Virus	Percentage
E-mail attachments	87%
Disks from home	4%
Disks (other)	2%
Unknown	2%
Download (from internal or external sources)	2%
Distribution CD	1%
Disk (sales demo)	< 1%
Automated software distribution	< 1%
Disk (shrink-wrapped)	< 1%
Disk (from LAN manager)	< 1%
Malicious person	< 1%
Browsing WWW	0%
Disk (from repair person)	0%
Total survey respondents	299

Source: Data from ICSA Labs Computer Virus Prevalence Study.
Note: Because respondents to the survey may have indicated more than one means of infection, the totals exceed 100%.

❶ A computer virus is a program that is specifically and maliciously designed to attack a computer system, destroying data. ❷ As businesses have become increasingly dependent on computers, e-mail, and the Internet, concern over the potential destructiveness of such viruses has also grown. ❸ Table 5 shows the most common sources of infection for U.S. businesses. ❹ As can be seen, in a great majority of cases, the entry point of the virus infection can be detected, with e-mail attachments being responsible for nearly 9 out of 10 viruses. ❺ This very high percentage is increasingly alarming, especially since with a certain amount of caution such infections are largely preventable. ❻ In consequence, e-mail users should be wary of all attachments, even those from a trusted colleague or a known sender. ❼ In addition, all computers used for e-mail need to have a current version of a good antivirus program whose virus definitions are updated regularly. ❽ While it may be possible to lessen the likelihood of downloading an infected file, businesses are still vulnerable to computer virus problems because of human error and the threat of new, quickly spreading viruses that cannot be identified by antivirus software.

1. Where does the data commentary actually start?

2. What are the purposes of sentences 1 and 2?

3. Do you consider this commentary a problem-solution text?

4. What are some of the features of this text that make it an example of written academic English? Look back to pages 18–24 if you need some help with this question.

5. Which sentence contains the author's key point?

6. After Task One we listed five common purposes for data commentaries. In which category (or categories) does this one fall?

7. The author has chosen to comment only on e-mail attachments. Why? Do you think this is enough? If not, what else should be discussed?

8. E-mail attachments constitute 87% of the total. In sentence 4, this is expressed as "nearly 9 out of 10." What do you think about this and about the following alternatives?

   a. about 90%

   b. just under 90%

   c. as much as 87% of all

   d. nearly all

Structure of Data Commentary

Data commentaries usually have the following elements in the following order.

1. Location elements and/or summary statements

2. Highlighting statements

3. Discussions of implications, problems, exceptions, recommendations, etc.

Here is the data commentary from Task Two again, with these elements marked.

Location +   Linking *as*-clause
indicative summary   and highlight

❸ Table 5 shows the most common sources of infection for U.S. businesses. ❹ As can be seen, in a great majority of cases, the entry point of the virus infection can be detected, with e-mail attachments being responsible for nearly 9 out of 10 viruses. ❺ This very high percentage is increasingly alarming, especially since with a certain amount of caution such infections are largely preventable. ❻ In conseqence, e-mail users should be wary of all attachments, even those from a trusted colleague. ❼ In addition, all computers used for e-mail need to have a current version of a good antivirus program whose virus definitions are updated regularly. ❽ While it may be possible to lessen the likelihood of downloading an infected file, businesses are still vulnerable to computer virus problems because of human error and the threat of new, quickly spreading viruses that cannot be identified by antivirus software.

Implications

TASK THREE

Table 6 provides some additional data on the sources of computer virus infections. With your partner, consider what data you might highlight. How can you account for the change in percentages over time?

Table 6   Source of Computer Virus Infections, 1992, 1996–2000

Source of Virus	1992	1996	1997	1998	1999	2000
E-mail attachments	0%	9%	26%	32%	56%	87%
Disks from home	43%	36%	42%	36%	25%	4%
Disks (other)	4%	21%	27%	21%	9%	2%
Unknown	29%	15%	7%	5%	7%	2%
Download (from internal or external sources)	7%	12%	18%	12%	13%	2%
Distribution CD	0%	0%	1%	2%	0%	1%
Disk (sales demo)	6%	11%	8%	4%	2%	<1%
Automated software distribution	0%	0%	2%	1%	0%	<1%
Disk (shrink-wrapped)	3%	2%	4%	2%	0%	<1%
Disk (from LAN manager)	1%	1%	3%	1%	0%	<1%
Disk from Malicious person	1%	0%	1%	1%	0%	<1%
Browsing WWW	0%	0%	5%	2%	3%	0%
Disk (from repair person)	6%	3%	3%	3%	2%	0%
Total survey respondents						299

Source: Data from 1992 IEEE and ICSA Labs Computer Virus Prevalence Study (2001).

Note: Because respondents to the survey may have indicated more than one means of infection, the totals exceed 100%.

We will now look at location elements and summaries in more detail.

Location Elements and Summaries

Many data commentary sections begin with a sentence containing a location element and a brief summary, as shown in Table 7. Location elements refer readers to important information in a table, chart, graph, or other figure. They are considered to be a form of *metadiscourse*—sentences or phrases that help readers make their way through a text by revealing such things as organization, referring readers to relevant parts of a text, or establishing logical connections. Metadiscourse is a noticeable feature of academic writing, although its value and frequency of use varies from one writing culture to another.

Table 7   Starting a Data Commentary

Location Element	Summary
a. Table 5 shows	the points of entry of computer viruses for U.S. businesses.
b. Table 2 provides	details of the fertilizer used.
c. Figure 2 plots	the two series for the last five years.
d. Figure 4.2 gives	the results of the second experiment.

The passive can also be used, as demonstrated by Table 8.

Table 8   Passives in Starting a Data Commentary

Summary	Location Element
a. The most common modes of computer infection for U.S. businesses	are shown in Table 5.
b. The details of the fertilizer used	are provided in Table 2.
c. The two series for the last five years	are plotted in Figure 2.
d. The results of the second experiment	are given in Figure 4.2.

We bring two points to your attention here. First, note the consistent use of the present tense. This occurs because the author is talking about his or her present paper. Second, in English the active forms are just as appropriate as the passive versions. (However, in a number of languages it may not be natural to say that a graph or other inanimate object *reveals, gives,* or *suggests.*)

Now notice that all the examples provide general summaries of the data. We have been told nothing yet about what the common modes of infection might be, which fertilizers were actually used, or what the results of the second experiment were. Alternatively, the writer could have highlighted a key piece of the data, as in the following.[1]

a. Table 5 shows that home disks are the major source of computer viruses.

b. Table 2 gives the active ingredients in the fertilizer.

c. Figure 4.2 suggests that the experimental results confirm the hypothesis.

---

[1] Notice the use of *that* in examples *a* and *c.* Sentences containing *that*-clauses do not easily go into the passive.

These two ways of writing the location element are similar to a two-way classification often used to categorize journal article abstracts. *Indicative* abstracts merely indicate what kind of research has been done; *informative* abstracts additionally give the main results. The parallel, we believe, is close, and therefore we can describe location elements as either indicative or informative.

❖ Language Focus: Verbs in Indicative and Informative Summaries

There are about a dozen verbs commonly used to make reference to nonverbal material. Some can be used with both types of summary statement. *Show* is one such verb.

> Table 5 *shows* the most common sources of infection. (indicative, general summary)

> Table 5 *shows that* e-mail attachments are the most common source of infection. (informative, highlight of a specific aspect of the data)

Notice that the summary after the *that*-clause is a full sentence.

Some verbs can be used with only one type of summary statement. *Provide,* for example, can only be used in an indicative summary and cannot be used with a *that*-clause. (The ☻ here indicates incorrect usage.)

> Table 5 *provides* demographic information for the study participants.

> *not*

> ☻ Table 5 *provides that* most study participants were over age 45.

TASK FOUR

Complete Table 9. Decide whether the verb can be used for an indicative (general) summary, an informative summary (highlighting a specific aspect of the data), or both. Use the three sentences following the table to help you make your decision. Mark each box in the table with a *Y* for *Yes* if the usage is possible and an *N* for *No* if impossible. The first two have already been done.

Table 9   Indicative and Informative Verbs

	Indicative	Informative
show	Y	Y
provide	Y	N
give		
present		
summarize		
illustrate		
reveal		
display		
demonstrate		
indicate		
suggest		

Table 1 _____ the frequency distribution of virus encounters.

Table 1 _____ that 99% of all companies had at least one virus encounter during the survey period.

Table 1 _____ that computer virus encounters are a major problem for businesses.

We took a look at Ken Hyland's corpus of 80,000 words from 80 research articles in biology, physics, electrical engineering, mechanical engineering, marketing, applied linguistics, sociology, and philosophy to determine which verbs are most frequently used in full sentences to refer to figures and tables (Hyland 2000). Table 10 shows the results of our analysis. All of the verbs in the table were in the present tense.

Table 10   Active Verbs Following Reference to a Visual

	Reference to Figure	Reference to Table	Total
shows	31	15	46
presents	6	7	13
illustrates	7	3	10
summarizes	2	4	6
demonstrates	2	3	5
contains	0	5	5
provides	0	3	3
depicts	2	0	2
lists	0	2	2
reports	0	2	2
Total			94

We then looked at verbs in the passive voice in references to figures and tables. The results are given in Table 11.

TABLE 11   Passive Verbs in References to a Visual

	Reference to Figure	Reference to Table	Total
shown in	21	23	44
illustrated in	29	5	34
presented in	2	10	12
given in	2	4	6
listed in	0	6	6
seen in	3	1	4
provided in	1	3	4
summarized in	1	3	4
seen from	3	0	3
Total			117

TASK FIVE

Take a look at an article, preferably in your field of study, and underline all of the verbs used in full sentences that refer to tables, figures, or illustrations. How do the results in our tables compare to verb use in references to figures or tables in your field?

❖ Language Focus: Linking as-Clauses

So far, we have used sentences in which the reference to nonverbal data is either the subject or the agent in the main clause. However, a more common structure for introducing informative statements is the linking *as*-clause. Here are three examples.

> As shown in Fig. 1 and Fig. 2, the companies used in this survey varied significantly in geographical location, size, and method of operation.

> As can be seen in Table 5, the overall rate of recall, while low, also showed considerable variation.

> Shallow junction GM APDs, peripheral area test structures, and gate-controlled diodes, as shown in Figs. 1(a), 1(b), and 1(c), were manufactured in p-type epitaxially grown bulk silicon using a conventional 1.5 μm CMOS process reported previously.

These linking clauses (where *as* does not equal *since* or *because*) are exceptional in English grammar. In the passive, these linking clauses have no subjects. Compare the following sentences.

> a. As it has been proved, the theory may have practical importance.

> b. As has been proved, the theory may have practical importance.

In sentence *a* there is a causal relationship between the *as*-clause and the main clause. Because the theory has been proved, it may have practical importance. In sentence *b* the *as*-clause serves to suggest that the practical importance of the theory (not just the theory) has been established. Although you may find examples that run contrary to this advice, remember, then, *not* to use subjects in passive linking *as*-clauses.

Finally, using prepositions with this type of linking statement can be tricky. Here are some of the main standard uses.

in   As shown *in* Table 1 . . .

by   As predicted *by* the model . . .

on   As described *on* the previous page . . .

TASK SIX

Fill in the blank with an appropriate preposition.

1. As can be seen _____ Figure 4, earnings have decreased.

2. As revealed _____ Figure 2, the lightweight materials outperformed traditional metals.

3. As described _____ the previous section, there are two common types of abstracts.

4. As defined _____ section 1, fraud is a form of intentional deception resulting in injury.

5. As described _____ the previous unit, passives are common in process descriptions.

6. As can be seen _____ a comparison of the two tables, household income is a more reliable predictor than level of education.

7. As has been demonstrated previously _____ materials _____ this type, small cracks pose a serious problem.

8. As has been demonstrated _____ many experiments, these materials have several advantages.

9. As shown _____ the line of best fit, there is no clear statistical relationship between fiscal costs and crisis length.

10. As explained _____ the above discussion, international one-year migrants were excluded from the sample.

TASK SEVEN

The following data commentary, which is based on Dr. Akiko Okamura's research on how Japanese researchers learn to write in English in their chosen field, is missing references to the nonverbal data given in Table 12. Expand the commentary by first starting with a summary statement and then adding a suitable linking *as*-clause. Review the material presented up to this point before you begin.

Table 12   Strategies Used by Japanese Scientists When Writing in English

Writing Strategy	Percentage
Think mainly in Japanese but write in English	61%
Think in Japanese and English but write in English	16%
Think in English and write in English	23%

Slightly more than three-fourths of the scientists surveyed adopted writing strategies that involved the use of their first language. Moreover, less than a quarter appear capable of writing directly in English. Overall, the figures would appear to suggest that most Japanese scientists have difficulties and frustrations when preparing papers for English-medium journals.

Highlighting Statements

The central sections of data commentaries consist of highlighting statements. Highlighting statements are generalizations that you can draw from the details of the data display. We have already seen some examples in the text that accompanies Task Two. Highlighting statements need good judgment. They are an opportunity to show your intelligence. In particular, they are an opportunity for you to demonstrate

- that you can spot trends or regularities in the data,

- that you can separate more important findings from less important ones, and

- that you can make claims of appropriate strength.

So, do *not*

- simply repeat all the details in words,

- attempt to cover all the information, or

- claim more than is reasonable or defensible.

Language Focus: Qualifications and Strength of Claim

We said that highlighting statements need good judgment. They also need good presentation of judgment. Thus, they have two requirements. One is the need to be cautious—and sometimes critical—about the data. As Skelton (1988) neatly observed, "It is important for students to learn to be confidently uncertain." The other requirement is to have the linguistic resources to express this caution. In this section, therefore, we deal with ways of qualifying or moderating a claim.

TASK EIGHT

Read through the following texts. Underline the words or phrases that seem to moderate, soften, or qualify the claims.

A. According to our results, impulsive buying is on the rise. Further, our survey data suggest that buying goods to improve one's self-image is probably a motivation that plays some role in most buying behavior, but it might be particularly important when people make unplanned or "spur of the moment" purchases. These unplanned purchases may well be regretted later and can lead to financial difficulty. (Dittmar and Drury 2000)

B. Currently, satellite launches cost approximately $10,000 for each pound lifted into space. However, this may soon change as a result of microelectromechanical systems (MEMS) devices, which could greatly reduce the size, weight, power requirements, complexity, and, eventually, the costs of space systems. For example, because of MEMs miniaturization it may be possible to construct a 1kg satellite that is highly resistant to radiation and vibration and therefore more reliable than a traditional satellite. Preliminary tests of MEMS subjected to accelerations over 20,000 times gravitational acceleration have shown promising results. (Cass 2001)

Now let's take a look at some specific ways of moderating or qualifying a claim.

Probability

There are many ways of expressing probability in written academic English. One simple way is to use a modal auxiliary, as you saw in Task One. Notice how the claim progressively weakens in these three sentences.

> Sleeping 7–9 hours each day *will* result in better academic performance.

> Sleeping 7–9 hours each day *may* result in better academic performance.

> Sleeping 7–9 hours each day *might/could* result in better academic performance.

In these further examples, the phrases weaken in strength.

Stronger It is certain that . . .
It is almost certain that . . .
It is very probable/highly likely that . . .
It is probable/likely that . . .
It is possible that . . .
It is unlikely that . . .
Weaker It is very/highly unlikely that . . .

sleeping 7–9 hours each day will result in better academic performance.

Stronger There is a definite possibility that . . .
There is a strong possibility that . . .
There is a good possibility that . . .
There is a slight possibility that . . .
Weaker There is little possibility that . . .

sleeping 7–9 hours each day will result in better academic performance.

Distance

Distance is another way of removing yourself from a strong—and possibly unjustified—claim. Compare the following.

Strong claim: The factory *has benefited from* the recent technology upgrade.

The factory *seems to have benefited from* the recent technology upgrade.

The factory *appears to have benefited from* the recent technology upgrade.

It seems that the factory has benefited from the recent technology upgrade.

It has been said that the factory *seems to have benefited from* the recent technology upgrade.

An alternative strategy is to distance yourself from the data by showing in some way that it is "soft." Here are a few examples.

Based on the limited data available,

In the view of some experts,

According to this preliminary study,

Based on an informal survey of nine department managers,

different employees react to the same situations differently.

Generalization

One classic verb for qualifying (or defending) a generalization is the verb *tend*.

Children living in poverty have a history of health problems.

Children living in poverty *tend to* have a history of health problems.

Another way of to defending a generalization is to qualify the subject.

Many children living in poverty have a history of health problems.

A majority of children living in poverty have a history of health problems.

In most parts of the world children living in poverty have a history of health problems.

A third alternative is to add exceptions.

With the exception of	a small number of countries such as Japan, Sweden, and Thailand, student loan schemes are almost exclusively reserved for higher education.
Apart from	
Except for	

Weaker Verbs

Finally, claims can be reduced in strength by choosing a weaker verb. At the beginning of this unit, we compared the following.

Unsound policies of the IMF *led to* the financial crisis. (stronger)

Unsound policies of the IMF *contributed to* the financial crisis. (weaker)

TASK NINE

Underline the verb making the *weaker* claim.

1. The results indicate/establish that there is a link between smoking and lung cancer.

2. Table 9 suggests/shows that the number of articles written and published by nonnative speakers will continue to increase.

3. The latest series of studies question/challenge the conclusions of much previous research.

4. The results given in Figure 4 validate/support the second hypothesis.

5. The quantities displayed in the table have been assumed/shown to be about 98% accurate.

6. The test results create/suggest a basis for product modification.

7. Changes in ambient temperature may have influenced/distorted the test results.

8. In their earlier work, they failed/neglected to take ambient temperature into account.

9. As shown in Table 3, the new tax laws have encouraged/ stimulated industrial investment.

10. Figure 12 depicts/clarifies the relationship between these two systems.

Combined Qualifications

Often, of course, several types of qualification are combined in order to construct a defensible highlighting statement. Here is an example. We start with a big claim.

> The use of seat belts prevents physical injuries in car accidents.

Now see what happens when the following qualifications are added.

prevents → reduces	(weaker verb)
reduces → may reduce	(adding probability)
+ in some circumstances	(weakening the generalization)
+ certain types of injury	(weakening the generalization)
+ according to simulation studies	(adding distance)

So we now have:

> According to simulation studies, in some circumstances the use of seat belts may reduce certain types of physical injuries in car accidents.

This sentence is a nice example of the writer being "confidently uncertain." But don't overdo it. Excessive qualification may result in your saying almost nothing, as in the following example from a journal in anthropology.

> It could be concluded that some evidence seems to suggest that at least certain villagers might not have traded their pottery with others outside the community.

TASK TEN

Now, see what you can do with any four of the following. Make the sentences academically respectable and defensible.

1. Attractive people have more favorable personal attributes than unattractive people.

2. Economic sanctions are ineffective.

3. Alcohol causes people to become violent.

4. Passive smoking causes cancer.

5. Recycling is the best solution to the waste disposal problem.

6. Physical exercise prevents depression.

7. Deep tunnels are safer and less vulnerable to earthquake shaking than are shallow tunnels.

8. Private schools provide a better education than do public schools.

Organization

Highlighting statements are usually ordered from general to specific. In other words, major claims are followed by minor claims. We saw this pattern, for example, in the short commentary on the Japanese scientists in Task Seven.

However, decisions about organization become more complex with comparative data. Consider the following case. You are taking a graduate course in the social sciences. You have been studying differences in parental behavior with regard to their adolescent children. Your instructor suggests that, contrary to popular belief, American parents may be stricter with their teenage sons than they are with their daughters. You are given Table 13, which is based on a survey conducted among suburban families in a midsize midwestern U.S. city, and asked to prepare for the next class a short commentary on the main findings.

TASK ELEVEN

Three students wrote the following incomplete data commentaries on Table 13. They include only the location statements and the highlighting sections. What are the differences among the three? Which do you think makes the best highlighting statement? Why?

Table 13   Percentage of Adolescents Reporting the Following Parental Restrictions on Their Lives (N = 200)‡

	Girls	Boys
Limitations on		
Opportunities to go out at night[1]	56%	35%
Use of the family car[2]	15%	40%
Time of expected return[3]	30%	61%
Interference in		
Choice of friends[4]	19%	23%
Future education choices[5]	18%	52%
Spending of self-earned money[6]	12%	27%

Note: Data is not authentic
Key [1] E.g., may be allowed to go out only two nights a week.
     [2] E.g., may be allowed to use the car only on special occasions.
     [3] Curfew is imposed; e.g., has to be back by 11 P.M.
     [4] E.g., girls are dissuaded from going out with older boys.
     [5] E.g., persuaded to study for a professional degree in college.
     [6] E.g., required to save 50% of earnings.

Student A

Table 13 shows the percentage of adolescents reporting parental restrictions on their lives. As can be seen, about one-fourth of female adolescents reported parental restrictions on average across the six categories. Restrictions were most common on going out at night (56%) and fewest on expenditure of self-earned money (12%). In contrast, 40% of the males reported restrictions on average across the six categories. Restrictions were most frequent for curfews (61%) and fewest for choice of friends.

Student B

Table 13 shows the percentage of adolescents reporting parental restrictions on their lives. As can be seen, boys tended to be more restricted than girls. Over the six categories, boys reported an average of 40% restrictions but girls only 25%. In fact, boys were more restricted in five of the six categories, the only exception being going out at night. In this category, 56% of girls reported restrictions but only 35% of the boys did so.

Student C

Table 13 shows the percentage of adolescents reporting parental restrictions on their lives. As can be seen, overall, boys tended to be more restricted by their parents than girls. However, the real difference lies in the rank order of the restrictions. The top three categories for boys were curfew, postsecondary education choice, and use of the family car; for girls, going out at night, curfew, and choice of friends. Although choice of friends occupied third place for girls, it was reported least by male adolescents.

✤ Language Focus: Qualifying Comparisons

There is another kind of qualification that can be usefully employed in data commentary. We can illustrate this by looking again at the data on parental restrictions in Table 13.

We have already said that it may not be a good idea to simply repeat the data in words. Therefore, it may not be a good strategy to make a series of statements like the following.

> Fifty-six percent of girls reported restrictions on going out late at night as opposed to 35% of boys.

A series of such statements seems to imply that the reader is unable to read the numbers.

Instead we might opt for comparative statements like the following.

> More girls reported restrictions on going out late at night than did boys.

> Fewer boys reported restrictions on going out late at night . . .

> Not as many boys reported restrictions on going out late at night.

One problem here is the vagueness of *more* or *fewer.* How much, for example, is "more"—2% or 10% or 50%? We could more exactly state,

> Twenty-one percent more girls reported restrictions on going out late at night.

While this statement is somewhat acceptable, it fails to convey the full magnitude of the comparison that you are trying to express. Just looking at the difference between the two data sets is not that informative. Some useful alternatives follow. Can you complete each sentence?

a. Almost exactly twice as many boys reported . . .

b. A marginally smaller percentage of girls reported . . .

c. Slightly over twice as many boys reported . . .

d. Close to three times as many boys reported . . .

e. Boys exceeded girls in the times they reported . . . by a ratio of 2.5 to 1.

The fact that you are indeed able to complete the sentences shows the usefulness of these expressions.

TASK TWELVE

Write a full data commentary for Table 13. Begin with a location element and summary. Choose whatever highlighting statements you want (you are of course free to construct your own). In Task Eleven, students A, B, and C did not offer any cautious explanations of the results. When you write your commentary, be sure to do so. Look back at the Language Focus on qualifications and strength of claim.

TASK THIRTEEN

You should find Table 14 particularly interesting—and encouraging. Examine the table and study the commentary. You should be able to analyze its organization by now.

Table 14   Years to Doctorate for Doctoral Programs at the University of Michigan, Ann Arbor, for Academic Years 1996–2001 (Numbers based on average values of time-to-degree data across the five-year period for Ph.D. recipients)

Division	U.S. Citizens/Permanent Residents—Mean Years to Ph.D.	International Students—Mean Years to Ph.D.
Biological and health sciences	7.0	5.8
Physical sciences and engineering	6.2	5.7
Social sciences and education	8.0	7.2
Humanities and the arts	7.2	5.9

Source: Data from Horace H. Rackham School of Graduate Studies 2002.

1 Table 14 shows the number of years to complete a doctoral program for both U.S. and international students at the University of Michigan. **2** As can be seen, international students on average complete doctoral programs in less time than U.S. students in all divisions. **3** The difference in years to completion ranges from a relatively low 0.5 years in physical sciences/engineering to a high of 1.3 years in the humanities and arts. **4** The consistent difference in time to degree is not fully understood at present. **5** However, one key factor may be motivation. **6** Many international students have considerable external pressures, including sponsorship/scholarship restrictions, family obligations, and employer demands, which could influence the length of time it takes to earn a doctorate.

Here are the instructor's comments on the commentary. The instructor is a professor of comparative higher education. Mark the comments as reasonable *(R)* or unreasonable *(U)* and discuss your choices with a partner. If you find some comments unreasonable, how would you edit the passage? There are no absolutely right or wrong answers here.

_____ 1. *In sentences 2, 3, and 4 you throw away the key finding that more rapid progress to degree is consistently in favor of international students in all divisions. You need to highlight this more.*

_____ 2. *You need to stress that based on present knowledge, we can only speculate about the explanations. As it stands I find sentence 5 hard to interpret. Is it just your idea, or do you have any evidence for this claim?*

_____ 3. *It is strange that you do not mention the English language factor. At least at first sight, this would seem to suggest that international students ought to be taking longer.*

_____ 4. *Don't you think you ought to finish by suggesting ways of getting at the real causes of this striking phenomenon? Case studies? Interviews with faculty and students?*

Concluding a Commentary

Concluding a commentary requires some original thinking. This is demonstrated in Table 15, which displays the typical elements of a conclusion in the order in which they generally appear.

Table 15   Concluding a Data Commentary or Results Section

Explanations and/or implications	Usually required
Unexpected results or unsatisfactory data	If necessary
Possible further research or possible future predictions	If appropriate

TASK FOURTEEN

Working with partners, first discuss how the following draft data commentary for Figure 5 can be revised, and then actually rewrite it. The grammar of the commentary is fine. However, you may want to think about such things as the points discussed in the commentary, the reference to the figure, and phrases that can link the discussion of the figure to the figure itself.

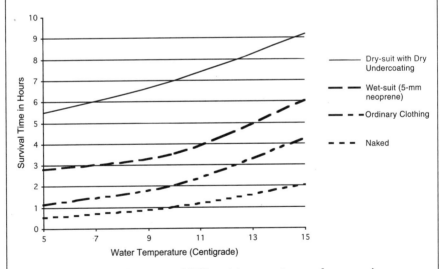

Fig. 5. Survival time in water of different temperatures when wearing different types of clothing. (Data from Noakes 2000).

The figure shows how long people can survive in water when they wear different kinds of clothing that have different levels of insulation. Clothing has an influence on how long a person can survive. The effect of clothing is greater at warmer temperatures. A person can survive the longest if they wear the right kind of clothing. A person wearing no clothing in cold water can survive only less than one hour.

TASK FIFTEEN

Here is an extended version of the commentary on the Japanese scientists in Task Seven. Label each sentence according to its function and list the qualifying words or phrases. The first one has been done for you.

❶ Slightly more than three-fourths of the scientists surveyed adopted writing strategies that involved the use of their first language. ❷ Moreover, less than a quarter appear capable of writing directly in English. ❸ Overall, the figures would appear to suggest that most Japanese scientists have difficulties and frustrations when preparing papers for English-medium journals. ❹ Given the well-known differences between scientific English and scientific Japanese (Okamura 2002), the heavy reliance on Japanese is somewhat unexpected. ❺ This phenomenon probably reflects a lack of confidence in English. ❻ Nevertheless, all the findings need to be treated with some caution since they are based on what scientists said they did, rather than on direct observations of their writing. ❼ Case studies of actual writing practices would be one possible direction for further research.

Sentence	Purpose	Qualifying Words or Phrases
1	Highlighting statement	*Slightly more than*
2		
3		
4		
5		
6		
7		

As in the case of Task Eleven, the data you are working with may not be perfect. In other words, it could contain some anomalies; or there may be discrepancies between the actual findings and the expected ones. Additionally, there may be obvious limitations in the study for which the data were collected. If any of these problems or limitations exist, usually the best strategy is to make a comment about them. You should try to explain why these unexpected results or errors occurred. Think back to Gene in Unit One. As you may recall, Gene was faced with a problem concerning the validity of his data. By bringing the problem out in the open, Gene was able to present himself as a perceptive and intelligent social scientist.

TASK SIXTEEN

Take a look at a journal article in your field, perhaps the one that you chose to analyze in Unit One, Task Seven. Does your article have a graph, chart, table, or other representation of data? If not, use a partner's article for analysis and discussion. Working with a partner or partners, examine your data commentaries for the following.

1. What kind of location statements are used—linking as-clauses, imperatives (see Table 1), or phrases (Fig. 1)?

2. What verb tense is used in the location statements?

3. Which verbs are used in the location statements? List them here.

4. In which section or sections of the article did you find the commentary on the data?

5. Do you see any instances of qualification or moderated claims in the commentary? List the phrases used to qualify or moderate.

6. Does the commentary have a statement indicating the source of the data? Does it have a legend explaining some aspect of the data?

❋ Language Focus: Dealing with "Problems"

Sometimes your data may not be quite what you expected. If this happens, your first reaction might be to ignore the data that doesn't fit. But instead you should try to find a way to discuss the data. In fact, such a discussion can help you position yourself as knowledgeable if you are able to offer a brief explanation and perhaps suggest what work could be done in the future to overcome problems with your data. The verb phrases in the following example sentences may be helpful as you discuss imperfect data.

> The difference between expected and obtained results *may be due to* fluctuations in the power supply.
>
> This discrepancy *can be attributed to* the small sample size.
>
> The anomaly in the observations *can probably be accounted for* by a defect in the camera.
>
> The lack of statistical significance *is probably a consequence of* weaknesses in the experimental design.
>
> The problem with dating this archaeological site *would seem to stem from* the limited amount of organic material available.

Now notice how *due to* is used in the following sentences. Only the first three uses are definitely correct.

1. The error *may be due to* improper installation of the program.

2. The error *may be due to the fact that* the program was not properly installed.

3. The error *may be due to* the program not being properly installed.

4. ☹ The error *may be due to* the program was not properly installed.

5. ?? The error *may be due to* not properly installing the program.

Sentence 4 is not well formed, while 5 is doubtful. While *due to* can sometimes be followed by an *-ing* clause, sentence 5 is problematic because of the lack of a clear agent. Notice that in the correct statements the verb phrase is followed by a noun phrase. If necessary, as in sentence 2, a noun phrase like *the fact that* could be added, even though *due to the fact that* is considered awkward by some instructors. Nevertheless, sometimes this is the only solution.

TASK SEVENTEEN

You are a teaching assistant for an introductory biology course with a total enrollment of 150. Exams are usually given in the evening to avoid losing valuable class time. Because some students have evening commitments, a makeup exam is always given. The professor has noticed a big discrepancy between the scores of the last regular exam and those of the makeup exam. Because you administered the last makeup exam, you have been asked to offer an explanation. You have prepared the data in Table 16. Now write a data commentary, either as a formal report or as an e-mail message (see Appendix Three) to your professor.

Table 16   A Comparison of the Regular and the Makeup Exam‡

	Regular exam	Makeup exam
Average score (out of 100)	86	72
Time administered	Wednesday, 7:00 PM	Friday, 4:00 PM
Difficulty of questions	average	average
Number of students	125	25
Proctor	professor	teaching assistant
Board examples	yes	no (not considered necessary)
Room environment	about 20°C	about 28°C

Dealing with Graphs

So far we have primarily focused on tables. Discussions of graphs essentially follow the same principles as those for tables, with one major difference. Much of the vocabulary used to comment on graphs is quite different.

TASK EIGHTEEN

Look at the graph in **Figure 6** and the accompanying data commentary written by one of our students. We have omitted certain words and phrases. Can you complete the passage? Work with a partner or with a group.

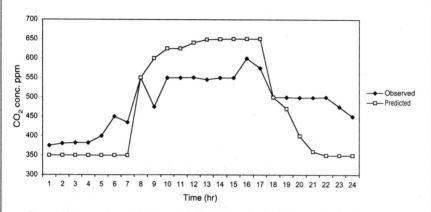

Fig. 6. Comparison of the actual CO_2 levels with the model predictions

The observed and predicted CO_2 levels for 24 hours in a commercial building _____ in Figure 6. The actual CO_2 concentrations were _____ directly from sites in the building by the CO_2 Trapping Method. The predicted concentrations were calculated by using one of the available indoor air quality models. In this case the "fully stirred and conservative reactor with internal source model" _____ since it was assumed that the air was completely replaced and mixed with fresh air every hour, and there was no degradation.

_____ shows that the predicted CO_2 concentrations increase sharply after 8 A.M. and _____ _____ steeply after 6 P.M. This is because the CO_2 levels were _____ to be dependent on the number of people in the building since people produce CO_2 as a result of respiration. However, the model overestimates the CO_2 levels during the occupancy periods (8 A.M.–5 P.M.) and _____

_____ .

The lower CO_2 levels found in the occupancy period _____
_____ several factors such as the presence of plants, which generate oxygen, while using CO_2. _____ , the predicted levels are lower than the _____ during the vacancy period because the model assumed that nobody was in the building after 6 P.M. and that the air was fully mixed. In fact, there might be overtime workers in the building after 6 P.M. or the ventilation rate _____ during the vacant period. Although the "fully stirred and conservative reactor with internal source model" tends to overestimate or underestimate _____ occupancy, overall, it performs well with a coefficient of 0.9 (r = 0.9). (Jiyoung Lee, minor editing)

Jiyoung has produced an excellent draft of a data commentary. But look at the last paragraph again. What changes would you suggest? Do you have any suggestions for changes in tense usage?

❖ Language Focus: Referring to Lines on Graphs

One feature of Jiyoung's data commentary in Task Eighteen is that she made little explicit reference to the lines on her graph, as many writers do when dealing with historical or technical data. As you know, graph lines have a special terminology. In fact, they have somewhat different terminologies depending on the discipline. We start this Language Focus with a graph providing data on hand temperature for two different kinds of soccer goalkeeping gloves (Fig. 7). The two sets of gloves were made of normal foam material (NFM) and phase control material (PCM), the latter being designed to change its physical state from solid to liquid to gas over a range of temperatures.

TASK NINETEEN

From the following list, choose a term that you think best describes the graph in Figure 7 at each of the following time periods.

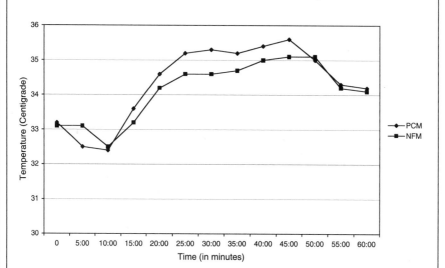

Fig. 7. Changes in mean hand temperature for PCM and NFM glove conditions during exercise. (Data from Purvis and Cable 2000.)

upward trend	peak	low point	sharp rise
steep fall	rise	leveling off	fell off
remained steady	spike	increase	decline

1. PCM 45 minutes _____

2. NFM 10 minutes _____

3. NFM 25–35 minutes _____

4. PCM 15–25 minutes _____

5. PCM 45–60 minutes _____

6. NFM 10–25 minutes _____

Can you think of other terms that could be used?

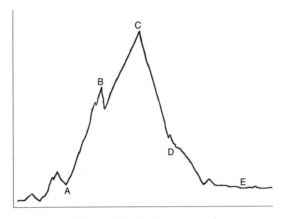

Fig. 8. Hard sciences graph

Now look at this graph from the physical sciences in Figure 8 and choose a term that best describes each letter. Some terms may be used more than once.

minimum   local dip/local minimum   local maximum
spike   maximum/peak   leveling off
kink   linear increase

A. _____   D. _____

B. _____   E. _____

C. _____

In what way are the terms for the physical sciences different?

Dealing with Chronological Data

The graph in Figure 7 has a time dimension. Such data often presents writers of data commentary with an organizational problem. On the one hand, writers want to follow the general-specific rule. On the other, they may want to respect the chronological order, that is, start with the earliest and finish with the latest.

TASK TWENTY

The sentences in this commentary expand on the information given in Figure 7. They are not in the correct order. Rearrange them in an appropriate order. Place *1* in front of the first sentence, *2* before the second, and so on. Work with a partner if possible.

_____ a. Hand temperatures for PCM were consistently higher during the 45-minute exercise period, reaching a maximum temperature of just under 36°.

_____ b. As can be seen, after an initial decrease, hand temperature increased in each condition.

_____ c. However, the increase in temperature was more pronounced for the PCM condition.

_____ d. The PCM gloves were designed to maintain a steady and comfortable hand temperature.

_____ e. Figure 7 displays the absolute skin temperature of the hand during exercise for both the PCM and NFM conditions.

_____ f. When exercise stopped at 45 minutes, hand temperatures for the two conditions fell at approximately the same rate.

_____ g. Thus, the PCM glove performance was inferior to that of traditional NFM and would not necessarily lead to enhanced goalkeeper performance.

_____ h. An overall increase in temperature is inevitable since goalkeeping gloves of any kind prevent heat loss and evaporation, leading to discomfort and a negative effect on performance.

_____ i. However, as can be seen, the PCM gloves did not perform as intended.

What can you conclude about how this data commentary is organized?

Language Focus: Prepositions of Time

The commentary in Task Twenty made few references to specific points at a particular time. However, it would have been possible to do so by including one or two sentences like the following.

From the 10th to the 45th minute, hand temperature increased.

During the first ten minutes, hand temperature dropped.

Hand temperature fluctuated *throughout* the period.

Hand temperature remained over 35°C *from* the 25th to the 50th minute for the PCM condition.

Hand temperature remained under 34°C *until* the 20th minute for the PCM condition.

The highest temperature occurred *in* the 45th minute for the PCM condition.

In the last ten minutes, hand temperature decreased for both conditions.

After 50 minutes had passed, hand temperature began to decrease.

At time 0, hand temperatures for both gloves was 33°C.

TASK TWENTY-ONE

Write a suitable data commentary for Figure 9 and Table 17. Find current data to supplement the information, if you can. Can you speculate about the future?

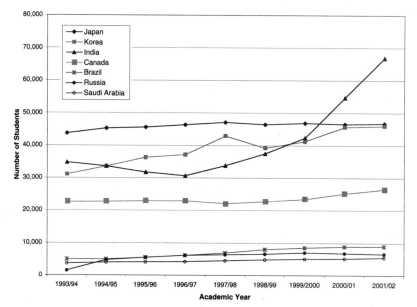

Fig. 9. Totals of international students from selected countries in U.S. colleges and universities, 1993–2002. (Data from *Open Doors,* http://opendoors.iienetwork.org/.)

Table 17   International Student Enrollment in the U.S., 1993–2002

Year	Total Enrollment
1993/94	449,749
1994/95	452,653
1995/96	453,787
1996/97	457,984
1997/98	481,280
1998/99	490,933
1999/2000	514,723
2000/2001	547,867
2001/2	582,996

Source: Data from: *Open Doors,* http://opendoors.iienetwork.org.

TASK TWENTY-TWO

Write a data commentary from your own field of study based on data that you select.

Unit Five

Writing Summaries

Of all the writing tasks so far, summary writing may well be the one you are most familiar with. We make summaries of many different things, including meetings, lectures, and readings. Our summaries may be quite elaborate, or they may only involve one or two key words, depending on our purpose for writing them. These summaries of what others have written or said may be for our own personal use. Most often we use this material for future reference. At the university especially, it can form an essential part of our preparation for an exam, a class discussion, a research paper, a thesis, or a dissertation. In these situations, we are free to concentrate on what we ourselves think is important or interesting about the source.

Summary writing may, alternatively, be part of a more public communication and an integral part of other work that you may do. For example, your advisor may ask you to summarize some recent literature that could be useful for your research group. Instructors may assign you to review or critique articles. In each of these cases, you are given the opportunity to "display" your understanding of some material. Summaries as part of a course assignment are relatively common in graduate student writing and may be a *foundation* for other, more complex writing tasks such as a literature review. Look back at the "Selling Cities" text on page 45 of Unit Two. Notice how by summarizing relevant portions of the text you can offer support to your response to the question on page 47.

In the first half of this textbook, you could successfully complete most of the writing tasks by relying either on information that you already possessed or on information that we provided. In the second half, we will pay more attention to writing that involves the use of sources. Unit Five deals with assignment summary writing. Unit Six expands our discussion of summary writing to the writing of critiques of or critical responses to source material, including book reviews. Finally, in the last two units, we move on to writing an entire research paper.

Writing an Assignment Summary

Assignment summaries can be extremely challenging to write. A good assignment summary has three principal requirements.

1. It should be focused on the relevant aspects of the source text or texts. (There may be no need to take information from every section or paragraph of the source texts.)

2. It should present the source material in an accurate fashion.

3. It should condense the source material and be presented in the summary writer's own words. (Summaries that consist of directly copied portions of the original rarely succeed. Such a summary may suggest that you can find potentially important information, but it does not reveal to what extent you have understood it. In addition, you may be engaging in plagiarism. See page 172.)

Notice that we have not said anything about the length of a summary, because this will often be determined by your instructor. Sometimes instructors will ask for a one-page summary of an article (or maybe a two-page summary of a book). They may also ask for a paragraph-length abstract (see Unit Eight) or even a minisummary of one to two sentences (as is typical of annotated bibliographies). Since the sample texts we provide here are quite short, we expect that the summaries you write will be half a page to a full page.

To do a good job, you must first thoroughly understand the source material you are working with. So, here are some preliminary steps in writing a summary.

1. Skim the text, noting in your mind the subheadings. If there are no subheadings, try to divide the text into sections.

2. Consider why you have been assigned the text. Determine what type of text you are dealing with, that is, the *genre* of the source text (e.g., a research paper) or perhaps the organization (problem-solution or general-specific). This can help you identify important information and focus your reading strategies.

3. Read the text, highlighting important information or taking notes.

4. In your own words, write down the main points of each section. Try to write a one-sentence summary of each section.

5. Write down the key support points for the main topic, but include minor detail only if necessary.

6. Go through the process again, making changes as appropriate.

TASK ONE

Read this adaptation of "Transformation of the Nile River Basin" and underline the information you think is significant and should be included in a summary. Next to each underlined section, briefly explain why you think the information is important. The first paragraph has been done for you. Then write in the margin, in as few words as possible, what each paragraph is about.

Transformation of the Nile River Basin

Reason for Highlighting

The Egyptian landscape has been changing for centuries. One area which has undergone dramatic change over the last 7,000 years is the Nile River basin. One of the most notable aspects of this transformation is the year-round irrigation of land for agricultural purposes, rather than a strict reliance on the annual flood.

This is the topic of the passage.

Conversion to continuous irrigation, which began around 1500 and was limited only by the level of technology, led to improved agricultural productivity. This in

The effect of the change in irrigation patterns is significant.

turn contributed to an increase in
the population of the area.

    Large-scale conversion of
agricultural land involving
perennial irrigation began in
1800 with the availability of more
modern technology. Water could be
retained, raised, and distributed
to summer crops with the aid of
barrages* constructed on the Nile
below Cairo and at sites on 30,000
km of new canals. Large dams
were built on the Nile at Aswan in
1902, 1912, and 1933. The final
transformation to continuous
irrigation was finished with the
completion of the Aswan Dam in
1960. This full-scale change
brought about a major shift and
expansion in agriculture. Cash
crops such as cotton, sugar cane,
and vegetables tended and still
tend to be produced at the expense
of subsistence crops.

---

*A barrage is a bank of earth or stones usually constructed over a river to provide
water for irrigation. (Based on Steven M. Goodman, Peter Meininger, et al., eds. *The
Birds of Egypt* [1989]. Used by permission of Oxford University Press.)

Because Egyptians have historically preferred to live within or near the cultivated land area, agricultural expansion has also had an impact on the environment and livelihood of the Nile population. As the amount of land available for agriculture increased, so did the population. Egypt's population has increased from 2.5 million in the early 1800s to 9.7 million in the late 1800s, 18.8 million in the 1940s, 37 million in the mid-70s, 46 million in 1984, and nearly 67 million in 2002. The population could reach over 100 million by the beginning of 2050. In 1907, urban dwellers constituted only approximately 17% of Egypt's population. By 2001, however, they were 45% of the total. Recent studies have indicated that approximately 1–2% of Egypt's arable land is lost annually to human encroachment.

TASK TWO

The "Nile" passage in Task One is fairly easy to summarize because it is factual, has three clear-cut sections, and follows a chronology. Take a look at some attempts at summarizing some of the details in the third paragraph. Which summary provides the right amount of detail? Explain your choice.

1. In the early 1800s the population of Egypt was 2.5 million. By the late 1800s it was 9.7 million. In the 40s the population reached 18.8 million; by the mid-70s it had reached 37 million. In 1984 the population was 46 million. In 2002 it was nearly 67 million. The population could reach over 100 million by 2050. One to two percent of Egypt's fertile land is disappearing annually as a result of the growth.

2. In the 1800s Egypt's population increased from 2.5 million to 9.7 million. In the 1900s it grew again, from 18.8 million in the 1940s to 46 million in 1984, reaching 67 million in 2002. By mid-century, the population will be almost double that in 1984. A result of this population growth is an annual 1–2% loss of agricultural land.

3. The Egyptian population has increased from 2.5 million in the early 1800s to 67 million in 2002. It could grow to approximately 100 million by mid-century. Along with this population growth, Egypt has also experienced a 1–2% loss in the amount of fertile land.

4. The Egyptian population has dramatically increased since the 1800s and is expected to continue to increase. A small percentage of agricultural land is lost each year because of the growth in population.

5. The Egyptian population in 2002 was approximately 30 times that in the early 1800s. By mid-century, it could grow to 100 million. Egypt is also losing agricultural land as a result of the population increase.

Now attempt your own summary of the third paragraph.

TASK THREE

Here is a slightly longer version of the "Selling Cities" passage from Unit Two. We have removed the citations in order to simplify our discussion. The "Selling Cities" text is somewhat more difficult to summarize than the "Nile" passage because it is less factual and more argumentative. Students in one of our courses were asked to use this passage to respond to the following questions: What is the potential impact of meetings tourism on a city? Does the meetings tourism market seem like a reasonable market for cities in economic trouble to pursue? With these questions in mind, read the passage, paying particular attention to the parts that have been underlined. Do you agree that the underlined sections are significant and for the reasons provided? Can you tell how the text is organized?

Selling Cities: Promoting New Images for Meetings Tourism

❶ <u>Meetings tourism, which we define as travel associated with attendance at corporate or association meetings, conferences, conventions or congresses or public or trade exhibitions, has emerged as a significant subsection of the tourist industry both in terms of volume of travel and expenditure generated.</u>

❷ "Meetings" demonstrate enormous variety, ranging from small business meetings of a few participants to large conventions of, for example, professional associations which might attract in excess of 20,000 delegates.

❸ The range of locations within which these meetings take place is also broad, including such sites as hotels, universities, sports venues, and specially built convention centers.

Meetings tourism may not be such a well known term, so I should include the definition along with something about its importance.

4 The meetings tourism market has been vigorously pursued by many former industrial cities in Europe and the U.S. as part of their strategies of post-industrial urban regeneration. **5** This market offers a number of obvious attractions to such cities, not least the rapidity of its growth during the 1970s and 1980s, the very period during which many cities were suffering contractions in their industrial base. **6** Figures for the U.S.A. suggest the business conference industry almost doubled during the 1980s. **7** The growth is particularly marked for international conferences, which bring the greatest financial returns for host cities. **8** In many European cities the economic contributions of business tourism outweigh those from leisure tourism by two to three times, making it both a seemingly appropriate and rewarding sector for former manufacturing cities to pursue.

9 Meetings tourists are high spending and hence the market is able to generate high levels of investment in cities and regions. **10** Although the myth of the bottomless expense account is somewhat exaggerated, meetings tourists are major users of the entertainment and accommodation facilities of the locations they visit.

This part further explains why meetings tourism is important.

This seems like good support for the idea of why meetings tourism is important—even more important than regular tourism.

This explains the impact of the spending by meetings tourists.

⑪ It has been estimated, for example, that the International Rotary Meeting at the International Convention Center in Birmingham, U.K., attracted 23,000 delegates resulting in spending of almost $40 million in the city during the meeting, much of which remained in the local market.

The specific example of how much meetings tourists spend is helpful.

⑫ The potential for direct and indirect job creation associated with meetings tourism has been recognized as high.

Here is a specific example of what the money generated by meetings tourism can do for a city.

⑬ A study of the potential job creation effects of a convention center in Birmingham, U.K., was crucial to the decision by the local authority to pursue the development. **⑭** The study estimated that while only 125 jobs would be created directly in the center itself, almost 2,000 indirect jobs would result from its development.

⑮ Success in this market also brings a number of nonfinancial rewards associated with image and profile enhancement, the improvement to decaying districts and city center landscapes and the generation of civic pride among residents.

This is another example of the impact of meetings tourism money.

⑯ The zeal with which some cities have developed facilities to attract meetings tourists during the 1980s suggests that it was seen as something of a panacea*

---

*A remedy or solution for all problems.

for the problems that had come to affect them. ⑰ <u>However, the pursuit of the meetings tourist market certainly incurs costs, for example, the long-term financial burden on local authorities</u> both to cover the costs of construction and to service the typical year-on-year financial deficits of such facilities. ⑱ It also brings with it potential problems, such as <u>a vulnerability to cut back during recession and the fact that at national levels, and sometimes regional levels, the competition between cities for meetings often results in enough profits to just cover expenses.</u> ⑲ <u>Despite potential risks, many city governments see meetings tourism as a good way to make the transition into a post-industrial economy.</u> (Adapted from Bradley, Hall, and Harrison 2002)

It's good to highlight the potential negative side of meetings tourism to provide a somewhat balanced discussion.

More on the potential drawbacks.

Overall it seems that meetings tourism is a good market for cities to pursue. This conclusion is important.

A preliminary summary of the passage in Task Three should probably include the definition along with some discussion of the advantages and disadvantages of meetings tourism. In the next step, these elements can be strung together to form the basis of a formal summary. Of course, special care has to be taken to ensure a logical flow of ideas. Here is a draft written in response to the two questions posed in Task Three.

Draft Summary

❶ Meetings tourism is travel associated with attendance at corporate or association meetings, conferences, conventions, or congresses or public or trade exhibitions. ❷ It has become a significant subsection of the tourist industry both in terms of the number of tourists and the money they spend. ❸ The meetings tourism market has been vigorously pursued by many former industrial cities that are aiming for urban regeneration. ❹ The meetings tourism market offers attractions to such cities, especially its growth during the 1970s and 1980s, when many cities were suffering from economic problems with their industrial base. ❺ The expansion in meetings tourism is especially outstanding for international conferences, which get the highest economic reward for entertaining cities. ❻ In many European cities the economic profits of business tourism are two to three times greater than those from leisure tourism.

❼ Because meetings tourists spend a lot of money, cities have funds to heavily invest in themselves. ❽ Meetings tourism has the potential for direct and indirect job creation. ❾ One study estimated that jobs can be created directly and indirectly from its development. ❿ Apart from generating funds, meetings tourism can also improve image and profile enhancement, improve decaying districts and city center landscapes, and generate civic pride among residents.

⓫ However, the meetings tourist market certainly takes some risk because cities have to pay for the construction and upkeep of facilities, a weak economy, and competition from other cities. ⓬ For example, there may not be a profit. ⓭ Many city governments see meetings tourism as a good way to make the transition into a post-industrial economy.

This is perhaps a reasonable beginning. The writer has retained the important parts of the text. Most of the sentences are short, as we would expect in a summary. However, this summary has three weaknesses.

1. It is probably a bit too long. The original contains 560 words, and the summary contains 335. It could be condensed further without any loss of meaning.

2. For the most part, too much of the text is written in the words of the original, although no whole sections were borrowed. It may very well be an example of plagiarism—work copied from a source without proper attribution. Notice that sentence 1 in the summary is very close to the first highlighted part of the original, sentences 2 and 3 use many of the same expressions as in the original, and so on.

3. The draft does not *display* a high level of understanding of the source passage. While it does show that the writer can pull out important information, it does not convince the reader that the

summary writer understands the information and how it is interrelated.

Overall, although this summary is a reasonable draft, it needs more work before it can be submitted as a written assignment.

Now, let us consider how this summary could be improved. One obvious approach would be to paraphrase the original. A paraphrase is a restatement (in your own words) of the ideas in the original. The most common strategy used to accomplish this involves replacing words in the source with synonyms and perhaps changing the grammar. Look again at sentence 4.

> ❹ The meetings tourism market has been vigorously pursued by many former industrial cities in Europe and the U.S. as part of their strategies of post-industrial urban regeneration.

A full paraphrase of this could be

> Many cities in the U.S. and Europe that once relied on heavy industry are now trying to revitalize themselves by developing a meetings tourism industry.

Note here that the language has been completely changed, although the sense of the original is fully maintained.

A paraphrase approach to summarizing can be somewhat successful, but if you do this sentence by sentence, you run the risk of not demonstrating your full understanding of the passage. You might miss an opportunity to highlight key points. Another possible danger is that the resulting summary may not be original enough and could be considered plagiarism by some. (See p. 172.)

Some students attempt to paraphrase by following a simple synonym substitution approach. However, this approach definitely has risks. If we take sentence 4 above and paraphrase using synonyms, we get something like the following.

> The meetings tourism industry has been energetically sought by several historically industrial cities in Europe and the U.S. as one element of their plan of post-industrial metropolitan rebuilding.

This paraphrase is somewhat difficult to understand. For one, *seek* does not have the same meaning as *pursue*. While an industry can be *pursued* in English, it generally cannot be *sought*. For another, *historically* does not give the sense that these cities are no longer industrial cities. Finally, the phrase *metropolitan rebuilding* requires some effort to understand because the common term in this context is *urban,* as in the original.

If you (understandably) feel that your paraphrasing ability is not so strong, you can copy some material and place it in quotation marks; however, a better but more difficult strategy would be to carefully consider the elements you have identified as important, put the original away, and write down what you have understood. This may allow you to condense the ideas in the source even further.

When you write a formal summary of someone else's ideas, you should keep in mind the following guidelines.

1. Always try to use your own words, except for technical terms.

2. Include enough support and detail so that the presentation is clear.

3. Do not try to paraphrase specialized vocabulary or technical terms.

4. Focus on the content of the original.

5. Make sure the summary reads smoothly. Use enough transition devices and supporting detail. You do not want a collection of sentences that do not flow.

TASK FOUR

Here again is the draft summary, which is now followed by some instructor comments. Discuss them with a partner and decide whether they are reasonable *(R)* or unreasonable *(U)*. If you are not sure, mark the comment with a question mark.

Draft Summary

❶ Meetings tourism is travel associated with attendance at corporate or association meetings, conferences, conventions, or congresses or public or trade exhibitions. ❷ It has become a significant subsection of the tourist industry both in terms of the number of tourists and the money they spend. ❸ The meetings tourism market has been vigorously pursued by many former industrial cities that are aiming for urban regeneration. ❹ The meetings tourism market offers attractions to such cities, especially its growth during the 1970s and 1980s, when many cities were suffering from economic problems with their industrial base. ❺ The expansion in meetings tourism is especially outstanding for international conferences, which get the highest economic reward for entertaining cities. ❻ In many European cities the economic profits of business tourism are two to three times greater than those from leisure tourism.

❼ Because meetings tourists spend a lot of money, cities have funds to heavily invest in themselves. ❽ Meetings tourism has the potential for direct and indirect job creation. ❾ One study estimated that jobs can be created directly and indirectly from its development. ❿ Apart from generating funds, meetings tourism can also improve image and profile enhancement, improve decaying districts and city center landscapes, and generate civic pride among residents.

⓫ However, the meetings tourist market certainly takes some risk because cities have to pay for the construction and upkeep of facilities, a weak economy, and competition from other cities. ⓬ For example, there may not be a profit. ⓭ Many city governments see meetings tourism as a good way to make the transition into a post-industrial economy.

Instructor Comments

I think you have a good start here. You have addressed the questions. You have hit the key points and for the most part expressed them clearly. Below are some suggestions for revision.

_____ 1. *Your first and second sentences are essentially copied from the source. Trying to write this definition in your own words may not be worth the effort. But since this is copied material, you need to place it in quotation marks and indicate the source.*

_____ 2. *Sentences 3, 4, and 13 are also quite close to the original. Try to put the points in your own words.*

_____ 3. *In sentence 5 you have made a good attempt at using your own words, but your synonym paraphrase approach has resulted in a somewhat awkward sentence. In particular, "entertaining cities" does not accurately convey the meaning of the original. Are you happy with "get"?*

_____ 4. "Profits" in sentence 6 doesn't seem quite right. The original says "contribution." Can you find another term?

_____ 5. You should identify the source somewhere in the discussion. This is standard practice in academic writing—even if your instructor has given the source. You could put this at the beginning or the end.

_____ 6. Sentence 7 looks good, but can you offer some support for the point?

_____ 7. You could clearly highlight how many benefits the article describes. For example, you could state that there are three benefits for cities that pursue meetings tourism.

_____ 8. Sentences 8 and 9 essentially say the same thing. Sometimes repetition is OK, but in this case nothing is gained.

_____ 9. The connection between sentences 11 and 12 is confusing. Is sentence 12 really an example?

_____ 10. Finally, as you revise and put things more in your words, see if you can reduce the overall length so that it is no more than one-third the length of the original.

_____ 11. You should perhaps indicate that this paper heavily relies on data that is rather old.

Since many of the summaries you write will be woven into your own original text, it is very important to identify at least the source author, if not the title as well. One of our students chose to identify the source in this way.

> According to Andrew meetings tourism can have an enormous effect on the economy of a city.

This is a reasonable first attempt, but you may be wondering who Andrew is. Andrew happens to be the first name of the first author of the "Selling Cities" article. When you refer to other authors, you should not use the given name alone. Family names alone are generally used. Also, since there is more than one author in our example, this needs to be acknowledged. We propose the following revision.

According to Bradley et al., meetings tourism can have an enormous effect on the economy of a city.

The following Language Focus provides some additional suggestions for how to refer to a source in your summary.

❖ Language Focus: Identifying the Source in a Summary

Most summaries will have a sentence near the beginning that contains two elements: the source and a main idea. Notice the use of the present tense in the later examples.

According to Boskin (2004) _____ .
                                                    (main idea)

Young and Song's 2004 paper on fluoridation discusses

_____ .

(main idea)

Bernstein (2004) states that _____ .
                     claims   (main idea)
                     argues
                     maintains

Barinaga (2004) suggests that _____ .
                     asserts   (main idea)
                     hypothesizes
                     states
                     concludes

In Tyson's article "Mapping Dark Matter with

Gravitational Lenses," _____ .
                                          (main idea)

There is a range of reporting verbs that you may use when referring to your source material. A recent study by Ken Hyland identified more than 400 different reporting verbs; however, nearly 50 percent of these were used only one time in his corpus of 80 research articles. A much smaller number of verbs tend to predominate. In Table 18 we show the most frequently used reporting verbs from a

Table 18   High-Frequency Reporting Verbs

Discipline	Verbs and Frequency					
Rank	1	2	3	4	5	6
Biology	describe	find	report	show	suggest	observe
Physics	develop	report	study	find	expand	
Electrical engineering	propose	use	describe	show	publish	develop
Mechanical engineering	describe	show	report	discuss	give	develop
Epidemiology	find	describe	suggest	report	examine	show
Nursing	show	report	demonstrate	observe	find	suggest
Marketing	suggest	argue	find	demonstrate	propose	show
Applied linguistics	suggest	argue	show	explain	find	point out
Psychology	find	show	suggest	report	demonstrate	focus
Sociology	argue	suggest	describe	note	analyze	discuss
Education	find	suggest	note	report	demonstrate	provide

Source: Data for biology, physics, electrical engineering, mechanical engineering, marketing, applied linguistics, and sociology from Hyland 1999, 341–67. Other data thanks to Carson Maynard.

variety of disciplines, with the most frequent on the left and the sixth most frequent on the far right. As you can see, there are some disciplinary differences.

TASK FIVE

Take the article from your field that you have been periodically examining (or another one, if you like) and underline all the reporting verbs. If your field is represented in Table 18, do your results match with those in the table? If your field is not represented, is there one field that is close to yours in its use of reporting verbs?

Although in theory summaries are supposed to be objective, this is not entirely true. A variety of reporting verbs can be used in summary writing to reveal your personal stance toward the source material. Notice how the reporting verbs in the following examples could allow the writer of the summary to convey his or her attitude.

> Campbell (2004) presumes that all parents are equally capable of helping their children with schoolwork.

> The authors speculate that people who scrap their old cars will immediately buy another, new(er) car.

Notice also how the addition of an adverb (in midposition, of course) can even more clearly reveal your stance, which you may want to do when writing in order to critique.

> The authors wrongly assume that patients will adhere to the treatment protocol.

TASK SIX

Some reporting verbs are less objective than others. In Table 19, can you identify which verbs seem to be objective and which verbs have the potential to be evaluative? The first answer has been provided for you.

Table 19 Objectivity of Reporting Verbs

	Objective	*Evaluative*
describe	X	
recommend		
claim		
assume		
contend		
propose		
theorize		
support		
examine		

Language Focus: Nominal that*-Clauses*

In formal academic English, many reporting verbs are followed by a *that*-clause containing both a subject and a verb. Can you identify the verbs in Table 19 that are not followed by *that?* List them here.

That-clauses have a variety of functions. In the following sentence the *that*-clause is the direct object of the verb *states.*

> Benfield and Howard (2000) state that many medical journals are now published in English because of a desire to attract greater readership and to attract better, more international manuscripts.

In spoken English *that* in clauses which function as direct objects is often omitted, as in the following example. Notice also that in this spoken English alternative the choice of verb is less formal.

> Benfield and Howard (2000) said many medical journals are published in English now because they want to attract greater readership and to attract better, more international manuscripts.

You may have wondered why we have not said anything about the verb *mention* in the opening sentence of a summary. Notice that if you were to use *mention* instead of one of the other verbs suggested, you would greatly change the importance of the information following.

> Benfield and Howard (2000) mention that many medical journals are now published in English because of a desire to attract greater readership and to attract better, more international manuscripts.

How does the preceding sentence compare to the first example presented in the preceding Language Focus?

Mention is used for information that was most likely given without detail or support. The example sentence using *mention* makes it seem as if the reason journals are now published in English is a minor point in the article. We suggest that you avoid using *mention* in summaries.

TASK SEVEN

Here are some introductory statements that students wrote for a summary of the "Nile" passage in Task One. Which, if any, would you prefer to have written? Why? Edit the weaker sentences.

1. Author Steven Goodman in "Transformation of the Nile River Basin" states that how the region has changed as a result of continuous irrigation.

2. "Transformation of the Nile River Basin" by Steven Goodman claims that changes in irrigation have led to an increase in population.

3. According to "Transformation of the Nile River Basin" Steven Goodman suggests that the Nile River basin has been changed.

4. Goodman in "Transformation of the Nile River Basin" mentions that irrigation has had an impact on the environment and the population.

5. In Goodman's "Transformation of the Nile River Basin" the Nile River basin has been transformed by the introduction of perennial irrigation.

If you are summarizing another author's work as part of a longer paper, you may make a reference to your source material following APA (American Psychological Association), MLA (Modern Language Association), IEEE (Institute of Electrical and Electronics Engineers), or another style, depending on your field of study. The APA and MLA systems refer to a source similarly, by author and date. The following references are in APA style.

a. Goodman (1989) has found a correlation between the increase in agricultural fertility and the shift away from traditional crops.

b. A correlation between the increase in agricultural fertility and the shift away from traditional crops has been identified (Goodman, 1989).

c. In his study of the Nile River basin, Goodman (1989) established a correlation between the increase in agricultural fertility and the shift away from traditional crops. Goodman also noticed . . .

How does the citation in sentence *b* differ from those in sentences *a* and *c?*

For a thorough discussion of APA and MLA styles, see the *Publication Manual of the American Psychological Association* and *The MLA Handbook for Writers of Research Papers.*

In engineering, it may be more common to use reference numbers.

Photorefractive crystals may be useful in the development of high-speed electrical signals.[1]

If you are in engineering, check the journals in your specific area to learn more about documentation for that area of engineering.

❊ Language Focus: Summary Reminder Phrases

In a longer summary, you may want to remind your reader that you are summarizing.

> The author goes on to say that . . .
>
> The article further states that . . .
>
> *(Author's surname here)* also states/maintains/argues that . . .
>
> *(Author's surname here)* also believes that . . .
>
> *(Author's surname here)* concludes that . . .
>
> In the second half of the paper, *(author's surname here)* presents . . .

In fact, if your summary is quite long, you may want to mention the source author's name at different points in your summary—the beginning, the middle, and/or the end. When you do mention the author in the middle or end of the summary, be sure to use the surname only.

> Goodman goes on to say . . .
>
> Bradley et al. also believe that . . .
>
> The author further argues that . . .

Some of the following sentence connectors may be useful in introducing additional information.

additionally	in addition to
also	furthermore
further	moreover

TASK EIGHT

Here are some summary reminder sentences written by our students. Which, if any, of these would you prefer to have written? Try to improve the weaker sentences.

1. Bradley finally says meetings tourism may not get rid of all of a city's economic problems.

2. In addition, the article also discusses about the problems that can come about.

3. In Bradley's article, he also points out that meetings tourism looks like a good idea.

4. Bradley and colleagues conclude that current strategies need to be reexamined.

5. Bradley and others conclude about the current risks that exist.

TASK NINE

Here is a summary of the "Selling Cities" passage in Task Three. Would it be improved by adding a reminder phrase? Where would you insert it?

Summary

1 According to Bradley et al., meetings tourism refers to "travel associated with attendance at a corporate or association meeting, conference, convention, or exhibitions, or congress or public or trade exhibitions." **2** The meetings tourism market has become increasingly important to cities that once depended on heavy industry for their economic strength. **3** Interest in meetings tourism has grown for three main reasons. **4** First, the average meetings tourist spends two to three times more money than the typical leisure tourist does. **5** If city hosts a "mega" meeting of tens of thousands of participants, the financial rewards can be considerable. **6** Second, meetings tourism can create jobs in a local economy. **7** For example, the meeting facilities require workers, while other jobs may be created in hotels, restaurants, and other entertainment facilities. **8** Finally, meetings tourism may lead to cities receiving a "facelift" with landscapes being improved and city centers being revitalized, which may in turn improve civic pride. **9** City improvements may also encourage meetings tourists to return to a host city at a future date for business, pleasure, or even a change in residence.

10 Despite these important advantages, investment in meetings tourism is not risk-free. **11** Investment in facilities may impose a long-term financial burden on cities that must face competition from many other cities in the market. **12** Thus, cities may invest heavily in meetings facilities, but may not reap the expected benefit. **13** Despite the potential concerns, a good meetings tourism strategy has the potential to revive an ailing post-industrial city. ⓮ As a result, this industry will likely continue to grow.

TASK TEN

Read "Reducing Air Pollution" and try to determine the text-type. Then read the summaries that follow. Decide which of the summaries you like best. Write one to two sentences after each summary, explaining what you like or dislike about each. Finally, discuss each of the summaries with a partner.

Reducing Air Pollution in Urban Areas:
The Role of Urban Planners

Yasufumi Iseki

Recently, increasingly significant problems regarding energy use have emerged. Enormous amounts of pollutants are being emitted from power plants, factories, and automobiles, which are worsening the condition of the Earth. This environmental degradation is a clear result of acid rain, increased levels of carbon dioxide (CO_2) in the atmosphere, and other forms of air pollution.

Acid rain and air pollution, for instance, are devastating forests, crops, and lakes over wide areas of Europe and North America. In fact, in Europe nearly 50 million hectares have been identified as damaged, representing 35% of the total forested area. In the United States, approximately 1,000 acidified and 3,000 marginally acidic lakes have been reported. Since the midcentury, CO_2 levels in the atmosphere have increased by 13%, setting the stage for global warming. As atmospheric temperatures rise, grain output may significantly decrease, making it more difficult for farmers to keep pace with the growth of population. In urban areas, air pollution is taking a toll on buildings and human health.

To reduce the amount of environmental damage in cities specifically, developed countries have devised technology to control the harmful emissions. However, as these countries already have an abundance of vehicles that continues to grow in number, the efficacy of these measures is diminished. Since cars and other vehicles create more air pollution than any other human activity, the most effective means to reduce pollution is to decrease the number of vehicles. A major shift away from automobile usage in urban areas may be possible with the aid of urban planning.

Summaries

1. According to Yasufumi Iseki, air pollution can be controlled through effective urban planning.

2. Yasufumi Iseki in "Reducing the Air Pollution in Urban Areas: The Role of Urban Planners" states that pollutants are worsening the condition of the Earth as a result of acid rain, increased levels of CO_2, and other forms of pollution. In fact, 35% of the total forested area in Europe has been damaged, and in the United States, approximately 1,000 acidified lakes and 3,000 marginally acidic lakes have been reported. Since the midcentury CO_2 levels have increased by 13%. Cars and other vehicles create more pollution than any other activity; thus, decreasing the number of vehicles is the most effective way to reduce pollution. This may be possible with urban planning.

3. Yasufumi Iseki states that because cars and other vehicles are the greatest single source of air pollution, a reduction in the number of vehicles in urban areas would be an effective approach to improving the urban environment. This reduction could be achieved through urban planning.

4. Yasufumi Iseki claims that urban planning can play a role in improving air quality in urban areas by prompting a shift away from heavy vehicle use. This will be difficult to achieve because of the overabundance of vehicles in developed countries.

Some Notes on Plagiarism

Plagiarism is best defined as a deliberate activity—as the conscious copying from the work of others. The concept of plagiarism has become an integral part of North American and Western European countries. It is based on a number of assumptions that may not hold true in all cultures. One is a rather romantic assumption that the writer is an original, individual, creative artist. Another is that original ideas and expressions are the acknowledged property of their creators (as is the case with a patent for an invention). Yet another is that it is a sign of disrespect—rather than respect—to copy without acknowledgment from the works of published authorities.

Of course, borrowing the words and phrases of others can be a useful language learning strategy. Certainly you would not be plagiarizing if you borrowed items that are commonly or frequently used in academic English or that are part of common knowledge.

Paris is the capital of France.

An increase in demand often leads to an increase in price.

The results from this experiment seem to suggest that . . .

These results are statistically significant.

But do not borrow "famous" phrases without at least putting them in quotation marks. Here, for example is a famous quotation by Louis Pasteur. It was originally in French.

Chance favors the prepared mind.

If you wanted to use this phrase, you should recognize its special status. We would encourage you to borrow standard phraseology of your field and skeletal phrases when appropriate, but not special expressions.

TASK ELEVEN

Here are some approaches to writing, beginning with a plagiarizing approach and ending with an acceptable quoting technique. Where does plagiarism stop? Draw a line between the last approach that would produce plagiarism and the first approach that would produce acceptable original work.

1. Copying a paragraph as it is from the source without any acknowledgment.

2. Copying a paragraph making only small changes, such as replacing a few verbs or adjectives with synonyms.

3. Cutting and pasting a paragraph by using the sentences of the original but leaving one or two out, or by putting one or two sentences in a different order.

4. Composing a paragraph by taking short standard phrases from a number of sources and putting them together with some words of your own.

5. Paraphrasing a paragraph by rewriting with substantial changes in language and organization, amount of detail, and examples.

6. Quoting a paragraph by placing it in block format with the source cited.

Finally, we recommend that you read through your university's plagiarism policy so that you are familiar with it.

TASK TWELVE

Complete your own summary of the "Nile" passage in Task One. Try to limit yourself to 150 words or less.

TASK THIRTEEN

Choose a short article or passage in an article from your field of study and write a summary.

Comparative Summaries

Comparative summaries are common in many graduate courses. They can be assignments on their own, part of a longer paper, or a response to an examination question. Comparative summaries can be more challenging to write than simple summaries, because they require you to analyze and use information from two or more sources rather than just one. In a comparative summary, you often need to infer and make explicit the relationships among your sources.

TASK FOURTEEN

The following are questions from the fields of neurobiology, economics, and epidemiology. How would you approach each of these tasks? What do you think are the instructor's expectations?

1. What do Alkon and Farley believe the role of seratonin to be in memory? In what ways do they fundamentally differ? How are they similar?

2. How do Winder & Gori and Agran view the political implications of recent evidence regarding occupational cancers?

3. Relate Kohl and Jaworski's recent article "Market Orientation: The Construct, Research Propositions, and Managerial Implications" to product and service quality. Consider the perspectives of Juran, Feigenbaum, Deming, and Crosby. What common themes emerge, and how do they differ?

Construct a similar task for your own field of study. How would you plan to answer it? Be prepared to explain your task and plan in class.

TASK FIFTEEN

In this task we return to a topic introduced in Unit Two—humor. Read the following two comparative summary drafts written in response to this question on a recent take-home examination in psychology:

> Discuss Wilson (1979) and Ziv (1984) as they relate to the social function of humor. In what ways are they similar? How do they differ?

Which of the responses do you prefer? Why? How might the response you prefer be improved?

1. In "Jokes: Form, Content, Use, and Function," Wilson states that humor has a variety of both personal and social functions. For example, it may be done to lower hostility levels, to rebel, or to raise sensitive issues. Regardless of the reason, the audience may actually choose whether to laugh. The broader, social function of joking is to simply maintain the status quo. People joke to reduce friction and anxiety as well as to ridicule others in a relatively safe way. Joking can be a way for minorities to release frustrations about being in less powerful positions. Wilson also notes that there is usually a pecking order or hierarchy in humor. Superiors joke about their subordinates. Those within a certain group joke about those outside the group. Joking is often directed at those in positions perceived as subordinate.

   Ziv, in "Personality and Sense of Humor" sees the social function of humor as one of control and maintaining or establishing rapport. Joking is a way to maintain social order. People joke about outsiders—people not in the mainstream. Jokes also arise when social norms have not been adhered to. People, therefore, act "appropriately" so as to not become the victim of a joke. Jokes are also a reflection of social hierarchy. People in "higher" positions joke about those in lower positions. While the former may freely joke about the latter, the latter may joke about the former only in private. For those in a "lower" position, then, humor is a way to relieve tensions and frustrations. Ziv goes on to say that joking can be a means of initiating and improving relationships with others. It is a way of narrowing social distance. The inside jokes of a group are a part of the identities of the individual members.

2. Wilson and Ziv both maintain that humor serves a social function. For one, jokes reveal the social hierarchy. The authors agree that superiors freely joke about those in lesser positions. Subordinates, including minority groups, can privately joke about those in "higher" positions in order to reduce tension and feelings of frustration. For another, humor is beneficial for a group. Although Ziv more clearly explains this point, Wilson would agree that joking about nongroup members can not only help unify a group, but can also play a role in establishing individual identities.

   While both Wilson and Ziv analyze joking in terms of relationships among individuals, Ziv has a somewhat broader view. Ziv argues that humor is a way to exert social control. Jokes frequently focus on situations where social norms have been broken. Therefore, in order to avoid becoming the victim of a joke, people tend to follow social conventions. (Adapted from Norrick, N.N. 1993. *Conversational Joking.* Indiana University Press 1993.)

The first summary in Task Fifteen, while accurate in terms of content, fails to highlight the similarities and/or differences between the two works. As such, it is a low-level discussion of two texts. The author has missed the opportunity to reveal a broader understanding, causing the reader more work to find the important information on his or her own. In the second summary, the writer has revealed an ability to see connections, overlapping views, and important differences in the two works. This is accomplished because the author has organized the discussion in terms of the topics addressed, rather according to the works at hand. It is difficult enough deciding what information to include in a summary of one article, but when working with two or more sources, clearly your job becomes even more complicated.

If you are writing a comparative summary of two or more texts, to begin you may want to set up a chart, table, diagram, or even spreadsheet that includes your articles and the key points they address. Once you have all of your key information before you, you may have an easier time of "eyeballing" the literature, making connections, and most importantly finding enough common threads. In short, you may be able to "see things that have not quite been seen before" and *display* this understanding to your reader (Swales and Feak 2000).

In writing a comparative summary, you may find it useful to incorporate some common language of comparison.

Language Focus: Showing Similarities and Differences

To show similarity

Similarly,

According to Fuhrman (2003), mothers generally believed that by the age of six most children should have their own money to spend. Similarly, Goy (2002) found that most fathers discussed the terms of receiving an allowance with their six-year-old children.

Likewise, . . .

According to Fuhrman (2003), mothers generally believed that by the age of six most children should have their own money to spend. Likewise, Goy (2002) found that most fathers discussed the terms of receiving an allowance with their six-year-old children.

In the same fashion, . . .

Mothers thought their daughters should spend their own money on makeup, hair care products, and nail polish. In the same fashion, mothers also felt that their sons should spend their own money on less essential items such as baseball cards.

As in X, in Y . . .

As in Fuhrman's study, in our study middle-class children generally thought that they should have to do some household chores in exchange for their allowance.

Like X, Y . . .

Like the middle-class children in Fuhrman's study, middle-class children in our study generally thought that they should have to do some household chores in exchange for their allowance.

the same . . .

Fuhrman found that most middle-class children thought that they should have to do some household chores in exchange for their allowance. The same was true for middle-class children in our sample.

To show contrast

In contrast, . . .

Over 75% of Britons feel children should receive money on special occasions. In contrast, only 20% of Germans think this is appropriate.

Unlike X, Y . . .

Unlike Germans, Britons feel no restrictions should be imposed on how children spend their money.

In contrast to . . .

In contrast to Germans, who believe that parents should have some say over how children spend their pocket money, Britons feel no restrictions should be imposed on a child's spending.

On the other hand, . . .

According to Fuhrman, Germans believe that parents should have some say over how children spend their pocket money. Britons, on the other hand, feel no restrictions should be imposed.

. . . ; however, . . .
. . . , but . . .

MacKenzie (2003) argues that our petroleum reserves will not make it through the next half century; however, Day (2003) believes that reserves will double in the next half century and will last another 100 years.

Whereas . . . , . . .
. . . , whereas . . .

Whereas MacKenzie (2003) argues that our petroleum reserves will not make it through the next half century, Day (2003) believes that reserves will double in the next half century and will last another 100 years.

While . . . , . . .
. . . , while . . .

While MacKenzie (2003) argues that our petroleum reserves will not make it through the next half century, Day (2003) believes that reserves will double in the next half century and will last another 100 years.

Verbal Expressions of Similarity

To show similarity

to be similar to	The conclusion that emerges from this
to resemble	study is similar to that in Lee et al. (2003).
to be comparable to	
to correspond to	

To show contrast

to differ from	The conclusion in this study differs from
to contrast with	that in Barber et al. (2002).
to be different from	

Take a look at the second summary of Wilson and Ziv in Task Fifteen. Find the devices used by the author to highlight similarity or difference.

TASK SIXTEEN

Find at least two articles on the same topic. Write a comparative summary.

Unit Six

Writing Critiques

In Unit Five, we worked on writing descriptive and comparative summaries. In this unit, we extend this work to the writing of critiques. *Critique* is a French word that means a critical assessment (positive, negative, or a mixture of both). Some common types of critique that you may be familiar with are film reviews in newspapers or book reviews in journals. Critiques may have various structures, but the simplest is a short summary followed by an evaluation. This unit will concentrate on the evaluation portion.

In our experience, critique assignments are employed somewhat variously in U.S. graduate programs. Certain instructors—from a wide range of programs—use them on a regular basis; certain others almost never do. In some fields of study, critiques are a regular part of take-home examinations; in other fields, they rarely are. Instructors may assign critiques for several reasons:

1. To try and ensure that students actually do reading assignments

2. To assess the students' understanding

3. To try and develop habits of analytical reading in their students

4. To train graduate students to integrate the assigned reading with other readings they have done, especially by making comparisons

5. To give graduate students a better sense of the scholarly expectations in their chosen field

The first four purposes are similar to those we have already seen for summaries. The fifth is somewhat different. Summaries focus on an accurate account of the content of the original article. Critiques require that students also learn to express their evaluative comments within their field's accepted standards of judgment.

It is important that critiques be "fair and reasonable." Part of being "fair" means that criteria that are reasonable in one field should not be applied to another field where they would be unreasonable. For example, in terms of how precise a measurement needs to be, psychology is not comparable to physics. Or, in terms of the expected size of an experimental group, research on language teaching methodology is not comparable to efforts to measure elementary school reading ability. The question of how "fair" criticism varies from one field to another is an issue that we will return to later.

We should also note at this stage that different fields are likely to impose different emphases on critiques. In the humanities, attention may focus on how "interesting" the arguments are; in the social sciences, on the methodology; and in the sciences and engineering, on the results and what they might (or might not) imply for the real world.

The final point we want to make here is that we have restricted this unit to the critiquing of written work. We know that students are sometimes asked to write critiques of other things: paintings, music, films, famous buildings, and so on. Critiques of works of art require special training and special writing conventions that lie outside the scope of this book.

One common critique assignment in the social sciences is the book review. In some fields, such as sociology, students may be asked to critique books as often as every two weeks. This can be particularly hard on nonnative speakers, who (understandably) may not be fast readers. Although you may not need to review books as part of your degree program, book reviews can help you gain an awareness of evaluative language, hedging, and scholarly expectations and values of your field. Thus, let's begin our discussion of critique writing by taking a look at book reviews.

Book Reviews

Book reviews have been an important part of academia for hundreds of years. Although early book reviews were largely an uncritical discussion or summary of the content of a book, they have evolved into a highly evaluative genre, which plays a major role in the softer sciences and a somewhat less important role in the sciences.

TASK ONE

What do you already know about book reviews? With a partner, discuss the following questions to determine whether you agree *(A)*, disagree *(D)*, or don't know (?).

____ 1. Published book reviews are usually strongly negative.

____ 2. Book reviews should always start with a summary of the book.

____ 3. The judgments expressed in a published book review could have career consequences.

____ 4. Published book reviews may be somewhat threatening for the author of the book being reviewed.

____ 5. Book reviews can be a good first publication for a graduate student or junior faculty member trying to build a publication record.

____ 6. Members of your field regularly read book reviews.

____ 7. Published book reviews may not only discuss issues of content, but other issues such as price or quality of production.

____ 8. On occasion book reviewers use the book under review as a springboard to air their own points of view on a topic.

____ 9. Book reviews may be written in a less formal style.

____ 10. Book reviews generally do not contain references to previous literature.

Unlike book reviews written for a class assignment, published book reviews can be a "direct, public, and often critical encounter with a text and therefore its author, who must be considered as a primary audience for the review" (Hyland 2000). Therefore, book reviewers must exercise some discretion when writing for publication. In addition, book reviewers should very carefully consider their broader journal audience, purpose, and strategy so as to display familiarity with the field, expertise, and intelligence.

The writers of book reviews have a certain freedom in the content and organization of their reviews, because, in the end, they are expressions of their own perspective or position. Even so, most book reviews provide an overview of the content of the book under review, either by chapter or larger section; general and specific evaluation; a discussion of the relevance of the book to their field; and an endorsement (despite shortcomings). In her investigation of 60 published book reviews in Economics, Chemistry, and Linguistics, Motta-Roth (1998) proposed a schematic description of the elements in book reviews, which we have adapted for you here.

General Aim		**Specifically Accomplishing that Aim**
Introducing the book	by	establishing the topic *and / or*
		describing potential readership *and / or*
		providing information about the authors *and / or*
		making generalizations about the topic (see Unit Two) *and / or*
		establishing the place of the book in the field
Outlining the book	by	highlighting the general organization of the book *and / or*
		describing the content of each chapter or section *and / or*
		referring specifically to nontext material such as graphs, tables, and appendices
Highlighting parts of the book	by	providing focused evaluation by making general, positive commentary *and / or*
		offering specific, negative commentary
Providing final commentary and recommendations	by	commenting on price or production standards (good binding, paper quality, size) *and / or*
		specifying the scope of the usefulness of the book *and / or*
		recommending (or not recommending) the book, despite limitations, if any

This, of course, is not an exhaustive list of things "to do" in a book review but, rather, a suggestion of the kinds of topic that you can address. Typical topics for praise and criticism are degree of originality, coherence of an argument, readability/style, extent or relevance of references, and even the author of the book under review (Hyland 2000). For a class assignment, some of these topics may be more relevant than others. Although it makes sense to us that you would introduce the book, summarize, and evaluate, it may not necessarily be worthwhile to comment on such things as price and the quality of the paper.

TASK TWO

Read the following book review, published in the *Journal of Ecological Engineering,* and discuss the questions that follow with a partner. The review deals with plants in wetlands or marshes. There is some technical vocabulary, which you will likely be unfamiliar with. You can look this terminology up in a dictionary or ignore it. Paragraph numbers have been added. See question 3 concerning the markings in paragraph 5.

Wetland Plants: Biology and Ecology, Julie K. Cronk and M. Siobhan Fennessey, Lewis Publishers, 2001, 462 pp., US $89.95, hardcover, ISBN: 1-56670-372-7

Stephen E. Davis, III
Department of Wildlife and Fisheries Sciences, Texas A&M University, 210 Nagle Hall, College Station, TX 77843-2258, USA

1   Wetland plants have gained considerable attention over the last few decades in response to our increased awareness of the systems they inhabit and the growing importance of wetland management and mitigation. However, there has been little synthetic work on the biology, physiology, and ecology of this unique and diverse group of plants. Cronk and Fennessey have filled a large gap in these areas with "Wetland Plants: Biology and Ecology." This book is a synthesis of recent literature from the field (including numerous studies from both authors) and, according to the authors, "is intended for wetland professionals, academicians, and students."

2   The table of contents literally and figuratively sets the stage for "Wetland Plants." I appreciated its detail and thought it served as a nice blueprint for each chapter as well as a user-friendly index. If anything, it demonstrated the authors' attention to detail and ability to link ideas and concepts throughout the book. This attention to detail was also reflected in numerous textual references directing the reader to more in-depth coverage of a particular topic as well as the overall number of references to recent, peer-reviewed literature (50 pages of more than 1200 references).

3   The body of the book is broken down into four sections, each containing two to three chapters. Each chapter ends with a chapter summary, and a number of them contain helpful case studies that pertain to topics covered in each chapter. Although the layout is sound, I felt the boundaries placed on the treatment of this topic were too restrictive. The focus is clearly on angiosperms, yet the authors acknowledge the vast areas of wetlands throughout the world that are dominated by gymnosperms, pteridophytes, mosses, and even algae. Along these lines, the book is also limited in its emphasis on temperate (inland and coastal) and tropical (coastal only) wetlands.

4   Part I of the book offers a well-organized introduction to wetland plants (types, distribution, etc.; Chapter 1), an overview of wetland communities (Chapter 2), and an introduction to the physico-chemical environment of wetlands (Chapter 3). These are basic topics, but most readers will find these chapters useful as a reference or a reminder. I found the section on the evolution of wetland plants in the first chapter particularly interesting.

5   Part II covers wetland plant adaptations to life in flooded or saturated conditions, focusing on plant strategies for dealing with oxygen stress, stabilization in water, salinity, submergence, and nutrient deficiency (Chapter 4). This was a well-written [co] review of current information, but the connection between nutrient stress, secondary compounds, and herbivory rates in wetland plants could have received greater coverage. [cr]. Part II also offers a thorough [co] overview of reproductive mechanisms and strategies

exhibited by wetland plants (Chapter 5). Although it is rare to see a synthesis of this information, I felt the authors' thoroughness <u>distracted</u> [CR] from the flow of the book at times. For example, over 12 pages are devoted to water pollination—a strategy the authors admit represents only 2% of abiotically pollinated hydrophytes.

6   The third part is a mixed bag of terminology and methods related to wetland plant productivity (Chapter 6) and biotic and abiotic factors affecting wetland plant community succession and composition (Chapter 7). Having worked in different disturbed and undisturbed south Florida wetlands, I was especially drawn to the chapter on invasive plant species in wetlands (Chapter 8), particularly the establishment of clear definitions related to the topic, the synthesis of information on the various approaches to controlling invasive species, and case studies of five noxious species in North America.

7   The final section of "Wetland Plants" covers applied topics: created, restored, and treatment wetlands (Chapter 9) and the use of wetland plants as biological indicators (Chapter 10). Given the authors' backgrounds, it comes as no surprise that this was an excellent synthesis of recent approaches and studies. Both chapters contained informative sections dealing with topics such as removal and retention of materials (nitrogen, phosphorus, heavy metals, etc.) and use of wetland plants as indicators of ecosystem integrity.

8   Cronk and Fennessey's coverage of wetland plants extends far beyond the botanical realm (as indicated by the title) to include aspects of physiology, community ecology, and wetland ecosystem dynamics. It is written in a manner suitable for an advanced undergraduate course, a graduate course, or merely as a reference. Aside from its minor limitations, this book is an important contribution to the field and will likely inspire and educate a multitude of people working in subdisciplines ranging from Ecology to Resource Management.
(Davis III 2003)

1. The review consists of eight short paragraphs. Explain the purpose of each. Use Motta-Roth's scheme, if possible.

2. In paragraph 6, what does the author mean by "a mixed bag of terminology and methods"?

3. Which of the sentences contain complimentary elements (CO) and which contain critical elements (CR)? Where do the criticisms appear? In the beginning, middle, end, or throughout? What parts of speech are mainly used? Paragraph 5 has been marked for you.

4. How serious do the cited weaknesses seem to be?

5. Hyland (2000) concludes that praise is global but criticism is specific. Does this hold true for the review here?

6. Has the author attempted to soften any of his negative evaluative comments? (See the discussion in Unit Four on qualifications.)

7. What tenses are used in the review?

8. The author uses *I* throughout. Does this seem appropriate? Why or why not?

9. Does the review give the impression of being fair?

10. How important do you think it is to cite weaknesses in what is by and large a good book? Is anything gained by doing so? (Consider "positioning," which was described in Unit One.)

TASK THREE

Find a published book review in a journal from your field. Bring it to class and be prepared to discuss such features as organization, style (as compared to a research article in the same journal), the nature of the praise and criticism, mitigation of criticism, and evaluative language.

❈ Language Focus: Evaluative Language

As you saw in the "Wetlands" review, writing a good review requires an awareness of evaluative language. According to Ken Hyland's study of 160 book reviews from eight disciplines[1] (2000), some evaluative terms cut across several disciplines, while other evaluative terms have a preferred status in one or two disciplines. Here is a summary of his findings.

Frequently used evaluative adjectives for all eight disciplines:	*useful, important, interesting*
Frequently used evaluative nouns in the "soft" fields:	*clarity, accessibility*
Frequently used evaluative adjectives in the hard sciences:	*detailed, up-to-date*

On a more specific level, philosophers and applied linguists often described books as *detailed,* while philosophers and marketing specialists praised books for being *insightful* and *significant.* Books in engineering were commended for being *comprehensive* and *practical.*

Of course, not all evaluation is positive. For all fields the most common negative adjective was *difficult.* In the softer fields books were criticized for being *inconsistent, restricted,* and *misleading.*

In our discussion so far, we have discussed issues of content, organization, and evaluative language. Although there is more to be said on each of these topics and we will return to some of these topics later in the unit, at this point we believe you have sufficient background to attempt your own short book review. You have had experience in writing an opening summary. You are familiar with the role and place of qualifications or "hedges." In addition, you have a growing sense of your instructor as audience and are learning to present yourself in your writing as a junior member of your chosen discipline.

---

[1]Cell biology, electrical engineering, mechanical engineering, physics, marketing, applied linguistics, philosophy, and sociology.

TASK FOUR

Write a review of a book from your field of study that you are currently engaged with. Alternatively, write your own review of one of the earlier units of this book. (Send your comments to the authors in care of the University of Michigan Press, if you like!)

As we said earlier, it is important to be fair when you critique. In the next task we ask you to read two sections from Diane Belcher's critique of the 1994 edition of *Academic Writing for Graduate Students (AWG)*. In this 2004 edition we did not respond to all past criticism of the book; therefore, it is very possible that the same criticisms would be valid for the 2nd edition.

TASK FIVE

Discuss with a partner whether the limitations highlighted by Diane Belcher in these two parts of her review hold true for this edition and whether they are reasonable or unreasonable. Do you see any attempts to mitigate the criticism? If so, where and how are these expressed?

A. Given *AWG*'s considerable strengths, it is surprising that its initial chapter does not provide more of the guidance and incentive which is so evident in the rest of the text. While Chapter 1 does begin by focusing on "macro" rather than on "micro" concerns—that is with audience and purpose considerations, rather than textual features—the "style" and "flow" of academic texts receive the greatest share of Swales and Feak's attention. Of course, as the authors note, new international students are "bombarded" with "mixed messages" regarding academic discourse, and no doubt are in need of explicit help in sorting out academic registers. Nevertheless, defining academic discourse largely in terms of "vocabulary shift" toward greater formality, the "most salient feature of academic writing" according to Swales and Feak, seems rather reductive.[1] Why not begin with a more intellectually compelling . . .perspective such as MacDonald's view of academic writing as a vehicle for constructing knowledge claims . . . ? In fact beyond its initial chapters, a much richer, more cognitively

[1]See p. 52 in Unit Two for a definition of reductionism.

adventurous and social interactionalist conception of academic writing does emerge in *AWG*, as students are led from descriptive to analytical discourse, and finally to creating their own research space.

B. Some teachers may question the wisdom of encouraging novices to begin the research paper at the Methods section [although other ESP specialists besides Swales and Feak, e.g. Jacoby, Leech and Holton (1995) do encourage the "Methods first" composing sequence]. A more general problem for teachers is whether students in the early stages of graduate school will have done any research that they can write up. Might not an extended literature review, a genre not covered in *AWG*, be a more useful and doable exercise for them, or perhaps a formal research proposal? Yet another question is how helpful the research paper chapters will be for students in fields such as history, economics, journalism, and other disciplines in which experimental research is less popular. To be fair, *AWG* does not claim to address the needs of all graduate students in all fields. No matter what textbook is used in a research writing course for graduate students, teachers should expect to deviate from and supplement it, as the *Commentary* recommends, and most of all to "negotiate the syllabus" (Frodeson 1995) with their students. (Belcher 1995)

Much of what we have said about published book reviews so far, of course, would apply to the writing of a book review for a class. In your book review your instructors will want to see some evidence that you are able to situate the book within ongoing discussions or debates or theoretical lineages in your field; that you can focus in on what is important at the macro and micro level; and that you can evaluate in a manner appropriate for your field.

Evaluating an Article

Graduate students in the United States (and elsewhere) are often expected and encouraged to evaluate journal articles. While the word *critique* may not be used, students are asked to analyze, examine, or investigate, with the underlying assumption that students will do these activities with a critical eye. Writing an article critique may be somewhat easier than writing a book review, since an article usually centers around a narrow research question or problem. However, as with book reviews, they can still be particularly challenging to write because they require you to take on an "unfamiliar persona"—that of a kind of authority (Dobson and Feak 2001). Another similarity to book reviews is that what you choose to examine will largely depend on your discipline. In a field such as history, you might evaluate conclusions by critiquing the evidence used to support those conclusions. In sociology, on the other hand, you may focus on the theoretical model employed in a study and the impact the model has on the conclusions. In psychology your critique may center on the instrument used to collect data, while in engineering you may notice that conclusions or explanations in a paper are not well supported and thus require further testing or more evidence.

In writing a critique, it may help to have a set of general questions in mind to guide your thinking as you read and provide the foundation for critical inquiry (Dobson and Feak 2001). We offer a few questions here for you to consider as you read an article.

1. Who is the audience?

2. What is the purpose of the article?

3. What research question(s) is (are) being addressed in the article?

    (Stating the research question as a *yes* or *no* question will help you identify the focus of a paper. In our experience, a question such as "Does herbal tea cause tooth decay?" can be more useful in guiding your thinking than can a simple statement establishing the topic, as with "This paper is about herbal tea and tooth decay.")

4. What conclusions does the author draw from the research? (Hint: Does the author answer *yes* or *no* to the research question?)

5. What kind of evidence is offered in support of the conclusions? Is there any evidence that could or should have been included but was not? How good is the evidence?

6. Are the author's conclusions valid or plausible based on the evidence? Why or why not?

7. Are there any important assumptions underlying the article? How do these influence the conclusions?

8. Does the research make an original contribution to the field? Why or why not?

TASK SIX

In this task we return to a text introduced in Unit Three. While you read it, consider the eight questions above.

The Role of English in Research and Scholarship

① There are many claims that a clear majority of the world's research papers are now published in English. **②** For example, in 1983 Eugene Garfield, President of the Institute for Scientific Information (ISI)[1], claimed that 80% of the world's scientific papers are written in English (Garfield 1983). **③** More recently comparable estimates have been produced for engineering, medicine, and nonclinical psychology.

④ It is not clear, however, whether such high percentages for English provide an accurate picture of languages chosen for publication by researchers around the world. **⑤** The major difficulty is bias in the databases from which these high percentages are typically derived. **⑥** The databases are those established by the major abstracting and indexing services, such as the ISI indexes and Medline, which are predominantly located in the United States. **⑦** As a result, these services have tended to preselect papers that *(a)* are written in English and *(b)* originate in the Northern Hemisphere. **⑧** For these two reasons, it is probable that research in languages other than English is somewhat underrepresented.[2] **⑨** Indeed, Najjar (1988) showed that no Arabic language science journal was consistently covered by the *Science Citation Index* in the mid-1980s.

⑩ We can hypothesize from the previous discussion that the role of English in research may be considerably inflated. **⑪** In fact, several early small-scale studies bear this out: Throgmartin (1980) produced English percentages in the 40% range for social sciences, and Velho

---

[1]The Institute for Scientific Information (ISI) publishes the *Science Citation Index (SCI), the Social Science Citation Index (SSCI),* and the *Arts and Humanities Citation Index (AHCI).*
[2]The ISI itself has concluded that it may underrepresent useful research from the lesser developing countries by a factor of two (Moravcsik 1985).

and Krige (1984) showed a clear preference for publication in Portuguese among Brazilian agricultural researchers. **⑫** A complete bibliography on schistosomiasis, a tropical disease, by Warren and Newhill (1978) revealed an English language percentage of only 45%. **⑬** These studies would seem to indicate that a more accurate percentage for English would be around 50% rather than around 80%.

⑭ However, so far no major international study exists to corroborate such a conclusion. **⑮** Until such a study is undertaken—perhaps by UNESCO—the true global picture of language use in research publication will remain open to doubt and disagreement. **⑯** Until such time, nonnative speakers of English will remain uncertain about how effective their publications are in their own languages.

In a critique, you may want to express criticism by saying what the author should have done but did not do. One example of this is present in the "Wetlands" book review, which contains an unreal conditional.

This was a well-written review of current information, but the connection between nutrient stress, secondary compounds, and herbivory rates in wetland plants *could have received* greater coverage.

For the "Role of English" passage, you could make the following observation.

The discussion would have been somewhat more relevant if the author had used more recent literature to support his views.

❖ *Language Focus: Unreal Conditionals*

Here are two additional examples of unreal conditional statements.

This article *would have been* more persuasive *if* the author *had related* the findings to previous work on the topic.

It *would have been* better *if* the authors *had given* their main findings in the form of a table.

Notice the structure of these conditionals:

would / might have + verb-$_{EN}$[2] + comparison + *if* + noun phrase + *had* verb-$_{EN}$

These conditionals refer to an unreal situation in the past. Past unreal conditionals are common in critiques because the texts being critiqued have already been put into final form—either published or turned in. There is no opportunity to revise the text in light of the criticism, because the time frame is closed. Since these conditionals express something that is impossible, linguists and philosophers often call them *counterfactuals*. In a critique, the *if*-clause in the past unreal conditional often occurs second. Why is this so?

Present unreal conditionals, on the other hand, describe a hypothetical situation in the present. In these, the simple past tense forms are used. In a consultation with your writing instructor, you may have heard a sentence such as this.

> Your paper *would be* stronger if you *included* some additional information.

In this sentence, it is clear that the possibility for revision still exists. The time frame is open. This type of sentence is sometimes called a *hypothetical conditional*.

TASK SEVEN

Complete and exchange these thoughts with a partner.

1. My grade on my last test would have been higher if . . .
   What about you?

2. My meeting with my advisor would have been more productive if . . .
   What about you?

3. The last talk in our department would have been better if . . .
   What do you think about the last talk in your department?

---

[2]EN is a convention used to refer to the past participle form of the verb, e.g., *write, wrote* (simple past-$_{ED}$, *written* (participle-$_{EN}$).

Now notice the italicized verb forms in the following.

> The author *should have provided* more data about her sample.

> Although this is an interesting and important paper, the authors *could have given* more attention to the fact that their model of consumer choice is based entirely on U.S. data.

Notice that *should* expresses a strongly negative comment, while *could* is less strong. *Should have* is a criticism, *could have* is more a suggestion, and *might have* is a weak suggestion.

The use of *could* and *might* in unreal conditionals also reminds us that it is important to make your points with appropriate amount of strength. Criticisms that are too strong and lack support will not help you position yourself, nor will evaluative comments that are expressed in too weak a manner.

❖ Language Focus: Evaluative Language Revisited

As you already know, the content parts of speech can be used for evaluation.

Nouns	success	failure
Verbs	succeed	fail
Adjectives	successful	unsuccessful
Adverbs	successfully	unsuccessfully

TASK EIGHT

Rate the adjectives as follows.

++ = very positive
+ = positive
0 = neutral, uncertain, ambiguous
− = negative
−− = very negative

In this _____ study, Jones and Wang attempt to show that . . .

___ unusual   ___ limited   ___ ambitious   ___ modest
___ small   ___ restricted   ___ important   ___ flawed

__ useful	__ significant	__ innovative	__ interesting
__ careful	__ competent	__ impressive	__ elegant
__ simple	__ traditional	__ complex	__ small scale
__ exploratory	__ remarkable	__ preliminary	__ unsatisfactory

Sometimes, we can make contrasting pairs of adjectives. The pairing of a positive and a negative can certainly soften the criticism.

> In this ambitious but flawed study, Jones and Wang. . .

> In this flawed but ambitious study, Jones and Wang. . .

Notice how the emphasis changes depending on the information you place first. Can you create three other suitable combinations?

In addition to pairing adjectives, you can also make other pairings using other linking words and phrases, especially those used to express adversativity (see Unit One).

> *Although* the author suggests that journal articles written in languages other than English may have limited impact, he fails to see the advantages of more publications being available in English.

> The author suggests that journal articles written in languages other than English may have limited impact; *however,* he fails to see the advantages of more publications being available in English.

> *Despite* the many interesting citations in support of his view, the citations are dated and are not likely meaningful today.

Evaluative Adjectives across the Disciplines

Classes composed of students from several disciplines do not always agree about these adjectives. This is fully understandable. Take the case of the *simple/complex* contrast. Students in science and medicine, for example, think of *simple* as a positive and *complex* as a negative. For such students, *simple* equals "well planned" or "clearly designed," and *complex* equals "confused" or "messy." In contrast, social scientists equate *simple* with "unsophisticated" and *complex* with "sophisticated."

In an interesting study (note the evaluative adjective!), Becher (1987) surveyed adjectives of praise and blame among historians,

**Table 20   Adjectives of Praise and Blame among Historians,
Sociologists, and Physicists in Britain and the United States**

	Good Work	Average Work	Poor Work
Humanities	scholarly original	sound	thin
Social sciences	perceptive rigorous	scholarly	anecdotal
Physics	elegant economical	accurate	sloppy

sociologists, and physicists in Britain and the United States. He
found considerable differences among the three groups. Although the
preferences listed in table 20 only indicate general tendencies, they
are quite revealing.

List some typical evaluative adjectives (both good and bad) used
in your field. What about *neat* for example?

Critical Reading

In Task Nine, you will critically read a short report on a topic that you
may have some experience with—bullying. The brief research report
is taken from the *Journal of Adolescence.*

TASK NINE

Read the following report fairly quickly to get an idea of what it is
about. Answer the questions that follow the report with a partner or
in a small group.

BRIEF REPORT

Types of Bullying among Italian School Children
Anna C. Baldry and David P. Farrington

Introduction
The main aim of this research is to investigate the prevalence
of bullies and victims and the types of bullying and places
of bullying in a sample of school children in Rome. The first
extensive study on bullying in Italy was conducted in
Florence and Cosenza, two towns of central and southern

Italy, by Genta et al. (1996) with a sample of over 1000 students from primary (8- to 11-years-old) and middle schools (11- to 14-years-old). They found that about 30% of students from middle schools reported being bullied sometimes or more often, and 10% were bullied at least once a week in the previous 3 months. About 15% of all students reported bullying others sometimes or more often and about 5% reported bullying at least once a week.

According to Farrington (1993), Rivers and Smith (1994) and Smith and Sharp (1994), whereas boys bully more than girls on average, boys and girls report about the same prevalence of victimization. What differs, however, is the type of bullying in which students are involved. Studies conducted on aggression among peers by Bjorkvist et al. (1992), Lagerspetz et al. (1988) and Rivers and Smith (1994) have shown significant differences between boys and girls. Boys are more likely to inflict direct physical aggression with the intent of causing physical harm, whereas girls are more likely to inflict indirect forms of aggression with the intent of causing psychological harm. However, there were no significant gender differences in direct verbal aggression. Results from the study conducted in Sheffield by Whitney and Smith (1993) found that most of the bullying in secondary schools took place in the classroom. Children were also bullied in corridors or in other parts of the schools such as in the toilets. Similar results were reported in the Italian study (Genta et al., 1996), indicating that more than 50% of those children ever bullied were victimized in their own classroom.

Method

Sample
The sample consisted of 113 girls and 125 boys aged between 11 and 14 years (mean age = 12.7 years, s.d. = 1.1). Students came from a representative middle school in Rome. Nearly half (44%) of the fathers were skilled workers, 21% were unskilled workers, 20% were merchants or operators of other businesses and 15% were in professional or managerial jobs. Nearly half (42%) of the mothers were homemakers,

38% were skilled workers, 11% were merchants, 6% were in managerial or executive positions and 3% were unskilled workers.

Procedure

All students from the school participated in the study. Those missing on the day when the questionnaires were initially administered in a group were able to fill them in on another day. Students were approached in their own classes by one of the authors (A.C.B.). They were told that the research was about bullying in school. They were assured of anonymity and confidentiality and informed that all information would be used only for research purposes. Students were asked to sit separately to allow no conferring, talking or helping when filling in the questionnaire. The following definition of "bullying" was read to students followed by a short discussion to ensure a common understanding of what constitutes "bullying". "Students bully weaker peers at school by deliberately and repeatedly hurting and upsetting them in several ways; by calling them names, hitting or threatening them and playing nasty games. It is not bullying when two students of about the same strength quarrel or have a fight".

Measures

The questionnaire was based on the Italian version (Genta et al., 1996) of the original questionnaire developed by Olweus (1993) for the Scandinavian population, subsequently translated and validated in English by Smith and his colleagues (Whitney and Smith, 1993; Smith and Sharp, 1994). All questions on bullying referred to the 3-month period preceding the administration of the questionnaire. For all questions students were allowed to choose more than one of the alternatives if they applied.

Results

Prevalence of Bullying

Overall, 56.7% of all students had never been bullied in the last 3 months, 13.9% were bullied once or twice, 14.7% sometimes and 14.7% once a week or more often. Girls tended to be victimized more than boys; 34.5% of girls, compared with 24.8% of boys, had been victimized sometimes or more often. This relationship was not far off statistical significance ($\chi^2 = 2.70$, df $= 1, p < 0.10$). Overall, 47.5% of all students had never bullied others in the previous 3 months, 27.3% bullied once or twice, 17.6% sometimes and 7.6% once a week or more often. About one-third (31.2%) of boys had bullied at least sometimes in the previous 3 months, compared with 18.6% of girls ($\chi^2 = 5.01$, df $= 1, p < 0.05$).

Types of Bullying

Table 1 shows that most students were directly victimized by being called nasty names or being physically hurt, or were indirectly victimized by being rejected or having rumours spread about them. Boys were significantly more likely to suffer from types of direct bullying, whereas girls were slightly more likely to suffer from indirect forms of bullying (e.g. being rejected, rumours spread about them). Significant differences emerged for types of direct bullying, especially for being threatened and marginally for being physically hurt. There were no significant gender differences in direct verbal bullying or indirect bullying; boys were almost as likely as girls to suffer indirect bullying. Both boys (69.3%) and girls (72.2%) were most likely to be bullied by one or several boys. Girls (9.3%) and boys (10.2%) were equally likely to be bullied by one or several girls, and 18.5% of girls, compared to 20.4% of boys, admitted being bullied by both girls and boys. Both girls (86.8%) and boys (75.0%) tended to be bullied by other children in the same class. However, boys were more likely to be bullied by older children (29.2% as opposed to 15.0%; ($\chi^2 = 2.89$, df $= 1, p < 0.09$) and by children in the same year but in a different class (16.7% as opposed to 7.5%; n.s.). Neither boys (4.2%) nor girls (3.8%) tended to be bullied by younger children. Bullying most commonly took place in the classroom (Table 1). This is in conformity with the fact that most bullies were in the same class as the victims. Other common places for bullying were in the corridors and in the playground. Boys were significantly more likely to be bullied in the toilets.

Discussion

Bullying among Italian pupils is quite prevalent. Over half of all students had bullied others, and nearly half had been

TABLE 1. Types and Places of Bullying

	% Girls (n = 54)†	% Boys (n = 49)†
Types of Bullying		
Called nasty names	59.3	71.3
Rejected	51.3	48.0
Physically hurt	18.5	34.0*
Rumours spread	27.8	23.4
Had belongings taken away	16.7	19.1
Other forms of bullying (e.g. teased)	14.8	10.6
Threatened	0.0	12.8{
No one would talk	3.7	6.4
Direct bullying‡	66.7	93.6{
Indirect bullying‡	74.1	68.8
Places of Bullying		
In the classroom	79.6	66.7
In the corridors	24.1	33.3
In the playground	27.8	33.3
Other places (gym, lunch hall)	7.4	10.4
In the toilets	0.0	12.5}

* $\chi^2 = 3.17$, df = 1, $p < 0.07$; { $\chi^2 = 7.33$, df = 1, $p < 0.01$; { $\chi^2 = 11.08$, df = 1, $p < 0.01$; } $\chi^2 = 7.17$, df = 1, $p < 0.01$.
†Percentages refer to those students ever bullied. Total percentages exceed 100 because students could check multiple responses.
‡"Direct bullying" includes called nasty names, physically hurt, belongings taken away, threatened, others (e.g. teasing). "Indirect bullying" includes being rejected, rumours spread, no one would talk.

bullied. Boys bullied more than girls, and girls were somewhat more likely than boys to be bullied sometimes or more often. In accordance with findings from other studies (Olweus, 1993; Smith and Sharp, 1994; Rigby, 1996), boys were more likely to suffer direct bullying such as being threatened or physically hurt. Surprisingly, boys were almost as likely as girls to suffer indirect bullying such as being rejected and having rumours spread about them, in contrast to the findings of Bjorkqvist (1994). Contradicting results from previous studies (Whitney and Smith, 1993; Genta et al., 1996), which showed that boys were mainly bullied by other boys and girls by other girls, in our sample both boys and girls were bullied by one or several boys. Most of the bullying took place in the classroom, with lesser amounts in the corridors or playground. Boys were more likely than girls to be bullied in the toilets.

References

Bjorkqvist, K. (1994). Sex differences in physical, verbal and indirect aggression: a review of recent research. *Sex Roles,* 30, 177–188.

Bjorkqvist, K., Lagerspetz, K. M. J. and Kaukiainen, A. (1992). Do girls manipulate and boys fight? Developmental trends in regard to direct and indirect aggression. *Aggressive Behavior,* 18, 117–127.

Farrington, D. P. (1993). Understanding and preventing bullying. In *Crime and justice.* Vol. 17, M. Tonry (Ed.). Chicago: University of Chicago Press, pp. 381–458.

Genta, M. L., Menesini, E., Fonzi, A., Costabile, A. and Smith, P. K. (1996). Bullies and victims in schools in central and southern Italy. *European Journal of Psychology of Education,* 11, 97–110.

Lagerspetz, K. M. J., Bjorkqvist, K. and Peltonen, T. (1988). Is indirect aggression typical of females? Gender differences in aggressiveness in 11- to 12-years-old children. *Aggressive Behavior,* 14, 403–414.

Olweus, D. (1993). *Bullying at school: what we know and what we can do.* Oxford: Blackwell.

Rigby, K. (1996). *Bullying in schools and what to do about it.* London: Jessica Kingsley.

Rivers, I. & Smith, P. K. (1994). Types of bullying behavior and their correlates. *Aggressive Behavior,* 20, 359–368.

Smith, P. K. and Sharp, S. (1994). School Bullying: insights and perspectives. London: Routledge.

Whitney, I. and Smith, P. K. (1993). A survey of the nature and extent of bullying in junior/middle and secondary schools. *Educational Research,* 35, 3–25.

Journal of Adolescence 22, Anna C. Baldry and David P. Farrington, "Brief report: Types of bullying among Italian school children," 423–426, © 1999, with permission from Elsevier.

1. What research question is being addressed? (Try to state this as a yes-no question.)

2. What do the authors conclude?

3. How good is the data used as support for this conclusion? In particular, what do you think about the strong reliance on self-report data?

4. The authors state that their main aim is to "investigate the prevalence of bullies and victims and the types of bullying and places of bullying in a sample of school children in Rome." Have they achieved their goal? Why or why not?

5. The authors used the following definition of bullying: "Students bully weaker peers at school by deliberately and repeatedly hurting and upsetting them in several ways; by

calling them names, hitting or threatening them and playing nasty games. It is not bullying when two students of about the same strength quarrel or have a fight." Do you think this definition is adequate?

How might the results differ if the authors had defined bullying in this way: "*Persistent,* offensive, abusive, intimidating or insulting behaviour, abuse of power or unfair penal sanctions which makes the recipient feel upset, threatened, humiliated or vulnerable, which undermines their self-confidence and which may cause them to suffer stress" (http://www.bullyonline.org/workbully/defns.htm)?

6. The authors state that "most students were directly victimized by being called nasty names or being physically hurt, or were indirectly victimized by being rejected or having rumours spread about them." To which students are the authors referring—most of the 238 students in the study or only those that had been bullied?

7. Table 1 would seem to suggest that bullying is a serious problem in the school. Do you think this is the case? Why or why not?

8. In the Discussion section how well have the authors compared their results with those of other studies?

9. What are the limitations of the study, if any?

10. The authors provide no recommendations for addressing the bullying problem in the school. Should they have? Why or why not?

As you were reading the report in Task Nine, you might have thought of comments you would like to make about it. Before we critique the report, we need to be *fair.* After all, being seen as fair and reasonable is part of graduate student positioning. It is clear, we think, that Baldry and Farrington cannot be expected in a short communication (see Unit Seven) to provide all the background information readers might require or to offer an intervention to address bullying in the Rome school. Also, it is likely that the authors would undertake similar research in other schools to get a better picture of the problem. We would then expect the authors to publish a full article in either the *Journal of Adolescence* or some similar journal.

TASK TEN

Here are some criticisms of Baldry and Farrington made by our own classes. (Our students also had some positive comments.) Discuss the list and mark each criticism as *R* (reasonable) or *U* (unreasonable).

_____ 1. The school may not be a typical institution; therefore, the research should have been carried out across a range of schools.

_____ 2. The sample of 238 may be too small to really draw any good conclusions.

_____ 3. There should have been equal numbers of boys and girls as well as equal numbers in each age group.

_____ 4. It is important to know more about the specific ages of the students since this may affect the results.

_____ 5. The definition of bullying seems a bit too broad. Almost any kind of aggression seems to be called bullying.

_____ 6. If you look at the kind of bullying for the whole school, not just for students that were bullied, the amount of bullying activity does not seem so high.

Do you have any other criticisms of the report that you consider fair and reasonable? Work in a group to come up with at least two more. Be prepared to offer them to the class.

TASK ELEVEN

Consider this draft critique of the report in Task Nine. Is there any positive evaluation? Underline the criticisms. Which of the criticisms do you accept as being "fair and reasonable" and which "unfair and unreasonable"? Can you offer any advice for improvement?

❶ According to Smith (1999) bullying in schools has become a serious problem in many countries over the past several decades. ❷ As a result, there is a growing body of literature on the causes, prevalence, and nature of the victims of bullying. ❸ Baldry and

Farrington add to this literature in their examination of bullying in one middle school in Rome, Italy. ❹ They administered a questionnaire on bullying to all 238 students in the school and found, unsurprisingly, that bullying exists in the school and that the most common form of bullying is calling someone a nasty name.

❺ The study by Baldry and Farrington mainly replicates the results of the much larger study ($N = 1000$) done by Genta et al. (1996). ❻ Thus, it adds little to our existing knowledge on bullying behavior. ❼ As a rather small study of one school environment, the results cannot be generalized. ❽ If in the future the authors extended their investigation to include more schools and more students, we could begin to gain a better understanding of bullying behavior in Italy and how this might compare to similar behavior in other countries.

❾ In addition to the problems listed above, this study has two major limitations, both of which negatively affected the results. ❿ First, the authors collected self reports of bullying behavior over a 3-month period using a questionnaire. ⓫ As is well known, self reports are not always reliable (Sudman 1977). ⓬ The authors should have undertaken observations in order to provide another source of data. ⓭ Minimally, additional questionnaire data from teachers and administrators should also have been collected. ⓮ Since bullying behavior is repeated in successive encounters with another person, the 3-month period is far too short to get a good glimpse of the problem in this school. ⓯ Second, an even more serious limitation centers on the definition of bullying employed in the study. ⓰ Although bullying is widely recognized as a serious problem, there is considerable debate as to what constitutes bullying. **❶** It is quite unfortunate that Baldry and Farrington have adopted a very broad definition of bullying. **❶** In fact, their definition is so broad that it would include everything from isolated instances of name calling to the more serious persistent acts intended to hurt another student. **❶** Their broad definition also fails to consider the importance of the imbalance in the power of the aggressor and that of the bullying target. **❷** Baldry and Farrington may therefore present percentages of bullying behavior that are too high but at the same time fail to capture the more serious, ongoing oppression of the individual victim (Smoith et al. 1999). **❷** It is the repeated psychological and physical oppression of the less powerful by the more powerful that needs to be identified and understood. **❷** The fact that the authors did not seriously consider this aspect of bullying completely undermines their work.

❷ This preliminary study confirms the existence of bullying behavior, but because of the serious limitations outlined above, it does not shed much new light on the issue.

As you may have noticed, the critique in Task Eleven is overall quite negative. However, only thinking negatively is probably ill-advised. After all, instructors rarely choose articles for critiquing because they think they are worthless. Further, you do not want to give the impression that you are only a "hatchet" person, someone who does nothing but criticize. It would be possible to structure the evaluation of the Baldry and Farrington report in this way.

Baldry and Farrington provide a small piece of research on an interesting topic.
                       (offer)   (preliminary)   (important)

However, the study	suffers from a number of limitations.
	exhibits several weaknesses.
	can be criticized on several counts.
	raises as many questions as it answers.

Since this is a short communication (see Unit Eight) perhaps to be fair, some of the conclusions should be qualified (see Unit Four). Here is an example.

However, *at least in its published form,* the study *apparently* suffers from a number of limitations.

TASK TWELVE

Now edit the draft of the critique from Task Eleven so that it is more balanced and fair.

✣ *Language Focus: Beginning the Critique*

Finding just the right sentence to begin your critique can indeed be a challenge. We read through several commentaries (critiques) published in *Behavioral and Brain Sciences,* one of the few journals that publishes expert responses to manuscripts. We found some very interesting opening sentences, which we have transformed into skeletal sentences for you.

[Author names] present a plausible case that . . . Less adequate is their discussion of . . .

[Author names] take on the difficult task of . . . Unfortunately, . . .

[Author names] present an important discussion of . . . Although we may not agree on all the issues raised in the article, we praise the authors for . . .

The article by [author names] is an ambitious feat of synthesis, encompassing diverse theories of . . . This effort, however, is not fully successful.

[Author names] have written an important and timely article on . . . Despite its many strengths there are a number of small, but important, weaknesses.

[Author names] present a compelling argument for . . . ; however, . . .

While the authors' position that . . . is attractive, there are a number of weaknesses in this concept.

Language Focus: Inversions

You already know that English usually requires an inverted word order for questions. You also probably know that a different word order is required if a "negative" word is used to open a sentence.

Not only has the author presented some valuable new information, he has also presented it in a very clear and coherent manner.

In no case do the authors provide any statistical information about their results.

Notice how the auxiliary verb precedes the subject, as in a question. Now look at this statement, first inverted, then in normal word order.

Particularly prominent were functional strategies . . .

Functional strategies . . . were particularly prominent.

This kind of inversion, even with simple adjectives or participles, is quite common in poetry ("Broken was the sword of the king"). However, in academic English, it only occurs with expressions that are emphatic (e.g., "particularly") or comparative (e.g., "even more"). The inversion is a strong highlighting device and should only be used for special emphasis, as when we want to single out *one* result/fault/problem/virtue from many others. Six typical expressions follow. Complete three of the five that have not been done for you.

1. Particularly important [+ *be* + noun phrase].
   was the discovery that many computer viruses have no known source.

2. Especially interesting _____ .

3. Much less expected _____ .

4. Rather more significant _____ .

5. Especially noteworthy _____ .

6. Of greater concern _____ .

TASK THIRTEEN

Now write a critique of a paper from your own field. Consider beginning with a brief summary and making sure that there is a good fit between your summary and critique.

❄ *Language Focus: Special Verb Agreements*

Notice the agreement of the subject and verb in this sentence.

A set of 200 questionnaires was distributed.

This sentence follows the standard rule whereby the verb agrees with the subject noun (in this case *set*) and not the second noun (in this case *questionnaires*). But note that this important rule does not apply in a few exceptional cases, such as when the first noun is a fraction, a proportion, or a percentage. In these special cases, the verb agrees with the noun *closest* to the verb.

A minority of the students *were* native speakers.

TASK FOURTEEN

Fill in the blank with either *was* or *were*.

1. The average score of all the results _____ 67.8%.

2. A total of 7,000 students _____ required to take the test.

3. Half of the students _____ asked to answer experimental questions.

4. Nearly 19% of the candidates _____ unable to complete the test within the time limit.

5. Approximately 46% of the test population _____ confident that they had clearly understood the directions.

6. One-quarter of the students _____ given extra time to complete the examination.

Another interesting grammar point arises in sentences beginning with *a . . . number of/the . . . number of.* Which form of *be* would you choose here?

> A small number of African students _____ included on an experimental basis.

> The small number of Japanese candidates _____ thought to be surprising.

Reaction Papers

Throughout this book, we have placed strong emphasis on formal style. We will continue to do so in Units Seven and Eight. However, in this section of Unit Six we would like to introduce you to two kinds of critique that permit—and encourage—a more personal and informal style of writing: reaction papers and reviews. These may be more common in the U.S. than elsewhere.

In a reaction paper students are encouraged to draw on their own experiences, feelings, and ideas as well as to make methodological and analytic comments. International students can often have an advantage here because they can incorporate observations and experiences that reflect their own special backgrounds, although this genre may be completely new to them and be particularly challenging to write. Often, the comments in a reaction paper will open instructors' eyes to things they had not thought of.

TASK FIFTEEN

Here are two short reaction papers on the "Bullying" report in Task Nine. Read the reactions and answer the questions that follow. Consider which of the two reactions you would prefer to have written and which would likely appeal to the instructor.

> A. ❶ The consequences of bullying are well known: stress, low self-esteem, depression, and even suicide. ❷ Although the findings of Baldry and Farrington are not new in my opinion, they remind us of how important it is to identify bullying behavior and intervene before too much damage has been done to an individual. ❸ Bullying, no matter what form it takes, hurts.

④ Unfortunately, the study did not investigate the impact that bullying had on the victim, who is often somehow "different" from many other children. ⑤ As a former elementary school teacher, I know that all too often school teachers and administrators look the other way when a child is bullied, thinking that name calling and other forms of aggression are just part of growing up. ⑥ They fail to notice that a child, once engaged and enthusiastic about school, has become withdrawn and afraid. ⑦ All schools need programs in place to address bullying and mitigate its effects. ⑧ I think that schools need to establish antibullying policies with the input of all school community members. ⑨ Not only should teachers and school administrators be involved in policymaking, but parents and students as well. ⑩ Antibullying policies should include a clear definition of bullying along with clear guidelines for dealing with bullying problems. ⑪ Antibullying agreements can also be drafted in which students agree to avoid bullying behavior themselves and to intervene when they see a peer being victimized. ⑫ Students can receive special training so that they have the confidence to intercede and protect. ⑬ We are all aware that many subtle forms of bullying can occur without detection. ⑭ Thus, I believe it is important for antibullying policies to encourage teachers to receive training that will heighten their awareness of the many forms that bullying can take and measures that can prevent opportunities for bullying. ⑮ Antibullying policies also need to clarify the penalties for bullying, if peer or teacher intervention is unsuccessful.

⑯ I think there is little doubt that well-formed antibullying policies can have a profound impact on the welfare of all school children. ⑰ There is no single approach to solving the bullying problem, but a good first step is for all schools to take a strong antibullying stance.

B. ① Since I lived in a very rural area, I went away to a state boarding school when I was 12. ② Certainly, there was a certain amount of bullying by the older and stronger boys, but my recollection is that this was really part of growing up. ③ Of course, extreme forms of bullying can be dangerous, but probably not as dangerous as the drugs, gangs, and weapons in some U.S. high schools.

④ So, my reaction to the Baldry and Farrington paper is not very favorable. ⑤ Some of the elements they describe as "bullying" in Table 1, such as spreading rumors, being ignored, or teasing, are certainly not always bullying. ❻ There must also be doubts about the methodology. ❼ If you ask somebody if they have had a bad experience of a particular sort, I think it is likely that they will remember (or perhaps misremember) such an experience. ❽ In the newspapers, a year or two ago, there were all those cases of false childhood memories of sexual abuse.

❾ More seriously, we are given no information in this paper about the race and religion of the kids in the study. ❿ We know that Italy no longer has the homogeneous population it once had, because of the new immigrants coming into the major Italian cities from Africa, the Middle East, etc. ⓫ Given that "bullying" is most likely to affect those who are "different," we really needed to know whether there were minority kids in the sample and whether they suffered more than the others.

⓬ While I recognize that this is a short report, I think as it stands the paper is still pretty "thin" and perhaps only marginally publishable. ⓭ Certainly, the authors have done a good job in their discussion of the previous research, but they have not done a brilliant job with their own!

1. Make a list of all the personal expressions used in the reaction papers.

2. How would you say the reactions are organized? Are they similar to a problem-solution text or general to specific?

3. In which sentence(s) do the authors make effective use of their own experiences?

4. The writer of reaction paper A has devoted her attention to the need for antibullying policies, which was not mentioned in the original article. Do you think her emphasis on antibullying policies has resulted in an effective response?

5. Compare one or both of the reaction papers to the critique on page 204. In what significant ways do the two types of paper differ?

❖ Language Focus: Scare Quotes

Earlier in this unit, we mentioned word inversion as a result of putting "negative" words at the beginning of sentences. The word *negative* in the previous sentence is in *scare quotes*. The use of scare quotes is a means of distancing the writer from the descriptor. The writer indicates by scare quotes that she or he does not necessarily believe that the concept is valid. For instance, the use of quotes around *negative* in our example suggests that *negative* is to be interpreted very broadly, since it will cover words like *hardly* and *scarcely* as well as "true" negatives (note the scare quotes!) such as *never*. Can you find the scare quotes in the reaction papers on bullying in Task Fifteen?

In critiques, scare quotes can also be a useful way to signal that you are not necessarily committed to the author's position. For example, you might write,

> The authors' position regarding English "dominance" in academia . . .

The scare quotes indicate that you have doubts about the validity of the author's position. Scare quotes are a useful demonstration of your sophistication. However, they tend to be used more in social sciences and humanities than in science and engineering.

TASK SIXTEEN

Now write a reaction paragraph to a paper from your own field. You may want to comment on why a particular methodology may or may not be useful for your own research. Alternatively, write a reaction paper to the "Bullying" brief report in Task Nine.

As it happens, an increasing number of journals are now printing readers' "reactions," "responses," or "discussions" to published articles. The published commentaries can be extremely interesting, as they often highlight key debates within your field. Do you know of such a journal in your field? If you can find and examine such a journal, you will see the large difference in style between the research article and the commentary.

A Few Thoughts on Manuscript Reviews

You may at some point be asked to review a manuscript that has been submitted for publication. Journals generally provide you guidelines by which to evaluate the manuscript. In your first few reviews, you may want to adhere to the guidelines, but as you gain more experience, you should also have confidence in your ability and develop your own reviewing style. In the guidelines of one journal with which John and Chris are very familiar, reviewers are asked to consider such things as the level of interest others in the field might have, the originality of the manuscript, the author's familiarity with the field, the appropriateness of the methodology and statistical analyses, the appropriateness of the conclusions, and writing style.

Regardless of the quality of the article that you are reviewing, as with all other forms of critique, it is important to be fair. Your job is not to find as much fault as possible with a manuscript. Instead, we suggest that you consider yourself as being in the role of a peer advisor engaged in a written dialogue with the author, albeit a dialogue that may be one-sided if you do not recommend the manuscript for publication.

Unit Seven

Constructing a Research Paper I

Units Seven and Eight consolidate many of the aspects of academic writing that we have stressed in earlier units. However, they also break new ground. They differ from the previous units in one important way. By this stage we think it possible that you may now be carrying out a research investigation of some kind. The purpose of these units, therefore, is to prepare you for and help you with writing up your own research. But before we get to this, we need to narrow the ground somewhat. This narrowing is necessary because there are many types of research publication that appear in journals, not all of which we have the space to deal with in this book.

Types of Serial Research Publication

A first point is that not all research articles are empirical. In astrophysics, for example, experimentation is actually impossible: "One cannot experiment on a star or a galaxy in the way in which one can experiment on a chemical compound or a bean plant" (Tarone et al. 1998, 115). As a result, astrophysicists tend to publish logical argumentation papers that have a general-specific structure (see Unit Two). This form of argument moves typically from known principles, to observations, and then to equations designed to account for the observed phenomena. This kind of paper can be common in theoretical physics, in mathematics, and in those fields (economics, biostatistics, engineering) that use computer modeling. In such "theory papers," the standard Introduction-Methods-Results-Discussion (IMRD) pattern (used for most research papers) does not apply. Because such papers have no fixed structure, there is a considerable amount of *metadiscourse* (Unit Four) which "roadmaps" the organization of the paper. Because of their theoretical nature, the use of first-person pronouns is widely accepted. We will not deal with this type of paper in any detail in the last two units.

Another kind of serial publication that will not be discussed in detail here is the *review article,* or *meta-analysis* (as it has come to be called in medical research). Such articles are usually written by senior researchers, often at the invitation of editors. Because they are reviews, they also do not follow the IMRD pattern. According to Noguchi's (2001) study of 25 review articles published in the *Proceedings of the National Academy of Sciences,* such pieces are likely to have a primary focus of one of these four types:

a. History   Presenting a historical view of (part of) the field

b. Current work   Describing the current state of knowledge

c. Theory/model   Proposing a theory or model to account for the available data

d. Issue   Calling attention to some issue in the field

TASK ONE

Take a review article of relevance of you. Does it have one (or more) of the foci listed above? Or is the approach different? What kind of section headings does it have? How long is it? How many references does it have?

We will not be dealing with separate literature reviews in *AWG* (for these please consult *English in Today's Research World* Units Four and Five). However, in Unit Eight, we will be discussing references and citations *as part of* Introductions and Discussions.

There are three types of serially published pieces left. One consists of responses and reactions to earlier work. These are rare in most fields, and were covered at least in part in Unit Six. Then there are *short communications* (also sometimes called *brief reports* or *notes*) and standard empirical research papers (typically in IMRD format). The main focus of these last two units will be on the latter, but first we will examine short communications, especially because these, along with book reviews, may be one of the first items that junior researchers publish.

Short Communications (SCs)

This type of research communication is widespread and can be found in international as well as national or regional journals. Unlike major article-length research communications, which are increasingly being published in English, many SCs in national or regional journals are still being written in many academic languages as well as English. They cover all the field disciplines (biology, archaeology, geology, etc.) and such areas as folklore, architecture, and ethnomusicology. They include case reports in medicine and descriptions of technical improvements in engineering. Unlike research papers (RPs), SCs may start directly with the research being reported, as in this engineering note.

> This note analyzes and provides implementable solutions for stabilization and maneuver control of two nanosatellites subject to control and state constraints, bounded disturbance and measurement error.

According to our informant from aerospace engineering, such notes tend to be pieces that offer technical solutions to particular problems and will likely only be read by those concerned with those particular problems. This is equally true for the readership of SCs in other fields as well.

However, a principal function of many SCs is to report on a rare or unusual phenomenon, whether it is a rare rock formation, disease, dialectal usage, or organism of some kind. In effect, SCs are used for reportable discoveries. The example in Task Two is taken from a small regional journal called *Michigan Birds and Natural History*. This journal is edited by a professional biologist at one of the state's universities and is published four times a year. It contains many SCs. The "Short Note" describes and discusses the discovery of a bat—one which is rare in the state of Michigan.

TASK TWO

Read the passage and be prepared to answer the questions that follow. Discuss the questions with a partner if possible. (A few vocabulary glosses have been added and are indicated by superscript letters.)

Eastern Pipistrelle in Ottawa County, MI

William S. Martinus and Allen Kurta

The Eastern Pipistrelle *(Pipistrellus subflavus)* is a small (0.14 to 0.21 oz/4 to 6 g), insectivorous bat that is listed as a species of "special concern" by the Michigan Department of Natural Resources. A recent review of the status of this species in Michigan indicated that it was known from only 24 animals that were captured in just 5 counties (Unger and Kurta 1998). All except 1 of these bats were found hibernating in mines of the western Upper Peninsula or were captured at Tippy Dam, in Manistee County, the only known hibernaculum[a] for bats in the Lower Peninsula (Kurta et al. 1997, 1999). The only Eastern Pipistrelle that was not associated with a hibernaculum was discovered near Stevensville, Berrien County, in 1966. Herein, we report a new county record for the Eastern Pipistrelle and the second instance of this bat being found away from a known hibernation site in Michigan.

In mid-December, 1999, one of us (WSM) noticed an Eastern Pipistrelle roosting in a garage attached to an occupied house. The house was located 8.1 miles (13 km) S of Grand Haven, Ottawa County, Michigan, about 55 yards (50 m) from a bluff[b] overlooking Lake Michigan. The garage had finished walls and ceiling, but was unheated, and the bat was hanging from a piece of wooden molding, 8.2 ft (2.5 m) above the floor, next to the door that led to the residence. The bat was alive when first discovered, as indicated by small movements of wings and ears in response to indirect disturbance, such as slamming the door. The bat, however, was not handled until April 2000, and by then, it was dead. It had remained in the same location throughout winter, and exact date of death is not known.

The dead bat was stored in a freezer and not examined for almost 1 year. Consequently, the carcass was freeze-dried (mummified) in the typical roosting posture, with tail curved over the belly and up to the chest, and we are not able to sex the animal without damaging the specimen. The animal is an adult, however, as indicated by obviously fused phalangeal epiphyses[c] (Davis 1963). This bat is now preserved as a specimen (#36169) in the Michigan State University Museum.

During hibernation, an Eastern Pipistrelle often is found in a cave or cave-like structure that provides stable ambient temperatures above freezing and typically near 45 to 52°F (7 to 11°C) (Fujita and

Kunz 1984; Unger and Kurta 1998). An unheated garage that frequently experiences temperatures far below freezing is not a viable hibernaculum for any bat, so death of this animal is understandable. Eastern Pipistrelles in southern states may remain active into December (Barbour and Davis 1969), and mild temperatures during autumn 1999 in Michigan may have extended the period of activity for this bat. However, presence of this individual so far from any known hibernaculum (93.2 miles/150 km from Tippy Dam) in December is surprising.

To date, all records of Eastern Pipistrelles from the Lower Peninsula are from counties bordering Lake Michigan—Berrien, Ottawa, and Manistee. We speculate that Eastern Pipistrelles are using the lakeshore as a migratory aid (Timm 1989) and/or that they are attracted to the lakeshore because of its mild climate, relative to more inland areas (Keen 1993). Nevertheless, additional records of the Eastern Pipistrelle in the Lower Peninsula are needed before these hypotheses can be evaluated fully.

Literature Cited

Barbour, R. W., and W. H. Davis. 1969. *Bats of America*. Lexington: University Press of Kentucky.

Davis, W. H. 1963. Aging bats in winter. *Transactions of the Kentucky Academy of Science* 24:28–30.

Fujita, M. S., and T. H. Kunz. 1984. Pipistrellus subflavus. *Mammalian Species* 228:1–6.

Keen, R. A. 1993. *Michigan Weather*. Helena, Montana: American and World Geographic Publishing.

Kurta, A., J. Caryl, and T. Lipps. 1997. Bats and Tippy Dam: species composition, seasonal use, and environmental parameters. *Michigan Academician* 29:473–490.

Kurta, A., C. M. Schumacher, M. Kurta, and S. DeMers. 1999. Roosting sites of an Eastern Pipistrelle during late-summer swarming. *Bat Research News* 40:8–9.

Timm, R. M. 1989. Migration and molt patterns of red bats, Lasiurus borealis (Chiroptera: Vespertilionidae) in Illinois. *Bulletin of the Chicago Academy of Sciences* 14:1–7.

Unger, C. A., and A. Kurta. 1998. Status of the Eastern Pipistrelle (Mammalia: Chiroptera) in Michigan. *Michigan Academician* 30:423–437.

Glosses

[a]Winter resting place.
[b]Small cliff.
[c]Separately boned digits.

1. The paper has two authors. Which of them do you suppose did most of the writing?

2. Of the eight references cited, how many do you think are themselves SCs? What is your reasoning?

3. The paper has five paragraphs. How would you summarize (in a phrase or two) the main function or functions of each paragraph?

   1. _____

   2. _____

   3. _____

   4. _____

   5. _____

4. How and where do the authors first announce their new finding? How do they prepare for this announcement? And why?

5. What can you learn about Allen Kurta from this SC?

6. You are an editorial assistant for *Michigan Birds and Natural History.* The editor tells you that the SC is a bit long for what it has to say. She tells you that it would be better if it could be cut down to fit on one and a half pages. What are your thoughts on this?

TASK THREE

Compare an SC from your field with Martinus and Kurta, especially if there is one you have written yourself. What differences did you find? How would you explain them? Be prepared to explain your findings in class.

Longer Research Papers

We assume that you will be using a typical organizational pattern for your paper—in other words, the IMRD format or some variant of it. So, where do we stand? As can be seen from the following list, we have already made good progress toward carrying out the difficult task of writing a research paper.

Parts of the Research Paper	*Contributions So Far*
Title	
Abstract	Unit Five, Summary Writing
Introduction	Unit Two, General-specific
	Unit Three, Problem-solution
	Unit Six, Critiques
Methods	Unit Three, Process descriptions
Results	Unit Four, Highlighting statements
	Unit Four, Qualifications
Discussion	Unit Four, Explanations
	(of unexpected results, etc.)
	Unit Six, Literature comparisons
Acknowledgments	
References	

We can also see from the list that there is some more work to be done. The really difficult areas, especially Introductions and Discussions, need considerable attention. We also need to consider writing up the Methods and Results for RPs, as opposed to, say, lab reports. There are some smaller bits of business, such as Acknowledgments and titles, to be discussed. Even so, enough has been done to make it possible for you to write an RP.

When you read an RP, you may think that it is a fairly straight-forward account of an investigation. Indeed RPs are often designed to create this impression so that they can appear more convincing to their readers. However, we believe that such impressions are largely misleading. RP authors typically operate in a highly competitive environment. They need to establish that their research questions are sufficiently interesting for publication. They need to demonstrate that they are familiar with the relevant literature so that the research questions can be shown to have not already been answered. And they need to compete against other RPs for acceptance and recognition. As a result, RP authors are very much concerned with *positioning*—with showing that their studies are relevant and significant and have some new contribution to make.

Overview of the Research Paper

The overall rhetorical shape of a typical RP looks like this.

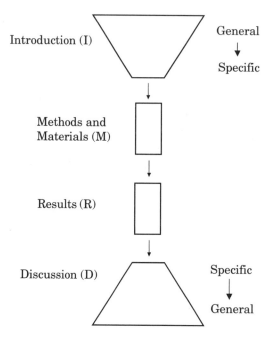

Fig. 10. Overall shape of a research paper

Figure 10 gives a useful indication of the out-in-out or general-specific-general movement of the typical RP. In addition, as the RP in English has developed over the last hundred years or so, the four different sections have become identified with four different purposes.

Introduction (I)   The main purpose of the Introduction is to provide the rationale for the paper, moving from general discussion of the topic to the particular question or hypothesis being investigated. A secondary purpose is to attract interest in the topic—and hence readers.

Methods (M)   The Methods section describes, in various degrees of detail, methodology, materials (or subjects), and procedures. This is the narrowest part of the RP.

Results (R)   In the Results section, the findings are described, accompanied by variable amounts of commentary.

Discussion (D)   The Discussion section offers an increasingly generalized account of what has been learned in the study. This is usually done through a series of "points," at least some of which refer back to statements made in the Introduction.

As a result of these different purposes, the four sections have taken on different linguistic characteristics. We summarize some of these in Table 21. The first line of the table shows, for instance, that the present tense is common in Introductions and Discussions but uncommon in Methods and Results.

Table 21   Frequencies of Selected Features in RP Sections

	Introduction	Methods	Results	Discussion
Present tense	high	low	low	high
Past tense	mid	high	high	mid
Passive voice	low	high	variable	variable
Citations	high	low	variable	high
Qualifications	mid	low	mid	high
Commentary	high	low	variable	high

As you can see from the table, there are similarities between the Introduction and Discussion, on the one hand, and between Methods and Results, on the other. In effect, we see a pattern of more "concrete" inner sections and more "conceptual" outer sections.

TASK FOUR

In 1993 Dorothea Thompson published a useful RP on Results sections in biochemistry articles. She was particularly interested in what kinds of comments researchers made in their Results sections and whether researchers followed the guidelines in manuals. Here are eight sentences from her paper. Based on Table 21 and on your own knowledge, can you guess from which of the sections they come? Mark each one I, M, R, or D. There are two from each section. Work with a partner if possible.

_____ 1. Only further research can determine the applicability of this study's findings to scientific disciplines outside biochemistry.

_____ 2. The data were analyzed both qualitatively and quantitatively.

_____ 3. Short communications and mini-reviews were excluded from the sample because these publications have different objectives and use a different format from that of the experimental research article.

_____ 4. The assumptions underlying this study are grounded largely in sociological accounts of the scientific enterprise (Knorr-Cetina 1981; Latour 1987; Latour and Woolgar 1979).

_____ 5. These style guides are, at best, superficial descriptions of the content of these sections.

_____ 6. In 15 of the sample articles, these methodological narratives included explicit justifications for the selection of certain technical procedures, laboratory equipment, or alternatives to standard protocols.

_____ 7. Scientific style manuals reinforce the conception that Results sections simply present experimental data in a "cold," purely objective, expository manner (Council of Biology Editors 1972; Day 1988; Mitchell 1968; Woodford 1968).

_____ 8. In 38% of the JBC Results sections sampled, Kornberg and his coauthors directly relate their findings to those of earlier studies, as the following illustrate.

Methods

You might have expected us to begin our discussion of RP sections with the Introduction. Instead, we are beginning with Methods. This is usually the easiest section to write and, in fact, is often the section that researchers write first.

Methods sections are very variable across the disciplines, and even the term *Methods* is not always used, as when authors use *The Study* as their section heading. In some fields, it is common to have subsections in Methods that might deal with materials, the apparatus used, definitions employed, the subjects or participants in the study, or the statistical procedures used. Methods also vary according to how much information and explanation they contain. At one extreme, they may be very *condensed;* at the other, elaborately *extended.* If they fall in between, they can be termed *intermediate.*

TASK FIVE

Now consider this first part of the methodology for a research paper written by a doctoral student in information and library science and then answer the questions that follow. The purpose of this research project is to study the effects on scientists of the new *collaboratories* (or dispersed virtual research communities); in this case the collaboratory is now called the Space Physics and Aeronomy Research Collaboratory, or SPARC (http://intel.si.umich.edu/sparc/).

Methodology

Data Collection

❶ Data used in this research consists of two parts: Survey data and data on coauthorship. ❷ Survey data were collected from 1993 to 1996. ❸ In the summer of 1993, a baseline survey was administered to a group of scientists who were likely users of UARC/SPARC. ❹ Prior to the commencement of data collection for the baseline survey, a letter was sent to every member of the group, notifying them of the forthcoming survey and informing them of its length, that their participation was confidential and anonymous, and that upon completion of the survey, they would be entered into a $100 cash incentive lottery. ❺ The sample size of the UARC/SPARC target group was 94 and the response rate was 65%. ❻ A questionnaire consisting of 32 items was sent to all of the participants. ❼ The items asked specifically about the scientists' communication behavior and social networks within the space science community. ❽ The questionnaire was designed to allow the participants to complete it within thirty minutes to an hour.

❾ After administration of the baseline surveys in 1993, the UARC/SPARC target group was surveyed annually from 1994 through 1996. ❿ The 1994 survey was also a mail survey. ⓫ In 1995, the survey was administered via telephone, which lasted 15 to 20 minutes. ⓬ In 1996, an email/web based survey was used in conjunction with a telephone interview. ⓭ In all years, the incentive scheme used was similar to that used in 1993. **⑭** In all years, scientists were asked questions about their research behavior, the use of the UARC/SPARC, and social networks within the space science community.

⑮ Coauthorship data were based on the examination of the publications of UARC/SPARC users from 1993 to 1996. **⑯** Data were collected from the *Science Citation Index*. **⑰** Data on whom the scientists were coauthoring with were examined.

1. Of the 17 sentences in this subsection, which is the shortest sentence and which the longest?

2. All the sentences are in the past tense except for one. Which is it?

3. Does the writer believe that *data* is singular or plural?

4. This is the "data collection" phase of her methodology. What do you think the next part contains: *(a)* description of the survey participants; *(b)* methods of analysis; *(c)* descriptions of the statistical procedures?

5. Where there is a potential choice, all the sentences are in the passive (see Unit Three). Suppose her advisor says to her, "We can use *we* sometimes too." Which three sentences in the Methods section do you think are particularly suitable for changing into the active. Why did you choose those three?

6. List all the phrases or clauses that come before the main clause. Also identify their sentence numbers. What kind of phrases and clauses are they? What does that tell us?

7. The text informs us in sentence 1 that two kinds of data were collected. The survey data is described in a quite *extended* manner, while the description of the coauthorship data is *condensed*. Her advisor is not very happy with this. He says that sentences 2–14 should be cut down and that sentences 15–17 should be extended. Revise either sentences 2–14 or sentences 15–17.

Variation in Methods Sections

We have already mentioned that Methods sections can be quite variable. In many of the social sciences, the methodology is very important and is often described in considerable detail. Indeed, in some cases in these areas, the main point of an RP will be to announce some development in method. However, in the natural sciences and engineering and in parts of medical research, standard practices and established methods are much more widely available. In these latter areas, then, sometimes methods may be largely taken for granted. At other times, however, it is the procedure that is newsworthy. We can put this variation in the form of a table (Table 22), with a "condensed" approach on the "hard" left and an "extended" approach on the "soft" right. We have chosen eight pairs of features to explore this variation.

Table 22   Variation in Methods Sections

Condensed	Extended
Assumes background knowledge	Sees need to provide background
Avoids named subsections	Several named subsections
Uses acronyms and citations as shorthand	Uses descriptions
Running series of verbs (e.g., *collected, stained, and stored*)	Usually one finite verb per clause
Few "by + verb-*ing*" "how" statements	A number of "how" statements
Few definitions and examples	More definitions and examples
Few justifications	Several justifications (often initial purpose clauses)
Few linking phrases	Wide range of linking phrases

Table 22 gives us a kind of rough "scorecard" for Methods sections, if we subtract a point for each element under *Condensed* and add a point for each one under *Extended*. For example, the coauthorship data (sentences 15–17) from the text in Task Five would score a -7 (every element in the Condensed column except for a running series of verbs).

TASK SIX

1. Using the "scorecard" in Table 22, what score would you give sentences 2–14 of the text in Task Five?

2. What score would you give the following extract?

Methods for Analysis and Functional Properties

The standard AOAC methods (AOAC, 1975) were used for the determination of total solids, nitrogen, crude fat, ash, and Vitamin C. Total sugars were determined by the method of Potter et al. (1968), and the total carbohydrates (in terms of glucose) were assayed according to the procedure of Dubois et al. (1956). The method of Kohler and Patten (1967) was followed for determining amino acid composition. (Quoted by Knorr-Cetina 1981, 157)

3. Score this extract from a botany paper.

To detect groups among the specimens and extract the variables that best diagnose the groups, we used principal components analysis (PCA). Before conducting the analysis, we standardized all measurements so that each variable would have a mean of 0 and a standard deviation of 1. For the PCA, we included only continuous characters. To avoid weighting characters, we excluded characters that are probably genetically redundant, as revealed by high values for the Pearson correlation coefficient between all possible pairs of characters. (Naczi, Reznicek, and Ford 1998, 435).

4. Now take a Methods section from a paper in your field and apply the "scorecard" to it. Be prepared to share your results with others.

Language Focus: Linking Phrases in Extended Methods

In question 6 in Task Five we asked you to identify the initial phrases or clauses coming before the main clause in the information science text. As was discovered, most of these were temporal, including the rather *fancy* "Prior to the commencement of data collection for the baseline survey . . ." Linking phrases in the short botany extract in Task Six included one temporal one ("Before conducting the analysis, . . ."), but there were also two *purposive* ones:

To detect groups among the specimens . . . , we used . . .

To avoid weighting characters, we excluded . . .

Many *extended* Methods have a number of such linking phrases that operate to tie the longer sections together and to add some stylistic variety. How many of these can you turn into complete sentences?

1. In an effort to reduce _____ , _____

   _____ .

2. In order to establish _____ , _____

   _____ .

3. For the purposes of this study, _____

   is defined as _____ .

4. Based on the feedback from the pilot study, _____

   _____ .

5. On the basis of the literature review described above, _____

   _____ .

6. With the exception of _____ ,

   _____ .

7. Of those who consented to participate, _____

   _____ .

8. During the data collection, _____ .

9. Prior to collecting this information, _____

   _____ .

10. In the interest of generating maximally useful data, _____

    _____ .

❖ Language Focus: Hyphens in Noun Phrases in Condensed Methods

Consider this opening sentence from a condensed Methods section written by one of our students: "Cells were cultured in 24-well plates." Hyphens are often used to clarify how complex noun phrases are to be interpreted. In this case, the hyphen indicates that the student was using plates containing 24 wells. Without the hyphen the phrase could be interpreted as 24 plates containing an unspecified number of wells. What differences can you see between the following pairs of noun phrases?

small-car factory/small car factory

blue-lined paper/blue lined paper

university-paid personnel/university paid personnel

Read the preceding pairs aloud. Can you make a distinction between them in terms of stress and intonation? Can you think of one or two similar pairs from your own field?

How would you indicate what you meant by the following noun phrases? All are ambiguous, at least out of context.

light gray laptop computer

artificial heart valve

dominant group member

traditional food programs

rapid release mechanism

strong acting director

Writing Up a Methods Section

As we saw in Unit Three (Task Sixteen), John interviewed a student planning her first research paper for her master's in social work. You may recall that Mei-Lan's research was on Chinese elderly living in the United States. She had chosen this topic because of some "prevailing myths" that the Chinese communities would always look after their elderly and that such elderly would not accept help from outsiders. She further noted that all the research to date had been conducted in the large Chinese communities in big cities on the east and west coasts and that therefore it would be useful to study smaller communities in the Midwest. John then asked her about her methodology. We repeat the discussion here for your convenience.

JS: How did you find your subjects?

ML: I used friends and friends of friends in the local Chinese community to introduce me.

JS: How did you collect your data?

ML: I used face-to-face interviews. I wanted one-on-one situations since I was afraid that if family members had been there, my interviewees might not have been truthful about their feelings and experiences.

JS: Did you have to get permission from the review board?

ML: Yes, because I was dealing with human subjects.

JS: Did you have any problems with this?

ML: No, not at all. Interview methods are usually quickly approved.

JS: How many people did you interview?

ML: I only managed to interview about ten. Not much time, and not all of my contacts worked out. I also got some refusals. So this was just a small-scale pilot study. There were not enough subjects for any statistical analysis.

JS: How long did the interviews last, and did you use a fixed list of questions?

ML: About an hour. I had some questions but did not always use them all. I guess my data could be said to be based on what sociologists call "semi-structured" interviews.

JS: Did you use English?

ML: The interviewees used whatever language they were most comfortable with—Mandarin, Taiwanese, or English. I think this was a strong point in my method.

TASK SEVEN

There is quite a lot of detail in the preceding interview. In terms of the expectations of your own discipline, make an ordered list of only the methodological points you would include. Further, are there aspects of the methodology that you would want to include but that were not brought out in the interview? (If you have a partner from the same field, work with him or her.) Be prepared to report your conclusions.

TASK EIGHT

Now write a Methods section of your own, paying close attention to how your field "scores" according to the "scorecard" in Table 22.

Results

The other section we will deal with in this unit is the Results section. As we will see, this section has much in common with the material that was covered in the unit on data commentary (Unit Four). Many of the concepts discussed there are directly relevant here, such as

- Judging the right strength of claim

- Using location statements

- Highlighting key findings from the data

- Rounding figures and making generalized comparisons

We will begin with our own "ministudy" of the use of sentence connectors in 12 articles from our field (see Appendix Four for further details). Task Nine presents the first part of the Results section as it now stands.

TASK NINE

Read the passage and answer the questions that follow.

Results

❶ A total of 467 sentence connectors were found, averaging just over two per page. **❷** Eleven of the 12 articles used connectors with some frequency, with totals ranging from 24 to 58. **❸** The one exception was the only article in the sample that dealt with literary texts, which used only nine connectors. **❹** The scarcity of connectors in this paper may be due to its heavy use of commentary on literary passages.

❺ Seventy different sentence connectors occurred in the sample. **❻** This large number is somewhat surprising, even taking into account our broad interpretation of "connector." **❼** Those that occurred more than ten times are listed in decreasing frequency of use in Table 23.

Table 23 Frequency of Connectors

Rank	Item	Total occurrence
1	however	62
2	first, second, etc.	52
3	thus	33
4	also	30
5	for example	29
6	in addition	20
7	finally	19
8	therefore	16
9	on the other hand	14
10	then	12
11	nevertheless for instance furthermore	11

(8) The heavy use of *however* and of enumerators such as *first* or *second* could have been predicted. (9) However, there are also a number of surprises in the frequency data. (10) Most people, for example, would not have anticipated that *thus* would be twice as common as *therefore*. (11) There was unexpectedly heavy use of the "informal" connectors *but* (9 instances) and *yet* (8 instances). (12) Although these are known to be frequent in newspapers and correspondence, we were somewhat surprised to find so many in refereed scholarly journals. (13) In contrast, the minimal use of "conclusives," such as *in conclusion,* was less unexpected. (14) In fact, under 2% of all the connectors fell into this category.

1. Is Table 23 in the right place in the text?

2. Leaving Table 23 aside, the three short paragraphs are full of numbers. Highlight all these numbers, whether written as words (twelve) or as digits (12). Can you work out the rules we followed in deciding whether to use words or digits? What are the "rules" in your field?

3. There are 14 sentences in this text. Decide into which of the following categories each sentence best belongs.

   Factual Description   Interpretation/Commentary   Unclear

4. Do your findings for question 3 surprise you? Do you approve?

5. In Table 23 only the 13 most frequent items are given; in the first edition, the list was twice as long, extending to those connectors that occurred four times or more. Which is preferable? (Is your choice affected by what is said in sentence 11?)

6. The sentences in this Results passage are rather short. Which pairs of sentences might be joined—and how?

Commentary in Results Sections

It is traditionally said that the Results section of an RP should simply report the data that has been collected; that is, it should focus exclusively on simply describing the actual results. However, as we have seen from Task Nine, at least one pair of authors seems to be behaving differently! So let us explore this issue a little further.

TASK TEN

Here are quotations from four textbooks and manuals. Read them and answer the questions that follow.

Woodford (1976, 28):

The best guide to offer is, perhaps, that the Results section must be comprehensible on its own and should indicate at least the *trend* of the author's reasoning, but any extended discussion of the observations or comparison with other's work is best deferred until the last section. (Original emphasis)

Björk and Räisänen (1996, 326):

Our advice is that you concentrate on *reporting* your results using factual statements, usually in the past tense, and that you only comment on these statements if they need immediate explanation, if they contain ambiguities or contradictions, or if comments facilitate the reader's understanding of the results. (Original emphasis)

Penrose and Katz (1998, 56):

Reducing the data, generalizing from the data, and highlighting specific cases are all highly interpretive processes. It should be clear by now that we don't let the data speak for themselves in research reports; in summarizing our results, we interpret them for the reader.

Swales and Feak (1994, 171)

Authors often include commentary because they are aware of their audience. They can *anticipate* that their readers may be thinking, "Why did they use this method rather than that one?" or "Isn't this result rather strange?" For obvious reasons, authors may not want to postpone responding to such imaginary questions and critical comments until the final section. (Original emphasis)

1. What differences do you see between the first quotation and the last two?

2. Do you think the 1996 Björk and Räisänen extract is more similar to Woodford's or to the last two?

3. Which of these extracts would you bring to the attention of a beginning graduate student in your field? (You can choose more than one.) And why?

The fact that the traditional distinction between Results and Discussions is not as sharp as commonly believed has been borne out by some recent research. As we have mentioned, Thompson (1993) studied the Results sections from 20 published biochemistry papers. Table 24 presents what she found.

Table 24   Commentary Found in Results Sections

Type of Commentary	Number of Papers (max. = 20)
Justifying the methodology	19
Interpreting the results	19
Citing agreement with previous studies	11
Commenting on the data	10
Admitting difficulties in interpretation	8
Pointing out discrepancies	4
Calling for further research	0

As can be seen, the first four types of commentary were used by half or more than half of her authors; indeed, only the "Calling for further research" category was universally postponed to the Discussion. Here is part of Thompson's conclusion.

> My research demonstrates that scientists—in this case biochemists—do not present results only in a factual expository manner; they also employ a variety of rhetorical moves to argue for the validity of scientific facts and knowledge claims. (126)

Broadly similar results were found by Brett (1994) for sociology, although Williams (1999) showed that in medicine *statements of findings* still tended to predominate.

TASK ELEVEN

Carefully read a Results section that you have written or read from your field, marking any commentary elements. In your estimation, which of the following types is the section most like?

Type 1
Gives straightforward description of the author's results; includes no commentary at all (no comparisons with the work of others, no justifications, no—or very few—obvious highlighting statements).

Type 2
Is mostly restricted to present findings, but includes a few minor uses of commentary.

Type 3
Consists of both description of findings and a number of commentary elements; uses several of the categories mentioned by Thompson.

Type 4
Makes heavy use of commentary; uses most of the categories found by Thompson; could almost be taken for a discussion.

Be prepared to discuss your findings in class. Bring your marked-up copy with you.

The Organization of Results Sections

Results sections may, or may not, have subsections. Some subsections may simply reflect the different stages or parts of the investigation. Consider the case of an article published in the *International Journal of Nursing Studies* entitled "Hospitalized Children's Descriptions of Their Experiences with Postsurgical Pain Relieving Methods." This article, which we will be exploring more closely a little later, has four subsections in the results:

5. Results

5.1. Children's self-initiated use of pain relieving methods

5.2 Nurses' use of pain relieving methods

5.3 Parents' use of pain relieving methods

5.4 Children's suggestions to nurses and parents

However, in another article from the same journal (entitled "Inflammatory Bowel Disease: Developing a Short Disease Specific Scale to Measure Health Related Quality of Life"), the subsections were very different:

3. Results

3.1 Disease specificity

3.2 Factor analysis

3.3 Reliability

3.4 Validity

Doubtless, in all fields the specifics of the investigation (including the methodology adopted) will determine subsection headings (if any).

The available research suggests that each aspect of the results will likely be treated in a general-specific manner (see Unit Two), the specifics variously being more exact data, cases or examples, or elements of commentary. However, Kanoksilapatham (2003) shows that at least for biochemistry Results sections, if there is a felt need for an explanation of procedure or a further justification of methodology, these will likely occur *before* general statements of results. Again we can see this as a strategy for anticipating potential reader concerns. Overall, one emerging pattern for handling a particular result looks like this:

Procedure/justification (optional)

Location statement (if the first of several)

Statement of general findings

More specific statements

Example/case/commentary (optional)

TASK TWELVE

Choose either A or B.

A. The following is the first subsection of Pölkki, Pietilä, and Vehviläinen-Julkenen's (2003) results on children's pain in a Finnish hospital. Suppose this was a draft, what kind of suggestions might you make for modification?

5. Results

5.1 Children's self-initiated use of pain relieving methods
   The children reported 13 successful types of self-initiated pain relieving methods. As shown in Table 2, most of the children reported using distraction, resting/sleeping, positioning/immobility and asking for pain medication or help from nurses when they experienced pain.

TABLE 2.   Children's Attempts to Manage Pain

"How have you tried to manage pain/what have you done to help yourself when you had pain?"

	N	%
Distraction	51	98
Resting/sleeping	42	81
Positioning/immobility	27	52
Asking for pain medications/help from nurses	27	52
Imagery	16	31
Walking/moving/doing exercises	11	21
Just being and trying to tolerate pain	10	19
Eating/drinking	6	12
Relaxation	4	8
Thought-stopping	1	2
Breathing technique	1	2
Thermal regulation (cold application)	1	2
Urinating often	1	2

The most common methods of distraction by which the children tried to focus their attention away from pain included reading, watching TV/videos and playing games. For example, a 10-yr-old boy described his experiences as follows:

> "I have read Donald Duck comics . . . this helps me forget the pain. I can also get my thoughts elsewhere by playing Nintendo games. When I concentrate on playing I don't have much time to think about anything else." (7)

Another method of drawing attention away from pain included the use of imagery in which the children reported thinking about some pleasant action/happening (e.g. getting home), important people (e.g. mother/father, friends) or pets in order to forget the pain. The method of thought-stopping was used by only one child. A 12-yr-old boy described this method as follows without utilizing specific replacement thoughts:

> "Then I have kept on thinking that I am not hurting, there is no pain, there is no pain." (11)

Children who used positioning typically associated this method with immobility or restricting movement, as one 12-yr-old girl described after undergoing an appendectomy:

> "I have attempted to determine the best possible position to be in . . . either on my side or in a crouched position. I have tried to be without moving so that it would not hurt more." (15)

All children reported using at least one self-initiated pain relieving method. The majority of them claimed to use four of these strategies during their hospitalization. The mean number of strategies identified was 3.8 with a range from 1 to 8.

B. You are completing a master's thesis in information science, and your topic is academic languages in the twentieth century. A contact in Finland has provided you with original data on the language of publication of doctoral dissertations in that country. The data will be summarized in Table 25 which follows.

Table 25   Language of Publication of Doctoral Dissertations in Finland

	Finnish	Swedish	German	English	Other	Number
1900–1910	20.6%	30.3%	41.2%	1.3%	6.6%	228
1911–20	30.4%	23.3%	39.1%	1.2%	5.9%	253
1921–30	30.0%	20.7%	41.3%	2.8%	5.2%	213
1931–40	27.7%	11.4%	52.5%	4.4%	4.0%	404
1941–50	34.1%	10.4%	32.7%	19.0%	3.7%	431
1951–60	24.4%	6.6%	19.5%	47.2%	2.3%	784
1961–70	21.9%	2.0%	5.8%	68.0%	2.2%	1249
1971–80	21.9%	3.0%	3.2%	71.3%	0.6%	2287
1981–90	18.6%	2.5%	1.1%	77.4%	0.3%	3434
1991–99	18.6%	1.6%	0.5%	77.8%	1.4%	6915

Source: Wilson 2002.

As you plan to write up this section of your results, which of the following points do you want to include? (Indicate your decisions by Y or N.)

_____ 1. Other languages might include Russian.

_____ 2. Finnish has been remarkably stable over the course of the 20th century.

_____ 3. The second official language in the country, Swedish, has virtually disappeared as a dissertation language.

_____ 4. The lowest numbers of dissertations completed occurred in the 1920s.

_____ 5. The number of dissertations has rapidly increased since 1960, doubling in the century's final decade.

_____ 6. The decline of German followed its defeat in the Second World War (1939–1945).

_____ 7. By the end of the century, the percentage of dissertations written in English had consolidated at over 75%.

_____ 8. By the end of the century, around 700 dissertations were being defended each year in Finland.

Decide the order of presentation of the points you have selected. Are there other descriptive or evaluative points you would like to make? Now write up this part of your Results section. Begin in the following manner.

3. Results

3.2 Language of publication of theses and dissertations

3.23. The situation in Finland.

Unlike the other countries so far investigated, the overall data for Finland is chronologically complete—even if it is not broken down into broad divisions, such as sciences versus humanities.

TASK THIRTEEN

Produce a Results section from your own work (or part of one if your work is extensive). If your results are not yet complete, create some findings for this task.

Unit Eight

Constructing a Research Paper II

In this final unit, we deal with the remaining parts of a research paper in the following order:

    Introduction sections

    Discussion sections

    Titles

    Abstracts

    Acknowledgments

Introduction Sections

It is widely recognized that writing introductions is slow, difficult, and troublesome for both native speakers as well as nonnative speakers. A very long time ago, the Greek philosopher Plato remarked, "The beginning is half of the whole." Indeed, eventually producing a good Introduction section always seems like a battle hard won.

    Writing the Introduction of an RP is particularly troublesome. In some kinds of texts, such as term papers or shorter communications (including case reports), it is possible to start immediately with a topic or thesis statement.

> The purpose of this paper is to . . .
>
> This paper describes and analyzes . . .
>
> My aim in this paper is to . . .
>
> In this paper, we report on . . .

However, this kind of opening is rare and unusual in longer and more substantial RPs (probably under 10 percent of published RPs start in this way). In fact, statements like these typically come at or near the end of an RP Introduction. Why is this? And what comes before?

We believe that the answer to these questions lies in two interconnected parts. The first half of the answer lies in the need to appeal to the readership. When a paper is written to fulfill a course requirement, the reader is set. (Indeed the reader is *required* to read and evaluate your paper!) On the other hand, a paper that is designed for the external world—if only in theory—needs to attract an audience. We can illustrate this by taking the case of one of those few published papers that actually does start by describing the present research. Here is the opening sentence of the Introduction:

> In this paper, we address the problem of scheduling and balancing sports competitions over multiple venues (Urban and Russell 2003).

The Urban and Russell paper, "Scheduling Sports Competitions on Multiple Venues," was published in a journal called the *European Journal of Operational Research,* a journal whose audience is researchers and practitioners working in the area of operational research/management science. Doubtless, the very specific opening to the Urban and Russell paper will appeal immediately to those researchers actively involved in this area. On the other hand, it may "turn off" many other readers of the journal—readers who have no direct interest in the actual scheduling of sporting events.

We believe that we can best explain the second half of the answer by using a metaphor—that of *competition* as it is used in ecology. Just as plants compete for light and space, so writers of RPs compete for acceptance and recognition. In order to obtain this acceptance and recognition, many writers will use an organizational pattern that contains the three "moves" as shown in Table 26, in the order given.

Creating a Research Space

The Introduction sections of RPs typically follow the pattern in Table 26 in response to two kinds of competition: competition for research space and competition for readers. We can call this rhetorical pattern the create-a-research-space (or CARS) model. In this Introduction

Table 26   Moves in Research Paper Introductions

Move 1   Establishing a research territory

    a. by showing that the general research area is important, central, interesting, problematic, or relevant in some way (optional)

    b. by introducing and reviewing items of previous research in the area (obligatory)

Move 2   Establishing a niche[a]

    a. by indicating a gap in the previous research, or by extending previous knowledge in some way (obligatory)

Move 3   Occupying the niche

    a. by outlining purposes or stating the nature of the present research (obligatory)

    b. by listing research questions or hypotheses (PISF[b])

    c. by announcing principal findings (PISF)

    d. by stating the value of the present research (PISF)

    e. by indicating the structure of the RP (PISF)

[a] In ecology, a niche is a particular microenvironment where a particular organism can thrive. In our case, a niche is a context where a particular piece of research makes particularly good sense.

[b] PISF = probable in some fields, but rare in others.

pattern, the work of others and/or what is known about the world is primary, and your own work is secondary. As we will see later, this background-foreground relationship is reversed in Discussions.

TASK ONE

We start with an Introduction to an RP from the humanities since we have not dealt with many humanities texts so far. (It has been adapted from a paper John wrote for a History of Art seminar he audited on Nineteenth-Century Realism.) Read it and answer the questions which follow.

Thomas Eakins and the "Marsh" Pictures

❶ Thomas Eakins (1844–1916) is now recognized as one of the greatest American painters, alongside Winslow Homer, Edward Hopper and Jackson Pollock. ❷ Over the last thirty years, there have been many studies of his life and work[a], and in 2002 there was a major

[a] Book-length studies include Hendricks (1974), Johns (1983), Fried (1987), Wilmerding (1993), Foster (1997) and Berger (2000).

exhibition devoted entirely to his art in his home city of Philadelphia. ❸ His best-known pictures include a number of rowing and sailing scenes, several domestic interiors, the two large canvasses showing the surgeons Gross and Agnew at work in the operating theater, and a long series of portraits, including several of his wife, Susan McDowell. ❹ The non-portraits are distinguished by compositional brilliance and attention to detail, while the portraits—most of which come from his later period—are thought to show deep insight into character or "psychological realism"[b]. ❺ In many ways, Eakins was a modern late nineteenth century figure since he was interested in science, in anatomy and in the fast-growing "manly sports" of rowing and boxing. ❻ In his best work, he painted what he knew and whom he knew, rather than being an artist-outsider to the scene in front of him. ❼ Among Eakins' pictures, there is a small series of scenes painted between 1873 and 1876 showing hunters preparing to shoot at the secretive marsh birds in the coastal marshes near Philadelphia. ❽ Apart from a chapter in Foster (1997), this series has been little discussed by critics or art historians. ❾ For example, these pictures were ignored by Johns in her pioneering 1983 monograph[c], perhaps because their overall *smallness* (physically, socially and psychologically) did not fit well with her book's title, *Thomas Eakins: The Heroism of Modern Life*. ❿ These pictures are usually thought to have come about simply because Thomas Eakins used to accompany his father on these hunting/shooting trips to the marshes[d]. ⓫ However, in this paper I will argue that Eakins focussed his attention on these featureless landscapes for a much more complex set of motives. ⓬ These included his wish to get inside the marsh landscape, to stress the hand-eye coordination between the shooter and "the pusher," and to capture the moment of concentration *before* any action takes place.

---

[b]The question of what actually makes a work of art "realistic" is, of course, one of the most discussed issues in the history of art, and will not be directly addressed in this paper. For analyses of realism, see, among others, Nochlin (1990).
[c]Johns' book is an example of the "new" art history with its detailed attention to the *social* conditions and circumstances that give rise to a particular form of art.
[d]Eakins contracted a bad case of malaria on one of these trips, and this brought his visits—and this series of paintings—to an end.

1. Divide the text into the three basic moves.

2. How many paragraphs would you divide the text into? And where would you put the paragraph boundaries?

3. Look at Table 26 again. Where in this Introduction would you divide Move 1 into 1a and 1b?

4. What kind of Move 2 does John use?

5. What kind of Move 3a does John use?

6. Underline or highlight any words or expressions in sentences 1 through 4 that have been used "to establish a research territory."

7. How many citations are there in the text and footnotes?

8. Footnotes and endnotes are widely used in the humanities. Consider carefully the four footnotes in this Introduction. Do you think that this information is rightly footnoted, or do you think sometimes it would have been better in the main text? Conversely, is there material in the main text that you would have put in footnotes? What do your decisions tell you about the use of notes?

In Unit Seven, we argued that RPs were not simple accounts of investigations. (This is also very true of our own mini-RP discussed in Appendix Four.) If you now look back at the Introduction to the Eakins paper, you will note that John does not explicitly state what his motive or rationale for carrying out the study was. Rather, the study seems to emerge as a natural and rational response to some kind of gap in the literature on Thomas Eakins.

In fact, this is not how the study started at all. The course John audited was the first History of Art course he had ever participated in, but he did already know something of Thomas Eakins. John is also a keen amateur bird-watcher. As he started to read the books on Eakins, he noticed that the critics sometimes misidentified and mislabeled the birds in Eakins' marsh pictures and sketches. This then was what made him focus on these pictures; however, he soon realized that the mistakes about the birds would not make a suitable main theme for a history of art paper—they could only be a small part of the story.

TASK TWO

Discuss the following issues with a group.

1. Do you think the "true" story behind John's paper should be built into the Introduction? If so, where and how?

2. Alternatively, do you think it should be made part of the Discussion? Or dropped in a footnote? Or could it be omitted altogether?

3. Do members of your group have comparable experiences to relate—perhaps stories about how pieces of research started almost by accident but are described as if they were planned? (See also Appendix Four.)

4. Finally, how would you answer the following question?

   In any investigation, certain events take place in a certain order. Do you think it is necessary to keep to that order when writing an RP, or is an author free to change that order to construct a more rhetorically effective paper?

TASK THREE

Here is an Introduction from a very different field. Can you reconstruct the sentences into their original order, numbering them from 1 to 11? Work with a partner if possible.

University-Community Agency Collaboration: Human Service Agency Workers' Views
Mọjisọla Tiamiyu

_____ a. Furthermore, governments, foundations, non-profit organizations, and other stakeholders continue to work on how to provide cost-effective community-based services to members of the society including the elderly.

_____ b. In particular, the study sought to provide an avenue for them to communicate their understanding of university-community agency collaborations, and identify how their agencies can work collaboratively with the university.

_____ c. According to the U.S. Bureau of the Census, it is anticipated that if this trend in growth continues, by the year 2030 there will be approximately 70 million Americans aged 65 or over.

_____ d. One approach has been an emphasis on community collaborations to address the planning and delivery of such services.

_____ e. Little is, however, known about participants' views of university-community collaborations.

_____ f. Several studies have examined issues related to the present and future provision and quality of community-based services for the elderly (Kelly, Knox & Gekoski, 1998; Buys & Rushworth, 1997; Damron-Rodriguez, Wallace, & Kington, 1994; Krout, 1994; Kuehne, 1992; Benjamin, 1988; Soldo & Agree, 1988; and Mahoney, 1978).

_____ g. Human-service agency workers are major participants of university-based collaborations; hence, the purpose of this study was to investigate their views of community-based services to the elderly in northwest Ohio.

_____ h. Funding agencies (e.g., U.S. Department of Housing and Urban Development [HUD]) have encouraged university-community collaborations.

_____ i. The growing size of America's population of seniors has drawn attention to their economic and social well-being.

_____ j. America's population is growing older.

_____ k. An example is HUD's Community Outreach Partnership Centers initiative, which involves university faculty, staff, students, and community residents and agencies/groups as partners in the development and implementation of research/community programs.

Which sentences were the most difficult to place? Why?

TASK FOUR

Examine a journal article from a journal in your field that is of interest to you. To what extent does the Introduction follow the CARS model presented in Table 26? Be prepared to discuss your Introduction with a partner in class.

TASK FIVE

There is a 2000 article in the *Journal of Economic Psychology* by Schwer and Daneshvary entitled "Keeping Up One's Appearance: Its Importance and the Choice of Type of Hair-grooming Establishment" (21: 207–222). Which of these three versions do you consider to be the most likely original opening sentence(s)? How did you (and your partner) arrive at your choice?

A. Americans have typically taken physical care of themselves by cosmetic improvements, exercise and attention to diet. Recently, this attention to appearance has increased with incremental expenditures (by both men and women) on personal grooming at beauty shops and the like.

B. Americans are taking care of themselves by exercising, eating nutritious foods, taking care of their skin, and enhancing their appearance including their hair via color, transplants, and permanents. In a quest to enhance their appearance, both women and men are spending more time and money on physical appearance, including personal grooming at beauty salons, beauty shops, and barbershops.

C. In comparison to past behaviors, both men and women in the U.S. today spend more money and time on their personal appearance.

In our experience, people overwhelmingly choose text A as the answer for Task Five, believing that text C is "too tame," and text B "too far out." (And we bet that you chose A too!) However, the real original opening is actually text B. Some of its linguistic features are worth examining a little further. Consider the following.

- The unusual use of the present continuous tense (*are taking care / are spending*) to create an impression of something happening everywhere, all the time

- The extremely heavy listing (four running *-ing* verbs) especially in the first sentence

- The rhetorically loaded use of *quest* in the second sentence

Language Focus: Claiming Centrality

In the "University-Community Agency Collaboration" passage, *claiming centrality* (Move 1a) was achieved by stressing the *growing* problem of coping with the elderly in sentences *j, c,* and *i.* In the Eakins text, centrality was created by stressing his growing status and the growing amount of literature devoted to his work (sentences 1–2).

In case you think that this kind of rhetoric would not be found in science or engineering, consider these two opening sentences from an aerospace RP. Pay particular attention to the phrases we have italicized.

> *The increasing interest* in high angle-of-attack aerodynamics *has heightened the need* for computational tools suitable to predict the flowfield and aerodynamic coefficients in this regime. *Of particular interest and complexity are* the symmetric and asymmetric separated vortex flows which develop about slender bodies as the angle of attack is increased. (Almosnino, 1985)

Note, too, that the second sentence opens with an emphatic inversion (see Unit Six).

Here are some further "skeletal" examples of these strong opening statements. Notice how many of them use the present perfect.

Recently, there has been growing interest in . . .

The possibility of . . . has generated wide interest in . . .

The development of . . . is a classic problem in . . .

The development of . . . has led to the hope that . . .

The . . . has become a favorite topic for analysis . . .

Knowledge of . . . has a great importance for . . .

The study of . . . has become an important aspect of . . .

A central issue in . . . is . . .

(The) . . . has been extensively studied in recent years.

Many investigators have recently turned to . . .

The relationship between . . . and . . . has been investigated by many researchers.

Many recent studies have focused on . . .

TASK SIX

Find a recent journal from your field of interest. Look at the openings of up to six articles. All the articles should come from the same journal. How many, if any, begin with a Move 1a? If any do, print the openings or write them down and bring them to class (or e-mail them to your instructor). This small piece of analysis should help you better understand this aspect of writing in your own area.

Reviewing the Literature

The CARS model states that Move 1b (introducing and reviewing items of previous research in the area) is obligatory. Why should it be obligatory?

TASK SEVEN

There are, in fact, a surprisingly large number of theories about the role and purpose of citations in academic texts. Six are given here. Discuss with a group the validity of each. Which do you think contribute most to our understanding of why citations are used in academic writing? Does your group have any other theories?

1. This theory is widely proposed in manuals and standard practice guides.

   Citations are used to recognize and acknowledge the intellectual property rights of authors. They are a matter of ethics and a defense against plagiarism (see "Some Notes on Plagiarism" in Unit Five).

2. This theory also has many supporters, especially in well-established fields like the sciences.

   Citations are used to show respect to previous scholars. They recognize the history of the field by acknowledging previous achievements.

The remaining theories have been proposed by individual authors.

3. Ravetz (1971):

   Citations operate as a kind of mutual reward system. Rather than pay other authors money for their contributions, writers "pay" them in citations.

4. Gilbert (1977):

   Citations are tools of persuasion; writers use citations to give their statements greater authority.

5. Bavelas (1978):

   Citations are used to supply evidence that the author qualifies as a member of the chosen scholarly community; citations are used to demonstrate familiarity with the field.

6. Swales (1990):

   Citations are used to create a research space for the citing author. By describing what has been done, citations point the way to what has not been done and so prepare a space for new research.

Now suppose that we have actually carried out a study of the reasons for using citations in academic texts and have begun to write an RP. This is the draft of the Introduction so far. Read it and consider the questions that follow.

M
O
V
E

1a

❶ Citations are widely recognized as being an important and distinctive property of academic texts. ❷ Indeed, the presence or absence of citations allows the casual reader to get an immediate sense of whether a text is an "academic" or "popular" one. ❸ Because citation is such an obvious surface phenomenon, it has been much discussed in the academic world. ❹ Indeed, there are several theories about the role and purpose of citations in academic texts.

We now have to write Move 1b.

1. How can we sequence our six theories (plus any others that have come up in your groups)? The key element in literature reviews is that *order* is imposed on the material, not so much order in your own mind, but order in the reader's mind.

2. Clearly we need to start with the two major traditional views (theories 1 and 2). How can we order the remaining four theories (3–6)?

3. Should we organize in the chronological order as presented? Is this—at least in this case—a weak kind of ordering? Is there another way?

4. One possibility might be to *categorize* theories 3–6. Do you consider the theories by Ravetz, Gilbert, Bavelas, and Swales to be economic theories? Sociological theories? Rhetorical theories?

We could then decide to take next the case where we have two members in the category. One plan could look like this.

Theory 1	Established major theories
Theory 2	

Rhetorical	Theories 4 and 6	
Economic	Theory 3	Theories associated with individual authors.
Sociological	Theory 5	

TASK EIGHT

Write either a short review of the citation literature (one paragraph) or a short review of at least five papers on the same topic (or similar ones) from your own field (one to two paragraphs). Use the reference system that you are most comfortable with. Refer back to Units Five and Six if you wish. If you review papers from your field, also hand in a rough diagram showing how you have imposed order on the material.

Language Focus: Citation and Tense

Tense choice in reviewing previous research is subtle and somewhat flexible. (It is also not very much like the "rules" you may have been taught in English classes.) The following, therefore, are only general guidelines for tense usage.

Several studies have shown that at least two-thirds of all citing statements fall into one of these three major patterns:

I. Past—researcher activity as agent

Jones (1997) *investigated* the causes of illiteracy.

The causes of illiteracy *were investigated* by Jones (1997).

II. Present Perfect—researcher activity not as agent

The causes of illiteracy *have been* widely *investigated* (Jones 1977, Ferrara 2000, Hyon 2004).

There *have been* several investigations into the causes of illiteracy (Jones 1997, Ferrara 2000, Hyon 2004).

Several researchers *have studied* the causes of illiteracy[1-3].

III. Present—no reference to researcher activity

The causes of illiteracy *are* complex (Jones 1997, Ferrara 2000, Hyon 2004).

Illiteracy *appears to have* a complex set of causes[1-3].

Note these common uses of these patterns:

Pattern I—reference to single studies—past

Pattern II—reference to areas of inquiry—present perfect

Pattern III—reference to state of current knowledge—present

Also note that in patterns I and II attention is given to what previous researchers did, while in pattern III the focus is on what has been found.

Finally, note that different areas of scholarship have somewhat different preferences. Patterns I and II are most common in the humanities and least common in science, engineering, and medical research. However, all three patterns tend to occur in many extensive literature reviews, since they add *variety* to the text.

We have said that these three patterns cover about two-thirds of the cases. The reason this proportion is not higher is because writers of literature reviews can have certain options in their choice of tenses. This is particularly true of pattern I. The main verbs in pattern I can refer to what a previous researcher *did* (*investigated, studied, analyzed,* etc.). By and large, in these cases the past is obligatory. However, the main verbs can also refer to what the previous researcher *wrote* or *thought* (*stated, concluded, claimed,* etc.). With this kind of reporting verb (see Unit Five), tense options are possible.

> Jones (1997) concluded that illiteracy can be related to . . .
>
> Jones (1997) has concluded that . . .
>
> Jones (1997) concludes that . . .

The differences among these tenses are subtle. In general, moves from past to present perfect and then to present indicate that the research reported is increasingly *close* to the writer in some way: close to the writer's own opinion, or close to the writer's own research, or close to the current state of knowledge.

The present tense choice is sometimes called the *citational present* and is also used with famous or important sources.

> Plato argues that . . .
>
> Confucius says . . .

The Bible says . . .

The Constitution states . . .

Comparable options exist in the subordinate clause.

Jones (1997) found that illiteracy *was* correlated most closely with poverty.

Jones (1997) found that illiteracy *is* correlated most closely with poverty.

The first sentence shows that the writer believes that the finding should be understood within the context of the single study. In the second, the writer implies that a wider generalization is possible.

Variation in Reviewing the Literature

In the Language Focus, we concentrated on the three main citation patterns. There are, of course, some others.

According to Jones (1997), the causes of illiteracy are closely related to poverty.

Jones' research shows that illiteracy and poverty are interrelated (Jones 1997).

Can you come up with some more?

Good writers of literature reviews employ a range of patterns in order to vary their sentences.

TASK NINE

Below is a review that uses only citation pattern I. As you can see, using the same structure all the time can cause the reader to lose interest. Rewrite the passage so that it has more variety. Your version will probably be shorter than the original—another advantage!

The Origins of the First Scientific Articles

The first scientific journal was started in London in 1665. Obviously, the first scientific articles had no direct models to build on, and several scholars have discussed possible influences. Ard (1983) and Valle (2000) suggest that the first articles developed from the scholarly letters that scientists were accustomed to sending to each other. Sutherland (1986) showed that early articles were also influenced by the newspaper reports of that time. Paradis (1987) described the influence of the philosophical essay. Shapin (1984) claimed that the scientific books of Robert Boyle were another model. Finally, Bazerman (1988, 1997) argued that discussion among the scientists themselves made its own contribution to the emergence of the scientific article.

Move 2—Establishing a Niche

In many ways, Move 2 is the key move in introductions to longer research papers. (However, this move may not be needed in shorter communications.) It is the hinge that connects Move 1 (what has been done) to Move 3 (what the present research is about). Move 2 thus establishes the motivation for the study. By the end of Move 2, the reader should have a good idea of what is going to come in Move 3.

Most Move 2s establish a niche by indicating a gap—by showing that the research story so far is not yet complete. Move 2s then function as a *mini-critique* (see Unit Six). Usually Move 2s are quite short, often consisting of no more than a sentence. Let us examine the Move 2s in the first two Introductions we have seen so far.

Thomas Eakins

Apart from a chapter in Foster (1997), this series *has been little discussed by critics or art historians.* For example, these pictures *were ignored by Johns* in her . . .

University-Community Agency Collaboration

Little is, however, known about participants' views of university-community collaborations.

❖ Language Focus: Negative Openings in Move 2

Probably the most common way to indicate a gap is to use a " quasi-negative" subject. Presumably, negative subjects are chosen because they signal immediately to the reader that Move 1 has come to an end. Note the following uses of *little* and *few*.

Little / few

Uncountable	However, little information . . .
	little attention . . .
	little work . . .
	little data . . .
	little research . . .
Countable	However, few studies . . .
	few investigations . . .
	few researchers . . .
	few attempts . . .

Note the differences in the following pairs.

There is little research. (negative, i.e., not enough)

There is a little research. (neutral, i.e., maybe enough)

The department has few computers. (negative, i.e., not enough)

The department has a few computers. (neutral, i.e., maybe enough)

Note the use of *no / none of.*

No studies/data/calculations . . .

Use *no* when your conclusion is based on but does not directly refer to the cited literature. If you want to refer directly to the previous research, use *none of.*

None of these studies/findings/calculations . . .

However, you may want to avoid using a full negative like "no studies"; chances are that somebody will find an exception to your strong statement!

TASK TEN

Here are some "negative" verbs and adjectives that tend to cluster in Move 2. Working with a partner, decide how "negative" they are. Mark them as definitely or strongly negative (- -) or neutral or slightly negative (-).

Verbs

However, previous research in this field has _____ .

____ a. concentrated on . . .   ____ g. neglected to consider . . .

____ b. disregarded . . .   ____ h. overestimated . . .

____ c. failed to consider . . .   ____ i. overlooked . . .

____ d. ignored . . .   ____ j. been restricted to . . .

____ e. been limited to . . .   ____ k. suffered from . . .

____ f. misinterpreted . . .   ____ l. underestimated . . .

Adjectives

Nevertheless, these attempts to establish a link between dental fillings and disease are at present _____ .

____ a. controversial   ____ e. questionable

____ b. incomplete   ____ f. unconvincing

____ c. inconclusive   ____ g. unsatisfactory

____ d. misguided

Of course, not all RP Introductions express Move 2 by indicating an obvious gap. You may prefer, for various reasons, to avoid negative or quasi-negative comment altogether. In such cases, a useful alternative is to use a contrastive statement.

The research has tended to focus on . . . , rather than on . . .

These studies have emphasized . . . , as opposed to . . .

Although considerable research has been devoted to . . . , rather less attention has been paid to . . .

Two other strategies are quite common, particularly in the "harder" areas. The first is raising a question, a hypothesis, or a need. Here are some skeletal examples.

> However, it remains unclear whether . . .

> It would thus be of interest to learn how . . .

> If these results could be confirmed, they would provide strong evidence for . . .

> The findings suggest that this approach might be less effective when . . .

> It would seem, therefore, that further investigations are needed in order to . . .

Note that in these cases, sentence connectors are not limited to the *however* type.

The alternative type of Move 2 was described in Table 26 as "extending previous knowledge in some way." This type may sometimes be appropriate for term papers or shorter communications. In longer RPs, it tends to be used by research groups who are following up their own research or that done by similar groups. The authors draw a conclusion from their survey of the previous research, indicating how some finding in the immediate research literature can be extended or applied in some way. Here are three examples.

> These recent developments in computer-aided design clearly have considerable potential. In this paper, we demonstrate . . .

> The literature shows that Rasch Analysis is a useful technique for validating multiple-choice tests. This paper uses Rasch Analysis to . . .

> Such active-R networks eliminate the need for any external passive reactance elements. This paper utilizes the active-R approach for the design of a circuit . . .

Sometimes, however, Move 2s can be quite complicated. Consider, for example, the Move 2s from the two other Introductions that we have introduced—first, the "Keeping Up One's Appearance" paper. After their opening paragraph discussed in Task Five, Schwer and Daneshvary (2000) devote the next five short paragraphs to a literature review, concluding that "there appears to be an economic incentive to appear attractive" (209). Now here is their seventh paragraph (our emphasis added).

> *Previous research has not addressed* whether or not people who are employed in some occupations rate the maintenance of overall appearance more important than do people who are employed in other occupations. *Moreover, research has not fully considered* the behavioral consequences of individuals putting more or less emphasis on physical appearance (e.g. does it affect grooming habits or maintenance rituals?). *Nor has it addressed if* they patronize a beauty shop, a barber shop, or a beauty salon in maintaining their appearance.

Notice the strategy here—as shown by the italicized stretches of text—of making negative statements about "previous research." Also, notice that as the three sentences progress, they increasingly narrow down to the precise research question that Schwer and Daneshvary are attempting to answer.

TASK ELEVEN

Now read the middle section of the Almosnino Introduction (containing Move 2) and then answer the questions that follow.

M O V E 2

❻ However, the previously mentioned methods suffer from some limitations mainly concerning the treatment of the vortex wake formation and its interaction with the body. ❼ The first group of methods[2–4] cannot treat 3D flows and is limited to very slender bodies. ❽ The second group of computational methods[5–8] is time consuming and therefore expensive, and its separation prediction is not sufficiently accurate. ❾ Both the methods in this group and the method in 9 suffer from the dependency on too many semi-empirical inputs and assumptions concerning the vortex wake and its separation. ❿ The steady 3D nonlinear vortex-lattice method, upon which the present method is based, eliminates many of these limitations by introducing a more consistent model, but it can treat only symmetrical flow cases. (Copyright © 1984 AIAA—reprinted with permission)

1. How many "critique" expressions can you find in the passage? Underline or highlight them.

2. Look back at Task Ten. What negative ratings would you give them?

3. What word signals that Move 1 has ended and Move 2 has started? What other words or expressions could also indicate this shift?

4. This Move 2 occupies as many as five sentences. Why do you think Almosnino has put these sentences in this particular order?

5. Can you now anticipate what the next sentence is going to be?

Occupying the Niche

The third and final step in the typical RP Introduction is to make an offer to fill the gap (or extend the tradition) that has been created in Move 2. The first element in Move 3 is obligatory. It has two main variants:

Purposive (P) The author or authors indicate their main purpose or purposes

or

Descriptive (D) The author or authors describe the main feature of their research.

TASK TWELVE

Here are the beginning parts of ten opening Move 3 sentences. Decide in each case whether they are purposive or descriptive, and enter a *P* or a *D* in the blank. The first two have been done. One of them is from the Almosnino paper (see Move 2 in Task Eleven). Can you guess which one it is? Complete at least three of the sentences with your own words.

_P_ 1. The aim of the present paper is to give . . .

_D_ 2. This paper reports on the results obtained . . .

_____ 3. In this paper we give preliminary results for . . .

_____ 4. The main purpose of the experiment reported here was to . . .

_____ 5. This study was designed to evaluate . . .

_____ 6. The present work extends the use of the last model by . . .

_____ 7. We now report the interaction between . . .

_____ 8. The primary focus of this paper is on . . .

_____ 9. The aim of this investigation was to test . . .

_____ 10. Our primary objective in this paper is to provide . . .

Note that Move 3 is typically signaled by some reference to the present text, such as the uses of *this, the present, reported,* and *here.* If the conventions of the field or journal allow it, it is also common for the authors to switch from the impersonal to the personal by using *we* or, more rarely, *I.* Also note that these signals come early in the sentence. It is very unusual to find

> We present the results of three experiments *in this paper.*

rather than

> *In this paper* we present the results of three experiments.

❖ Language Focus: Tense and Purpose Statements

Students sometimes ask whether they should use *was* or *is* in purpose statements. Indeed, both were used in the phrases in Task Twelve. The answer to this question depends on how you refer to your work. You have two choices:

1. Referring to the type of *text*—paper, article, thesis, report, research note, etc.

2. Referring to the type of *investigation*—experiment, investigation, study, survey, etc.

If you choose to refer to the type of text, you must use the present tense. If you write, "The aim of this paper was to . . . ," it suggests that you are referring to an original aim that has now changed.

If you choose to refer to the type of investigation, you can use either *was* or *is*. However, there is an increasing tendency to choose the present, perhaps because it makes the research seem relevant and fresh and new. The "safe rule," then, is to opt for the present.

Completing an Introduction

Sometimes a second sentence is necessary to complete Move 3a, as in sentence B from the nursing paper in Task Three. Here, for example, is Almosnino's Move 3.

M	⓫ The present work extends the use of the last model to asymmetric,
O	body-vortex cases, thus increasing the range of flow patterns that can
V	be investigated. ⓬ In addition, an effort is made to improve the
	numerical procedure to accelerate the convergence of the iterative
E	solution and to get a better rollup of the vortex lines representing the
3	wake. (Copyright © 1984 AIAA—reprinted with permission)

These secondary statements are often introduced by such language as

In addition, . . .

Additionally, . . .

A secondary aim . . .

A further reason for . . .

In Table 26 (p. 244) we listed four other elements that can be found at the end of introductions. (There can be others, such as a depiction of the statistical measures employed.) The list order of the four elements is also the most likely order of occurrence:

3b. by listing research questions or hypotheses

3c. by announcing principal findings

3d. by stating the value of the present research

3e. by indicating the structure of the RP

In all cases we added the acronym PISF (probable in some fields but not in others).

In your field, is it probable or improbable that an RP would have any or all the elements listed under 3b–d? If you are unsure, how might you find out? Be prepared to discuss your position.

Listing Research Questions

Of the four introductions we have been considering, only the "Keeping Up One's Appearance" paper includes this element. The authors write:

> (Move 3a) This paper uses a sample to investigate whether one's a) occupational status influences the importance one attributes to maintaining overall appearance, and b) occupation influences one's choice of type of hairgrooming establishment. (Move 3b) Specifically, we test two hypotheses:
>
> Hypothesis 1. . . .
>
> Hypothesis 2. . . .

Announcing Principal Findings

There is some confusion as to whether RP Introductions should close with a statement of the principal results. One investigation (Swales and Najjar 1987) found that physicists do this about half the time but that educational researchers hardly ever include such statements. One useful guideline is to ask yourself whether the RP will open with an Abstract. If there is an Abstract, do you need to give the main findings three times: in the Abstract, in the Introduction, and in the Results? We think not. If there is no Abstract, you may wish to reconsider. Another suggestion would be to follow standard practice in your field—or ask your advisor.

Stating Value

You may also want to consider whether you want to mention at this stage anything about the contribution your research will make. Of course, you will do this in the Discussion section in any case. Note that as is typical of many engineering papers, Almosnino squeezes a value statement into his Introduction.

> . . . , thus increasing the range of flow problems that can be investigated.

If you opt for a value statement, it would be wise to be cautious and to use qualifications (see Unit Four).

Outlining the Structure of the Text

A final option is to consider whether you need to explain how your text is organized. This element is obligatory in dissertations and theses but is only included in RPs under certain circumstances. One such circumstance arises when your text is unusual in some way, such as not using a standard IMRD format. Such a field would be economics. Another arises if you are working in a relatively new field. Cooper (1985) found, for example, that outlining the RP structure was quite common in computer technology, and this practice continues today. Ask yourself, therefore, whether your anticipated readers need to have the organization of the RP explained.

Here is a useful example of a textual outline, well-motivated by the unusual structure of the paper. Notice how it uses a good variety of sentence structures. The paper is about currency rates in the European Common Market and was written by one of our students.

> The plan of this paper is as follows. Section II describes the current arrangements for regulating exchange rates within the EC. In Section III a theoretical model is constructed which is designed to capture these arrangements. Experimental parameters are then tested in Section IV. Finally, Section V offers some suggestions for the modification of the current mechanisms. (Pierre Martin, unedited)

TASK FOURTEEN

Below is a textual outline by another of our students. Notice how this time it lacks variety. Can you rewrite it?

> The rest of the paper is organized as follows. Section 2 presents the theoretical concept. Section 3 presents the empirical specification, the implementation of the model. Section 4 presents the results of statistical and other computational analyses. Section 5 summarizes the findings and provides a brief discussion concerning the shortcomings of the methods employed. Finally, an appendix presenting the detailed algebraic works is presented at the end of the paper. (Abdul Malik, unedited)

TASK FIFTEEN

We started this section with a complete introduction from the humanities. Now here is one from biostatistics published in a journal called *Controlled Clinical Trials*. Read it and answer the questions that follow.

Fraud in Medical Research: An International Survey of Biostatisticians

J. Ranstam, M. Buyse, S. L. George, S. Evans, N. L. Geller,
B. Scherrer, E. Lesaffre, G. Murray, L. Edler, J. L. Hutton, T. Colton,
and P. Lachenbruch

❶ The public awareness of scientific fraud has increased remarkably since the late 1980s when a controversy made front-page news, in which a paper investigated for fraud had as coauthor a Nobel laureate [1]. ❷ During the 1990s scientific fraud was disclosed on numerous occasions [2]. ❸ In fact, it was recently suggested that fraud now is "endemic in many scientific disciplines and in most countries" [3]. ❹ However, the clandestine character and consequential lack of reliable information make it difficult to study scientific fraud. ❺ The characteristics and frequency of scientific fraud, therefore, are generally unknown, and its impact on medical research is unclear.

❻ Biostatisticians routinely work closely with physicians and scientists in many branches of medical research and have unique insight into data. ❼ In addition, they have the methodological competence to detect fraud and could be expected to have a special professional interest in the validity of results. ❽ Biostatisticians therefore could provide unique and reliable information on the characteristics of fraud in medical research.

❾ The objective of this study was to assess the characteristics of fraud in medical research by surveying members of the International Society of Clinical Biostatistics (ISCB).

1. Underline all words and phrases that help "establish territory" in the first three sentences.

2. What does *clandestine* in sentence 4 mean?

3. Identify all of the linking words and phrases in this short introduction. What are their functions?

4. Where and how is the gap established?

5. Using the analysis in Table 26, it is quite easy to show how all of the sentences, except for sentences 6–8, fit into the model. How would you interpret those three sentences?

TASK SIXTEEN

Now write or rewrite an RP Introduction of your own.

Discussion Sections

It is not so easy to provide useful guidelines for writing Discussion or Conclusion sections. (We will not distinguish between these two terms since the difference is partly conventional, depending on traditions in particular fields and journals.) See what is done in your own field.

The problem is that Discussions vary considerably, depending on a number of factors. Despite some recent research on Discussions (especially Lewin et al. 2001), not all these factors are understood. Obviously there is disciplinary variation. For example, some scientists, perhaps especially those in the life sciences, believe that a long Discussion implies weak methods and results, while social scientists and humanists may well believe the opposite. Another important set of factors concerns the kind of research question that a study attempts to answer, and how successful was that quest. A final factor that leads to variation is the position of the Discussion section in the RP. By the time readers reach the Discussion, authors can assume a fair amount of shared knowledge. They can assume (if not always correctly) that the reader has understood the purpose of the study, obtained a sense of the methodology, and followed along with the results. Authors can use this understanding to pick and choose what to concentrate on in the Discussion. As a result, they typically have greater freedom than in the Introduction.

Overall, if Results deal with *facts*, then Discussions deal with *points;* facts are *descriptive*, while points are *interpretive*. Effective discussion sections are similar to effective lectures, which, as Olsen and Huckin (1990) note, are based on points, rather than on facts. Further, authors of Discussions have some flexibility in deciding which of their possible points to include and then which to highlight.

Discussions, then, should be more than summaries. They should go beyond the results. They should be

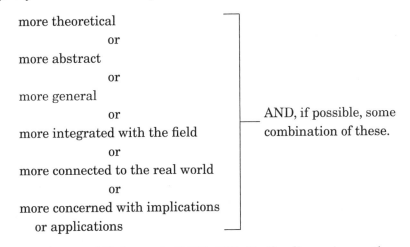

more theoretical

or

more abstract

or

more general

or   AND, if possible, some

more integrated with the field   combination of these.

or

more connected to the real world

or

more concerned with implications

or applications

As Weissberg and Buker note (1990, 160), "in the discussion section you should step back and take a broad look at your findings and your study as a whole."

We have said that Discussions can be viewed as presenting a series of points. While this is true, Discussions may start with a general reorientation to the study as a whole—especially if the authors believe that their readers may not have been fully attentive to the substance of the earlier sections. Some of the common "skeletal" formulations for this optional move are as follows:

In this paper we have investigated . . .

The main purpose of this paper has been to . . .

The survey reported on in this study has produced a wealth of data.

Typically, the points are arranged as in Table 27.

Table 27   Discussion Moves

Move 1	Points to consolidate your research space (obligatory)
Move 2	Points to indicate the limitations of your study (optional but common)
Move 3	Points to recommend a course of action and/or to identify useful areas of further research (optional and only common in some areas)

Move 1 is usually quite extensive, and Moves 2 and 3 are often quite short. At this point, you might want to observe that Move 1 and the later moves seem self-contradictory. Why, you may ask, would authors build up something in order to apparently attack it later? However, if we remember *positioning,* we can see that authors can present themselves very effectively by both

1. highlighting intelligently the strengths of the study

   and

2. highlighting intelligently its weaknesses.

Indeed, Moves 2 and 3 can also be used to identify and open up future research space for authors and their colleagues. In a study of 60 research articles from biochemistry, Kanoksilapatham (2003) found that all 60 had a consolidation move (or series of moves), 45 had a Move 2, and 32 had a Move 3.

Opening a Discussion Section

As we have already suggested, there are many options in opening a discussion. Consider the case of the following data. We studied Discussion openings in 15 articles from a small U.S. regional journal of natural history research. We found great variation even within one journal. Four Discussions did open with the *main results.* This was the largest category but was still less than 30 percent of the total.

Three begin with a *discussion of the literature*. Here are two "skeletal" examples.

1. Graikowski et al. (1986) recovered . . . toxin from . . . and found that . . . suffered 100% mortality when. . . .

2. Food shortages, social stress . . . within . . . are causes of dispersal among . . . (Fritz and Mech 1981, Messier 1985, Mech 1987, Packard and Mech 1980).

Two sections start in a more dramatic way by offering a general conclusion.

3. Apparently, we are witness to the early phases of a classic population explosion.

4. From this data, it is clear that . . . are not major consumers of commercially important fish-species in. . . .

The remaining types of opening occur only once in the sample. We were surprised, for example, to find only *one* opening that reminds the reader of the *original purpose*.

5. The objective of the survey was to quantify the number of . . . within. . . .

In another case, the author opens with a *summary*.

6. This report brings together all known records of . . . since 1959.

In another, the authors raise the level of discussion by referring to *theory*.

7. The interrelationship of bird populations and the environment is extremely complex.

One author starts with a comment about *methodology*.

8. There is a bias associated with using either ground or aerial counts, exclusively.

Another author begins his discussion by highlighting the special importance of his *research site*.

9. . . . is one of the few sites in North America where the presence of a significant number of migrating . . . has been documented.

And in the final case, the author actually begins by discussing the *limitations* of the data.

10. The census figure of . . . is expected to be an underestimate of the total population of. . . .

This small survey shows some of the many strategies that can be adopted for opening a Discussion section. The choice of strategy clearly depends in part on how the authors view their work. We will briefly comment on the last three cases. In opening 8 the author begins with a methodology critique of previous work, because one of his main points is that he has taken the trouble to "combine both aerial and ground surveys." In opening 9 the researcher begins by stressing the point that the location of his research site offers exceptional advantages. Finally, take the case of opening 10. It might appear that the author of this opening has adopted a very risky strategy, but in this particular context it is not. It soon emerges that carrying out a complete census of this particular species would be very difficult. Therefore, the author presumably felt on safe ground when he opened in this way. Indeed, he can go on to claim that his numbers are much larger than anybody else has so far been able to report!

TASK SEVENTEEN

Survey and classify the openings of at least six Discussion sections from a journal in your field. Bring your findings to class.

Despite all this talk about variation, the available research (e.g., Lewin et al. 2001) does point to a number of useful suggestions. As we have seen, Move 1 can be preceded by a statement reminding the readers of what you have done. Then we might find the elements listed in Table 28.

In order to see this in action, we return, in Task Eighteen, to the "children's pain" paper discussed in Unit Seven.

Table 28   Details of the Opening Move

Move 1a	Report your accomplishments by highlighting major findings.
Move 1b	Relate and evaluate your data in the light of previous research.
Move 1c	Interpret your data by making suggestions as to why your results are the way they are.
Move 1d	Anticipate and deal with potential criticisms (only if necessary).

TASK EIGHTEEN

Read the opening and closing paragraphs of the first Discussion subsection from Pölkki et al. 2003 (40–42), then answer the questions that follow.

1 This interview study indicated that hospitalized children, aged 8–12 yr old, are capable of describing the methods for relieving pain. **2** The results are consistent with earlier studies conducted among pediatric patients (Savedra et al. 1982; Pölkki et al. 1999; Pederson et al. 2000). **3** In order to achieve the children's own perspective, however, the children should be asked about the methods that could potentially alleviate their pain, as well as their suggestions regarding the implementation of pain relief measures. **4** Due to their tendency to be independent, school-aged children may conceal their pain and be reluctant to request help from others (cf. Lutz, 1986; Woodgate and Kristjanson, 1995). **5** This phenomenon in the children requires specific attention, despite the fact that a certain level of cognitive maturity is achieved during the school-aged period, and a much broader array of non-pharmacological methods are appropriate to use at this age (Vessey and Carlson, 1996). . . .

6 Many children had suggestions to the nurses, but only a few to the parents concerning the implementation of surgical pain relief measures. **7** This may indicate that the children expect the nurses to know how to care for them and relieve their pain (cf. Alex and Ritchie, 1992), whereas the children do not have specific expectations of their parents other than simply to "stay with me more." **8** In order to improve nursing care for children with postoperative pain the recommendations provided by children to nurses, such as creating a more comfortable environment (especially minimizing noise problems), giving more or stronger pain medication without delay, as well as visiting regularly or staying with the child more, should be taken seriously into account in nursing practice.

1. How many of the eight sentences make reference to the previous literature?

2. What does *cf.* mean?

3. What differences do you see between these two paragraphs and the Results paragraphs given in Unit Seven, Task Twelve A?

4. What do you assume to be the purposes of sentences 3–5?

5. What do think were the topics of the two missing paragraphs (paragraphs 2 and 3)? (Table 2 in Unit Seven, Task Twelve A, p. 238 may help you here.)

6. The discussion has three titled subsections. The second is called "Reliability and Validity," and the third "Challenges for Future Research." What do you think the first subsection was called?

Language Focus: Levels of Generalization

In the Results sections, statements may be quite specific and closely tied to the data.

> As can be seen in Table 1, 84% of the students performed above the 12th-grade level.

> Seven out of eight experimental samples resisted corrosion longer than the controls.

On the other hand, in the Abstract or in a Summary, space restrictions may lead to a high level of generality.

> The results indicate that the students performed above the 12th-grade level.

> The experimental samples resisted corrosion longer than the controls.

In the Discussion, we usually expect something in between these two levels. One common device is to use one of the following "phrases of generality."

> Overall, . . .

> In general, . . .

On the whole, . . .

In the main, . . .

With . . . exception(s), . . .

The overall results indicate . . .

The results indicate, overall, that . . .

In general, the experimental samples resisted . . .

With one exception, the experimental samples resisted . . .

Limitations in Discussions

We saw in Introduction Move 2s (see pp. 257–62) that extensive "negative" language was a possible option. In contrast, Discussion Move 2s tend to use less elaborate negative language. The main reason is obvious; it is now your own research that you are talking about. Another reason is that many limitation statements in Discussions are not so much about the weaknesses in the research as about what *cannot be concluded* from the study in question. Producing statements of this kind provides an excellent opportunity for the writer to show that he or she understands how evidence is evaluated in the particular field.

❈ Language Focus: Expressions of Limitation

Here are some typical formulations for stating limitations in one's research scope.

It should be noted that this study has been primarily concerned with. . . .

This analysis has concentrated on. . . .

The findings of this study are restricted to. . . .

This study has addressed only the question of. . . .

The limitations of this study are clear: . . . .

We would like to point out that we have not. . . .

Below are some typical openings for statements that firmly state that certain conclusions should *not* be drawn.

> However, the findings do not imply. . . .

> The results of this study cannot be taken as evidence for. . . .

> Unfortunately, we are unable to determine from this data. . . .

> The lack of . . . means that we cannot be certain. . . .

We said earlier that Move 2s are optional in Discussions. If you feel it is unnecessary to comment on your work in either of the above two ways, a useful alternative is to place the limitation in an opening phrase. At least, it does express a becoming academic modesty.

> Notwithstanding its limitations, this study does suggest. . . .

> Despite its preliminary character, the research reported here would seem to indicate. . . .

> However exploratory, this study may offer some insight into. . . .

TASK NINETEEN

Read the following extracts from the second section of the Discussion from the "children's pain" paper, and then complete the tasks that follow.

❶ Use of the interview as a data collection method allowed the children to express their own perspectives regarding the methods of relieving their pain in the hospital; however, there were some defects that may potentially prevent the attainment of purpose. ❷ First, some children may have tried to provide favorable answers during the interview even though the researcher reminded them that there were no right or wrong answers. ❸ Secondly, there were practical problems that may have disturbed some children's ability to concentrate on relating their experiences. ❹ For example, ... ❺ The use of triangulation, such as observing children during their hospitalization, may have increased the validity of the results. . . . ❻ In order to improve validity and reliability of the study the researcher attempted to establish a confidential relationship with the child and minimized noise problems during the interview.

1. Is this a problem-solution text?

2. What is the sequence in the opening sentence? Good news → bad news, or the reverse? Why did the authors choose the pattern they did?

3. How are the "problems" hedged or qualified in the first three sentences?

4. Write an appropriate completion for sentence 4.

5. In sentence 6 the first author, having earlier demonstrated her awareness of the problems with self-report data, now starts to show how she managed to reduce possible inaccuracies. In the remaining four sentences of the subsection, she says what else she did. Can you guess two of the things she did?

Cycles of Moves

Finally, we should point out that many Discussion sections run through the Move 1-2-3 sequence (or part of it) more than once. Commonly, each cycle occupies one paragraph. Further, the more research questions there are to be discussed, the more this cycling is likely to occur. Such cycling can also occur in Introductions, but it tends to be less common there, especially in shorter RPs.

If you wish to write a longer discussion, follow the shape recommended in Figure 11. Begin with specifics and then move toward the more general.

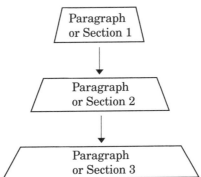

Fig. 11. Shape of a longer discussion

TASK TWENTY

Write or rewrite a Discussion section for your own research. If you are working with others, collaborate with them. If your original paper lacked a Move 2 and/or a Move 3, add these to your new draft.

Unfinished Business

Although we have now gone through the four main sections of the RP, there remain some other matters to be attended to. Obviously, there is the question of a title. Then there is an Abstract. You may need a short Acknowledgments section. Finally, the references have to be in good order.

Titles

Although the title comes first in an RP, it may sometimes be written last. Its final form may be long delayed and much thought about and argued over. Authors know that titles are important, they know that the RP will be known by its title, and they know that a successful title will attract readers while an unsuccessful one will discourage readers.

What, then, are the requirements for good RP titles? In general, we suggest the following three.

1. The title should indicate the topic of the study.

2. The title should indicate the scope of the study (i.e., neither overstating nor understating its significance).

3. The title should be self-explanatory to readers in the chosen area.

In some cases it may be helpful to also indicate the nature of the study (experiment, case report, survey, etc.), but this is not always required.

Notice that we have so far not mentioned the length of the title. The expected length of RP titles is very much a disciplinary matter. In some areas, such as the life sciences, titles are becoming longer and looking more and more like full sentences. In others, the preferred style is for short titles containing mostly nouns and prepositions.

Finally, at this stage in your career, we advise against "clever," "joke," or "trick" titles. These can be very successful for undergraduates and for senior scholars, but in your case, such titles may simply be interpreted as mistakes. An example of such a title follows. The author of the paper is Professor Hartley, a well-known professor of psychology who conducted many experiments on what makes English texts easy or difficult to read. In this instance, he has been comparing texts that have "ragged right" margins at the end of the lines with those that have straight, or "justified," margins. Here is the title.

> Unjustified Experiments in Typographical Research and Instructional Design (*British Journal of Educational Technology* [1973] 2: 120–31)

In this case, we can assume that Professor Hartley is making a joke. But if you wrote it?

As it happens, we have in this textbook already referred to a fair number of written texts, some written by our students, but most from published sources. Look again at the titles of eight of them. How many of these can you remember?

1. University-Community Agency Collaboration: Human Service Agency Workers' Views (Tiamiyu, p. 247)

2. Reducing Air Pollution in Urban Areas: The Role of Urban Planners (Iseki, p. 170)

3. Selling Cities: Promoting New Images for Meetings Tourism (Bradley, Hall, and Harrison, p. 45)

4. On the Use of the Passive in Two Astrophysics Journal Papers (Tarone et al., p. 215)

5. The Position of Sentence Connectors in Academic English (Swales and Feak, p. 232)

6. Arguing for Experimental "Facts" in Science: A Study of Research Article Results Sections in Biochemistry (Thompson, p. 223)

7. Hospitalized Children's Descriptions of Their Experiences with Postsurgical Pain Relieving Methods (Pölkki p. 326)

8. High Angle-of-Attack Calculations of the Sub-sonic Vortex Flow in Slender Bodies (Almosnino, p. 250)

TASK TWENTY-ONE

Use Table 29 to complete an analysis of the eight titles listed on page 279. The first one has been done for you.

Table 29   RP Title Analysis

Title	Number of words	Any verbs	Punctuation	Field
1	9	No	Colon	Nursing
2				
3				
4				
5				
6				
7				
8				

Can you determine the system of capitalization that has been used in these titles? Is it the same as in your field? (Changes in capitalization occur in the reference list; see the notes at the beginning of our references on p. 323.)

As it happens, only one of these eight titles used a qualification. Number 4 uses *on*. What differences do you see between the following pairs of titles?

1a. On the Use of the Passive in Journal Articles
1b. The Use of the Passive in Journal Articles

2a. A Study of Research Article Results Sections
2b. A Preliminary Study of Research Article Results Sections

3a. An Analysis of Errors in Period Placement

3b. Toward an Analysis of Errors in Period Placement

4a. The Role of Urban Planners

4b. The Potential Role of Urban Planners

4c. A Possible Role for Urban Planners

Depending on your field, you may wish to consider using qualifications in your titles. In nearly all cases, the process of arriving at the final form of a title is one of narrowing it down and making it more specific. Qualifications can be helpful in this process.

Table 29, in Task Twenty-One, reveals that three of the eight titles use a colon.

2. Reducing Air Pollution in Urban Areas: The Role of Urban Planners

3. Selling Cities: Promoting New Images for Meetings Tourism

6. Arguing for Experimental "Facts" in Science: A Study of Research Article Results Sections in Biochemistry

Colons are widely used in titles. One of the colon's typical functions is to separate ideas in such combinations as the following.

Pre-Colon	Post-Colon
Problem:	Solution
General:	Specific
Topic:	Method
Major:	Minor

Maybe you can think of others.

TASK TWENTY-TWO

Bring the title of one of your papers to class and be prepared to discuss its final form and how it got there.

Abstracts

Unless you are in the true humanities, your RP will probably require an abstract. RP Abstracts usually consist of a single paragraph containing from about 4 to 10 full sentences. This kind of Abstract is more important for the reader than for the writer. By this we mean that an unsatisfactory RP Abstract is not likely to affect whether the paper is finally accepted for publication (although the editors may suggest changes to it). It may, however, affect the number of people that will read your paper. We know from many studies that readers of academic journals employ a vast amount of skimming and scanning. If they like your Abstract, they may read your paper—or at least part of it. If they do not like it, they may not.

There are two main approaches to writing RP Abstracts. One we will call the *results-driven* Abstract, because it concentrates on the research findings and what might be concluded from them. The other approach is to offer an *RP summary* Abstract in which you provide one- or two-sentence synopses of each of the four sections. Most RP Abstracts should aim to be *informative* rather than *indicative* (i.e., they should include the main findings). However, this may not be possible with very complex papers or with very theoretical ones (as in mathematics). We should also note that structured Abstracts have been spreading outside the medical field (Hartley 1997). Structured Abstracts have subheadings as a paper would, such as

Background

Aim

Method

Results

Conclusion

TASK TWENTY-THREE

Read the following two drafts of an Abstract for our mini-RP (refer to Appendix Four if necessary), then answer the questions that follow.

Version A

A count of sentence connectors in 12 academic papers produced 70 different connectors. These varied in frequency from 62 tokens (*however*) to single occurrences. Seventy-five percent of the 467 examples appeared in sentence-initial position. However, individual connectors varied considerably in position preference. Some (e.g., *in addition*) always occurred initially; in other cases (e.g., *for example, therefore*), they were placed after the subject more than 50% of the time. These findings suggest that a search for general rules for connector position may not be fruitful.

Version B

Although sentence connectors are a well-recognized feature of academic writing, little research has been undertaken on their positioning. In this study, we analyze the position of 467 connectors found in a sample of 12 research papers. Seventy-five percent of the connectors occurred at the beginning of sentences. However, individual connectors varied greatly in positional preference. Some, such as *in addition,* only occurred initially; others, such as *therefore,* occurred initially in only 40% of the cases. These preliminary findings suggest that general rules for connector position will prove elusive.

1. The journal requirements state that the abstracts accompanying papers should not exceed 100 words. Do versions A and B qualify?

2. Which version is *results driven* and which is an *RP summary?*

3. Compare the tense usage in versions A and B.

4. Which version do you prefer? And why?

5. Some journals also ask for a list of *key words.* Choose three or four suitable key words.

It seems clear that tense usage in Abstracts is fairly complicated. First, the conclusions are nearly always in the present. Second, RP summary Abstracts often use the present or present perfect for their opening statements. Third, there appears to be considerable disciplinary and individual tense variation with sentences dealing with results.

In the two versions used in Task Twenty-Three, the results were all expressed through the past tense. Nevertheless, it is not difficult to find exceptions to this pattern. Here is a short abstract from the "Rapid Communications" section of the journal *Physical Review A.*

Nuclear-Structure Correction to the Lamb Shift

K. Pachucki, D. Leibfried, and T. W. Hänsch

In this paper the second-order nuclear-structure correction to the energy of hydrogen-like systems is estimated and previous results are corrected. Both deuterium and hydrogen are considered. In the case of deuterium the correction is proportional to the nuclear polarizability and amounts to about -19kHz for the 1S state. For hydrogen the resulting energy shift is about -60Hz.

Our investigations suggest that the shift to the present tense is more likely to occur in physical sciences, such as physics, chemistry, and astrophysics, and less likely to occur in the social sciences. We also found that physicists and chemists were—perhaps surprisingly— more likely to adopt a personal stance. Indeed, we have found occasional Abstracts, particularly in astrophysics, which contain sequences of sentence openings like the following.

We discuss . . .   We compute . . .   We conclude . . .

It would therefore seem that choice of tense and person may again be partly a strategic matter in Abstracts. Choosing the present tense option—if permitted—can produce an effect of liveliness and contemporary relevance. Choosing *we* can add pace, by making the Abstract a little shorter.

TASK TWENTY-FOUR

Choose one of the following. Analyze five Abstracts from a central journal in your field in terms of their use of tense. Be prepared to summarize your findings in class, perhaps in the form of a table. Alternatively, draft an Abstract for your own RP.

Acknowledgments

Acknowledgments have become an integral part of most RPs. Indeed, one well-known professor of our acquaintance reported to us that he always reads the Acknowledgments section of an RP first. When we asked him why, he replied, "Oh, the first thing I want to know is who has been talking to whom." While we do not think that this is standard reading behavior, it does show that Acknowledgments can be more than a display of necessary politeness.

Acknowledgments occur either at the bottom of the first page, following the Discussion, or sometimes at the end of the RP. They provide an opportunity for you to show that you are a member of a community and have benefited from that membership. The Acknowledgments, therefore, allow you to "repay your debts" (Giannoni 2002). At the same time, however, they allow you to highlight that you are also "intellectually responsible" for the content of the publication (Giannoni 2002). Here we list some of the common elements in Acknowledgments.

1. Financial support

   Support for this work was provided by [sponsor].

   This research was partially supported by a grant from [sponsor].

   This research was funded by Contract (number) from [sponsor].

2. Thanks

   We would like to thank A, B, and C for their help. . . .

   I wish to thank A for his encouragement and guidance throughout this project.

   We are indebted to B for . . .

   We are also grateful to D for . . .

3. Disclaimers (following element 1 or 2)

   However, the opinions expressed here do not necessarily reflect the policy of [sponsor].

   The interpretations in this paper remain my own.

   None, however, is responsible for any remaining errors.

   However, any mistakes that remain are my own.

We believe that, if permitted, Acknowledgments should be written in the first person—using *I* for a single author and *we* for coauthors.

It is possible to find phrases like "the present authors," but we consider them too formal for this situation.

As far as we can see, financial support tends to come first, followed by thanks. Disclaimers seem optional. Mentions of other matters, such as permissions or sources of materials, may also occur. (Acknowledgments in dissertations are treated in some detail in *English in Today's Research World,* Unit Six.)

TASK TWENTY-FIVE

Write a suitable Acknowledgments section for one of your pieces of work. If necessary, invent some forms of assistance to expand the section.

Appendixes

Appendix One

Articles in Academic Writing

Three of the most common words in the English language are also three of the most difficult to use. We are referring to the articles *a, an,* and *the.* We will not attempt here to give you every rule of article use in English, but we will provide you with a quick review of some basic rules to guide you in your choice of *a, an, the,* and Ø (no article needed). For a much more complete discussion of article use in academic writing, we suggest you look at Peter Master's publications on article use.

1. Countability

Before deciding if you should use an article, you should determine whether the noun in question is countable or uncountable and whether it is generic (representative or symbolic) or specific (actual). Let us first take a look at specific nouns and countability. We will take a look at generic use in section 5 of this appendix.

TASK ONE

Mark the following nouns as either countable *(C)* or uncountable *(U).*

commodity	____	money	____
complication	____	problem	____
computer	____	progress	____
device	____	proposal	____
discrepancy	____	research	____
energy	____	research project	____
equipment	____	researcher	____

fracture	____	society	____
information	____	theory	____
knowledge	____	traffic	____
machinery	____	vegetation	____
model	____	work	____

Determining whether a noun is countable may not be as easy as it seems. First, you cannot tell whether a noun is countable simply by looking at it. Some nouns that you intuitively think can be counted may not be countable. Money, for example, can be counted; however, the noun *money* itself is uncountable. If you do not know whether a noun is countable, you can either ask a native speaker or check a dictionary. (If a plural form is given, it is usually countable.)

Second, a noun that is countable in one language may not be countable in another and vice versa. *Information,* for example, is uncountable in English but countable in most of its European equivalents. The following nouns are usually uncountable in English.

Names for languages—Chinese, Korean, French, Arabic . . .

Names for areas of study—physics, biology, economics . . .

Names for solids—coal, steel, marble . . .

Names for liquids—water, nitric acid, oil . . .

Names for gases—oxygen, hydrogen, methane . . .

Names for powders—salt, sugar, sand . . .

Third, although you may have learned that nouns are either countable or uncountable, this is not the whole story. There are quite a number of nouns that can be either. These can be referred to as *double nouns.* There may even be considerable differences in meaning between the countable noun and its uncountable counterpart. Table 30 lists some double nouns.

Table 30   Double Nouns

Uncountable	Countable
analysis (in general)	an analysis (a particular one)
calculation (in general)	a calculation (a particular one)
diamond (the hard substance)	a diamond (a precious stone)
iron (the substance)	an iron (a device for ironing)
science (in general)	a science (a particular one)
grain (in general), i.e., cereal	a grain (a particular one), i.e., a grain of salt

An important group of nouns in this category refers to concepts that can be measured or quantified. Examples of these are *temperature, pressure, voltage, growth, density,* and *velocity.* Can you describe the difference between *temperature* and *a temperature?*

A thermometer measures *temperature.*

Temperature is expressed in degrees.

A temperature of over 120°C was recorded.

The patient ran *a* high *temperature* for several days.

Fourth, some nouns that are almost always uncountable in everyday English may have countable uses in technical English. Can you explain the difference in usage between the italicized nouns in the following sentences?

Rice is a staple food around the world.

A rice that can resist certain types of diseases should be introduced to the farmers of the region.

Steel is critical for the construction of skyscrapers.

The use of *a* light-weight *steel* would improve fuel efficiency.

There are at least two possible explanations for the difference. One is that the second sentence of each set involves a highly specialized use of the term that would most likely only be used by experts in the field who may find it necessary to make such fine distinctions. For example, while most nonexperts would make a distinction between rice and wheat or between steel and aluminum, they would not necessarily distinguish between different types of rice or steel. Experts, however, can and do. Another reason may be for purposes of conciseness. It is simply more efficient for experts to talk of *steels* rather than *different types of steel*. (However, we recommend that you do not shift uncountable nouns to countable unless you have seen examples from your field of study.)

Finally, some nouns in English are perhaps in the process of shifting from uncountable to countable. For instance, although *work* has long been an uncountable noun, it is not unusual to hear students say that they have "a lot of homeworks to do." Further, *research* is an uncountable noun for the vast majority of native speakers; however, it is not at all inconceivable that it may someday become countable— perhaps as a result of pressure from nonnative speakers.

Once you have determined what type of noun you are using, you then can make some further decisions regarding your choice (or omission) of article.

2. The Indefinite Article and Ø

A(n) and *one* are related but not identical. As you know, *a(n)* indicates that the noun is *any* single item, rather than a specific one. *A(n)*, therefore, can *never* be used with plural or uncountable nouns. *A* is used before consonant sounds, while *an* is used before vowel sounds. Sound, not spelling, is important here. Notice the difference between *an uprising* and *a university*.

A(n) is typically used with the first mention of a singular countable noun, but not always. There are a number of linguistic contexts that require the use of *the*. (See section 3.)

Usually, no article (Ø) is necessary for the first mention of a plural or an uncountable noun where none of the special conditions for definite article use apply. (See section 3.)

3. The Definite Article

The use of the definite article is far more problematic than the use of the indefinite, because the definite article is used in a number of different ways. The most important of these, however, is to specify a particular noun, to make clear that reference is being made to a particular singular or plural noun. The definite article should be used in the following contexts.

- Second mention (either explicit or implicit)

  a. The surface is covered by *a thin oxide film. The film* protects the surface from corrosion.

  b. A very lightweight car was developed, but *the vehicle* performed poorly in crash tests.

  c. A new computer was purchased to complete the process, but *the hard drive* was damaged.

- Superlatives or ordinals

  a. *The most-controlled therapy* yielded the best results.

  b. *The first studies* were conducted in early 1993.

  c. *The last security conference* was termed a success.

- Specifiers (e.g., *same, sole, only, chief, principal . . .*)

  a. *The same subjects* were retested at two-week intervals.

  b. *The only research* previously done in this area yielded mixed results.

  c. *The principal causes* of the disaster have yet to be discovered.

- Shared knowledge or unique reference

  a. *The sun* rises in the east and sets in the west.

  b. *The oxygen balance* in the atmosphere is maintained by photosynthesis.

  c. *The stars* are fueled by fusion reactions.

- *Of*-phrases or other forms of postmodification (but not with first mention of partitive[1] *of*-phrases such as *a molecule of oxygen, a layer of silicon,* or *a piece of information*)

  a. *The behavior of this species* varies.

  b. *The price of gold* fluctuates.

  c. *The results of the investigation* were inconclusive.

---

[1]A partitive phrase is a construction which denotes part of a whole.

- Partitive *of*-phrases with plurals

  a. *None of the projects* was satisfactory.

  b. *Some of the subjects* had adverse reactions.

  c. *All of the questionnaires* were returned.

- Names of theories, effects, devices, scales, and so on modified by a proper name used as an adjective

  a. *the Doppler* effect

  b. *the Heisenberg* uncertainty principle

  c. *the Hubble* telescope

  d. *the Kelvin* scale

Note, however, that when a proper name is used in possessive form, no article is used.

  a. Coulomb's law

  b. Einstein's theory of relativity

  c. Broca's area

  d. Wegener's hypothesis

4. Acronyms and Abbreviations

Acronyms and abbreviations follow the same rules as nouns that are spelled out. Review the guidelines in sections 1–3 and then look at the following examples. (Note the use of *an*. As with other nouns, if the first *sound* is a vowel sound, then *an* is used.)

a / an / Ø

> This device contains *an LED*.[2]

> *A TFT* was used.

> This computer has *a CD-ROM*.

> *R&D* is a high priority.

> *NASA* is working on a space station.

---

[2]LED = light emitting diode, TFT = thin film transmitter, CD = compact disc, ROM = read only memory, R&D = research and development, NASA = National Aeronautics and Space Administration.

the

Taxes in *the EU³ are relatively high.*

Some of the LEDs need to be replaced.

The LCD in this computer is of high quality.

The GNP of the United States has fluctuated greatly.

It is difficult to say which is *the best PC.*

Notice that when acronyms and abbreviations are used as modifiers, you should focus on the head noun as you choose your article.

An EU response to this situation can be expected.

Many items had to be removed from *the NASA budget* submitted earlier this year.

A new R&D initiative was outlined by the president.

TASK TWO

Read this passage on writing and fill in the blanks with either *a, an, the,* or Ø.

_____ writing is _____ complex sociocognitive process involving _____ construction of _____ recorded messages on _____ paper or some other material and, more recently, on _____ computer screen. _____ skills needed to write range from making _____ appropriate graphic marks, through utilizing _____ resources of _____ chosen language, to anticipating _____ reactions of _____ intended readers. _____ writing as composing needs to be distinguished from _____ simpler task of _____ copying. _____ writing is slower than _____ other skills

---

³EU = European Union, LCD = liquid crystal display, GNP = gross national product, PC = personal computer.

of _____ listening, _____ reading, and _____ speaking. It is further slowed by _____ processes of _____ thinking, _____ rereading what has been written, and _____ revising. _____ writing is not _____ natural ability like _____ speaking but has to be acquired through _____ years of _____ training or _____ schooling. Although _____ writing systems have been in existence for about 5,000 years, even today, only _____ minority of _____ world's population knows how to write.

TASK THREE

Read this passage on hearing aids and fill in the blanks with either *a, an, the,* or Ø.

As _____ average population of _____ United States has increased, so too has _____ number of _____ hearing impaired individuals. Approximately _____ 20 million hearing aids are now in use, and this number is expected to rise. Although there have been _____ considerable advances in _____ hearing aid technology, they still have _____ number of _____ drawbacks, one of _____ most notable ones being problems in dealing with _____ important environmental sounds. For example, _____ people who are deaf in both ears are unable to determine _____ direction of _____ sound with _____ conventional hearing aid. This limitation could result in _____ accident or injury if _____ wearer cannot decide _____ direction of _____ siren or _____ other warning sound. _____ Another problem concerns _____ people suffering from _____ high-frequency hearing loss. This type of _____ hearing loss removes many consonants and other useful environmental noises,

such as _____ ringing of _____ telephone.

TASK FOUR

Now, edit the rest of the passage on hearing aids, inserting articles with a caret (^) as necessary. The first sentence has been done for you.

To overcome these limitations, researchers have been investigating the ^ possibility of multiprogrammable hearing device that could perform two functions. One would be to convert high frequency information to low frequencies that fall in range of normal hearing. Other would involve producing LED display that could indicate probable direction of sound. Since same device can perform two functions, it could be used by wider range of consumers than conventional devices. Prototypes of device are currently being tested. If successful, it should be commercially available within next five years.

5. Generics

So far, we have only discussed article use for specific nouns. Generic nouns, however, are equally important. Generics are as important as specific nouns for academic writing because

1. they more frequently occur in highly formal English;

2. they are more likely to occur in introductions and conclusions, because they are closely associated with generalizations (often of an abstract nature);

3. they are often associated (when they occur) with initial (and topic) sentences in paragraphs; and

4. they tend to occur in the subject position in sentences (either as the subject or following *of*-phrases).

Generic versus Specific Nouns

A generic noun or noun phrase can represent an entire class or can be one representative of a class of objects, people, quantities, or ideas. A generic noun is like an archetype in that it manifests what is typical for the class. For this reason, generics are used in formal definitions (see Unit Two).

Compare the specific and generic noun phrases in table 31.

Table 31   Specific versus Generic Noun Phrases

Specific	Generic
The *disinfectant* caused an allergic reaction.	A *disinfectant* is an agent capable of destroying disease-causing microorganisms.
The *solar car* engineered at the University of Michigan won the race.	A *solar* car would certainly result in a cleaner atmosphere.
The *computer* crashed in the middle of the program.	The *computer* has replaced *the typewriter.*
The *trees* in this region have suffered from the drought.	*Trees* are valuable in maintaining air quality.
Add *some water* to the solution.	*Water* is essential for all living beings.

The specific noun phrases refer to something real. The generic noun phrases, on the other hand, refer to either an entire class or a representative of the class. You may have noticed in Table 31 that there are different types of generic noun phrase. Can you describe the differences?

Abstract versus Concrete Generics

Generics can generally be divided into two different types: the abstract generic and the concrete generic. An abstract generic refers to *an entire class* of objects, while the concrete generic refers to a *representative* of a class. Look at the examples in Table 32. Abstract generics require *the,* while concrete generics use either *a* (with a singular countable noun) or Ø (for plural countables and uncountable nouns).

In each of the examples in Table 32, a generalization is being made. (See Unit Two.) The abstract generics refer to the entire class. Singular concrete generics, on the other hand, refer to a generalized

Table 32   Abstract Generic versus Concrete Generic

Abstract Generic: The Entire Class	Concrete Generic: A Representative of the Class
The wasp can detect unique volatile compounds over great distances.	A wasp can be trained to detect odors.
The laser has a great many uses in medicine.	A laser can be used by a surgeon to make very clean cuts.
The computer has been invaluable in scientific advancement.	Computers are playing a growing role in all aspects of university life.
	Concrete is relatively cheap.

instance of the class. Finally, plural concrete generics and uncountable generics do not allow for such a clear distinction between class and representative. They can, however, be used when referring to a generalized instance.

Verb Tenses with Generic Nouns

Because generics are used to make generalized statements, they are typically used only with the simple tenses, particularly the present. Nevertheless, they can sometimes be used with the present perfect or the continuous.

> The elephant *has come* dangerously close to extinction.

> Synthetic skin *is replacing* animal skin in the testing of cosmetic products.

These examples present a changing, not yet fully realized situation. In this context the use of the present perfect or the continuous is appropriate.

Choosing the Proper Generic Form

Given that there are many possible generic forms, how do you know which to use? Should you use an abstract or a concrete generic? Singular or plural? Although there is no absolute rule for your choice, there is a tendency in academic writing to use the abstract generic (*the* + a singular noun) more often than the concrete. Even so, generic use will often depend on your field of study and on the type of noun you are using.

In medicine and biology, generics are common: abstract reference is made to *the heart, the liver, the brain,* and other parts of the body. On the other hand, in medical English, the names of diseases tend *not* to involve generics, except for colloquialisms like *the flu.* In the sciences and engineering, plural concrete generic reference and Ø concrete generics are common in many contexts. Hence, we see *lasers, quantum wells, bonds, atoms, combustion, catalysis, ionization,* and so on. The abstract generic is mainly used with instruments and devices.

The optical scanner is in widespread use.

You should become familiar with the use of generics in your own field of study. By looking through some journal articles, you should begin to get a sense of how things are done in your field.

Generic noun phrases do not follow the same rules for article use as specific nouns do. It is sometimes possible to shift from Ø to *a* with generics and vice versa. However, it is not possible to shift from Ø to *the* or from *a* to *the.*

TASK FIVE

Read this passage and fill in the blanks with either *a, an, the,* or Ø.

Much has been learned about _____ brain in _____ last 150

years. _____ brain, _____ most complicated organ of _____

body, contains _____ ten billion nerve cells and is divided into

_____ two cerebral hemispheres—one on _____ right and one

on _____ left. Interestingly, _____ left hemisphere controls

_____ movements on _____ right side of _____ body, while

_____ right hemisphere controls _____ movements on _____

left.

_____ researchers also know that _____ specific abilities

and behaviors are localized; in _____ other words, they are

controlled by _____ specific areas of _____ brain. _____

language, it seems, is highly localized in _____ left hemisphere. In

_____ 1860s Dr. Paul Broca discovered that _____ damage to _____ front left part of _____ brain resulted in _____ telegraphic speech similar to that of young children. Soon thereafter, Karl Wernicke found that _____ damage to _____ back left part of _____ brain resulted in _____ speech with _____ little semantic meaning. These two regions in _____ brain are now referred to as _____ Broca's area and _____ Wernicke's area.

Although there is some debate surrounding _____ specialization of _____ brain, _____ researchers generally agree that _____ speech is controlled by _____ left side. There is no debate that in _____ great majority of cases, _____ injuries to _____ left side nearly always have _____ impact on _____ speech.

Appendix Two

Academic English and Latin Phrases

Nearly all academic languages make occasional use of foreign phrases and expressions, either to add technical precision or to add "color" to the text. English is no exception. Although in many fields the use of expressions or words from French or German may be declining in academic English, the tradition of incorporating bits of Latin remains surprisingly strong. For that reason, this appendix (*appendix* is a Latin word!) deals only with Latin. We include this appendix primarily to help you negotiate Latin expressions in your reading. You should consider the preferences of your field when deciding whether to use such expressions in your own writing.

Did you know that *per* in *percent* or *kilometers per hour* is a Latin preposition that originally meant *through* or *by? Per* is also used in the Latin expression *per se* meaning *through or of itself,* and hence "intrinsically."

> Although education conveys important economic benefits, it is also valuable *per se.*

As this example shows, Latin expressions are often set apart from the English language text by italics.

Did you know that all the following abbreviations derive from Latin? How many do you know? How many can you give the full form for?

1. e.g.
2. i.e.
3. N.B.
4. A.M.
5. P.M.
6. P.S.
7. etc.
8. A.D.
9. CV

We have divided this appendix into three sections.

1. Expressions Referring to Textual Matters

There are quite a number of these, which we display in Table 33.

Table 33 Common Latin Expressions

Expression	Full Form	Literal Meaning	Modern Use
cf.	confer	compare	compare
e.g.	exempli gratia	free example	for example
et al.	et alii	and others	and other authors
etc.	et cetera	and other things	and others
errata	errata	errors	list of typographical mistakes
ibid.	ibidem	in the same place	the same as the previous reference
i.e.	id est	that is	that is to say
infra	infra	below	see below
loc. cit.	loco citato	in the place cited	in the place cited
N.B.	nota bene	note well	take note
op. cit.	opere citato	in the work cited	in the work cited
passim	passim	here and there	the point is made in several places
P.S.	post scriptum	after writing	something added after the signature
sic	sic	thus	the error is in the original quote
supra	supra	above	see above
viz.	videlicet	obviously	namely

2. Latin Expressions Starting with a Preposition

a fortiori   with even stronger reason

a posteriori   reasoning based on past experience, or from effects to causes

a priori   deductive reasoning, or from causes to effects

ab initio   from the beginning

ad hoc   improvised, for a specific occasion, not based on regular principles (e.g., an *ad hoc* solution)

ad infinitum   to infinity, so for forever or without end

ad lib	at will, so to speak off the top of the head
ante meridiem	before noon, typically abbreviated A.M.
antebellum	before the war, usually before the American Civil War
circa (c. or ca.)	about, approximately, usually used with dates (e.g., c. 500 A.D.)
de facto	from the fact, so existing by fact, not by right (e.g., in a *de facto* government)
de jure	from the law, so existing by right
ex post facto	after the fact, so retrospectively
in memoriam	in the memory of a person
in situ	in its original or appointed place (e.g., research conducted *in situ*)
in toto	in its entirety
in vitro	in a glass (e.g., experiments conducted in vitro)
in vivo	in life, experiments conducted on living organisms
inter alia	among other things
per capita	per head, so a *per capita* income of $20,000
per diem	per day, so expenses allowed each day
post meridiem	after noon, usually abbreviated P.M.
postmortem	after death, an examination into the cause of death
pro rata	in proportion (e.g., *pro rata* payment for working part-time)
sine die	without a day, with no time fixed for the next meeting
sine qua non	without which not, hence an essential precondition for something

3. Other Expressions

Anno Domini (A.D.)	in the year of the Lord, or the number of years after the beginning of Christianity

bona fide	in good faith (e.g., a *bona fide* effort to solve a problem)
caveat	a caution or warning (e.g., *Caveat emptor,* "Let the buyer beware")
ceteris paribus	other things being equal (used by economists)
curriculum vitae	summary of one's education and academic accomplishments
ego	literally "I," the consciousness or projection of oneself
locus classicus	the standard or most authoritative source of an idea or reference
quid pro quo	something for something, to give or ask for something in return for a favor or service
status quo	things as they are, the normal or standard situation
sui generis	unique
viva (voce)	an oral examination

There are further uses of Latin that this appendix does not cover. Most obviously, it does not deal with the technical details of Latin names in the life sciences. However, we observe, in passing, that Latin names do not take generic articles (see Appendix One). Compare the following:

The Common Loon breeds in the northern part of Michigan.

Gavia immer breeds in the northern part of Michigan.

Finally, this appendix does not address the widespread use of Latin in British and American law.

Appendix Three

E-Mail

Writing e-mail messages is probably the most common writing task for any graduate student. E-mail has replaced phone calls, face-to-face interactions, and many forms of written messages; it has become part of the fabric of academic communication. Given the important role of e-mail, in this appendix we offer some general suggestions for e-mail communications with people you do not know well or to people of higher status, such as advisors or instructors. Messages to friends are your own personal business.

1. Respond to All Personal Messages Promptly

It is important to let the sender know that you have received an e-mail message sent to you. If you have nothing to reply or you are not sure how to reply, at least acknowledge the message. Here are two examples.

> I just read your question about the manuscript. I'll get back to you ASAP.

> I've read your message about applying for a fellowship. Thanks very much for the suggestion. I am thinking about it and will get back to you later.

(Do you know what the acronym ASAP means? FYI? BTW? If not, see the short list of common acronyms at the end of this appendix.)

2. Be Careful about Forwarding Personal Messages

Remember that personal e-mail messages have been sent to you—with you as all or part of the intended audience. Before forwarding a message to somebody else, ask yourself whether the sender would approve. If in doubt, do not.

3. Check that it is OK to send an attachment

Attachments are a very efficient means to exchange files that contain your homework or a manuscript. However, you should send them only if you've prearranged this with the receiver, especially since many people still prefer to read and comment on printed material. Also keep in mind that sending an attachment means you're asking them to do a bit of extra work, namely, the printing of the file.

If you do have the OK to send an attachment, make sure the files aren't too large or too many in number. Finally, when you do send an attachment, always include a message. We usually accept homework via attachment, but if it is early in the term and a student sends an attachment with no message identifying himself or herself, we will not open it.

4. Check Outgoing Messages before Posting Them

Once an e-mail message is sent, it is gone. You cannot get it back. Therefore, read through all the messages you write before sending them. If you think the tone is wrong (too critical, too direct, too apologetic, too weak, etc.), cancel the message and start again. You do not want a written record of a message that reflects poorly on you.

Suppose your advisor sends you this message:

> Please have a look at the Mills et al. paper in the latest issue of JACL. I suspect it may be relevant to your project. What do you think?

Why might you decide to *abandon* the following replies? (Remember that *positioning* also applies to e-mail—you want to present yourself as a credible graduate student/junior member of the club.)

    a. I am sorry to bother you. I have read the Mills paper, but I cannot understand it. Could you please help me by letting me know what you had in mind?

    b. I spent three hours in the library reading and rereading the Mills paper that you told me to read. Since it deals with wheat and my project concerns corn, I don't really see how it relates.

    c. Thanks for the excellent suggestion to read the paper by Mills et al. I just finished reading it and it

> was great. You always have such great ideas. I think
> I need to rethink the direction of my project before
> I go any farther with it. I know that you are really
> busy these days, but I would like to see you
> tomorrow to talk about how you think I can
> incorporate some parts of the paper into my work.

If you are unsure why you might want to abandon these replies, please see the end of this appendix.

5. Use the Subject Line to Clearly Indicate the Topic

Especially in sequences of e-mail messages, subject lines help receivers to recognize the topic (rather than making them search their memories). They also help to make the messages concise and precise. In the following message, notice how the student uses the subject line to avoid repeating herself.

> Subject: Guest Speaker for ED 817 "Int. & Comp. Ed"
> To: Sungjoon Cho
> From: Bob Wakefield
>
> How would you like to be one? Professor Walsh is looking for someone to spend an hour with our tiny seminar (about 8 people), and I suggested you. The class meets on Tuesdays from 4–7. Let me know if you're interested!
>
> Bob

We offer one note of caution, however: if your reader does not look at the heading, he or she will definitely be confused.

6. Do Not Overuse Conversational Openings and Closings

As we can see from the examples already given, e-mail language is a hybrid of speech and writing. Because of its speech elements, many international students tend to use conversational openings and closings from (phone) conversations. We often see messages that open and close like this:

Hi Chris! How are you? This is Fatima from your 321 class.
Can I change our appointment to Friday at 9:30? I have a test
on Wednesday. Have a good day.

Got to run. Bye, bye. Fatima.

Some recipients (like Chris) encourage students to adopt a more conversational style. However, it is very easy to misinterpret this informality or friendliness as "unbusinesslike" and perhaps somewhat naive.

Notice, too, that in many cases e-mail allows you to avoid the problem of determining how to address someone. You do *not* have to choose among such greetings as the following.

Dear Dr. Smith,

Dr. Roger Smith,

Dear Roger Smith,   I'm afraid I will be ten minutes late for our appointment.

Dear Roger,

Dear Advisor,

7. Express "Business" Requests Politely

E-mail language is typically informal. In many ways, this feature is very helpful for nonnative speakers. It helps to build relationships. It also allows people to use the system quickly and without worrying too much about typos, imperfect sentences, and so on. There is, however, one situation where this informality can be very problematic. When a student sends a request to a faculty or an administrator, informal language may be too direct and thus insufficiently polite.

Two examples follow. The first might be considered only a little offensive, the second rather more so. Of course, giving offense was not the intention of either writer.

> Subject: Pages
> To: Joan Robinson
> From: Keiko Ichiko
>
> Dear Professor Robinson,
>
> Finally, I have something for you to read. I will leave the draft of my paper in your mailbox soon, so please pick it up when you stop by.
>
> Keiko

This first message is problematic for two reasons. First, there is the vagueness of *soon*. (How many times will Professor Robinson have to check her mailbox before she finds Keiko's pages?) Second, the end of the message is completely unnecessary. Here is a simple "repair."

> Dear Professor Robinson,
>
> Finally, I have something for you to read. I will put the draft of my paper in your mailbox by noon tomorrow.

Here is the second example.

> Subject: Paper
> To: Henry Rabkin
> From: Kumar Bhatia
>
> I am currently working on a paper (approx 8/9 pages). I should be done on Mon. evening. Could you please go through it & give your comments by Wednesday?
>
> Kumar

Studies of politeness suggest three elements for polite requests.

1. Do not impose

2. Give options

3. Make the receiver feel good

Notice how Kumar breaks all three rules. Here is what he might have written instead.

> I am currently working on a paper (approx 8/9 pages). I should be done on Mon. evening. If you are not too busy, I would appreciate any comments you might have to make before I submit it. Unfortunately, it is due on Wed., so there isn't much time. If you can help, I'll bring you my draft as soon as it's done. If you can't, that's quite OK too.

This draft looks better in terms of the three elements, but what do you think of this message? Ask your instructor how he or she might react.

In contrast, here is a superb student request that John received.

> Subject: Article review
> To: John Swales
> From: JP Park
>
> I was wondering if you have an article that you want me to review yet. If you have something appropriate, next week would be a good time for me to get started on it. Don't want to sound anxious to get going on this, but I'll be around, so let me know. Thanks.

It is clear that JP really wants to get going on this assignment and perhaps believes that John has been a little slow off the mark. However, he presents himself as being very relaxed about it; notice in particular his use of the past continuous ("I was wondering") to give distance to the request. This message is a very good example of how to be informal and polite at the same time. (It was also immediately successful.)

8. Keep Your Messages as Brief as Possible

We would suggest that you don't burden your readers with messages that are very long (more than one screen's worth of text) or include information that is really unnecessary. If, for example, you need to cancel an appointment or miss class because you are ill, there is no need to describe the illness. A simple statement that you are ill and unable to get to class or an appointment is fine. In other situations, such as if you need to ask for an extension on a homework assignment, some explanation may be necessary.

9. Learn Common Abbreviations

Many terms and expressions are expressed as acronyms or as abbreviations in e-mail. For example, among those abbreviations we have used in this appendix are *ASAP* and *Mon.* Notice others as they scroll across your screen.

10. Do Not Worry Too Much about Capitalization

Some people relax or even completely abandon the normal rules for capitalization. Here is an extreme example.

> here's what i know about the next tesol conference. it's in atlanta from march 16 to 20—the hq hotel is the hilton.

You might not want to go this far. At the other extreme, don't write your messages in all capital letters. MOST PEOPLE FIND MESSAGES IN ALL CAPS rather threatening and imposing. It seems very much like shouting. If you need to add emphasis, however, you can use uppercase, instead of underlining.

11. Use Deletions Carefully

It is becoming usual to leave out certain articles and pronouns and various other bits and pieces of English grammar in e-mail.

Standard English

> I got your message about the manuscript. I will return it along with my comments to your mailbox on Friday.

Message with Deletions

> Got your message about the manuscript. Will return it along with comments to your mailbox Friday.

Unless your English grammar is very strong, we recommend that you do not use these deletions. You may teach yourself bad habits.

12. Avoid Conventions for Communicating Emotions (emoticons)

E-mail is a written medium but has many of the characteristics of speech. In speech, we can use voice inflection and gestures to communicate what we are feeling. Some e-mail users adopt special symbols to communicate their state of mind: :-) = happy, ^0^ = worried, :-(= unhappy. These devices are fine to use in e-mail for friends. They also seem more widely used by undergraduates than by graduates. We advise against using them in "business" messages.

A Final Word

In this appendix, we have provided some suggestions for using e-mail. We hope in this way to increase your confidence. We do not want in any way to make you anxious about this means of communication. Many nonnative speakers find e-mail to be an ideal way to improve their English, and therefore they participate in various e-mail groups and chat rooms. If you have the time to use e-mail to improve your English fluency, we strongly recommend it.

Some Common Acronyms

AKA = also known as   IMHO = in my humble opinion
ASAP = as soon as possible   IMO = in my opinion
BTW = by the way   LOL = laughing out loud
FYI = for your information   WRT = with respect to

Do an Internet search on e-mail, instant messaging, and Internet acronyms and emoticons if you'd like to learn more.

Some Thoughts on the Three Messages in Section 4

Possible reasons you should destroy the replies include the following.

a. You do indeed seem rather hopeless here. Even if you did not understand the paper, do you need to say so? Like this?

b. You seem rather irritated—and perhaps you missed the point. What if your advisor thinks that it is the methodology part that is relevant? Perhaps it would be wiser to respond with a question like "Could you be more specific about which parts of the paper are most relevant?"

c. You sound like you cannot think for yourself and are too eager to please you advisor.

Appendix Four

Writing Up a Small Research Project

This appendix gives an account of the writing up of a small research investigation of our own in the field of English for Academic Purposes. Among other things, we hope in this way to illustrate certain strategic aspects of RP writing.

Here is a summary of our mini-project. You will remember from Unit One that sentence connectors are words like *however* and *therefore*. We became interested in the position of sentence connectors in written academic English sentences. We became curious about this since we found that the standard grammars of English had little to say on this topic. We are currently writing up our small-scale investigation. Like many writers of research papers, we started with the Methods section, although we of course had some ideas of what might go in the Introduction.

Here is our draft of the Methods section. For this and the other IMRD sections, our drafts are followed by comments. These are designed partly to point out features of the drafts and partly to take you "behind the scenes" of our actual texts. We hope you will find the comments useful as you undertake the writing up of research projects of your own.

Methods

❶ In order to investigate the position of connectors, we examined their occurrence in academic papers published in three journals. ❷ The sample consisted of all the main articles appearing in the third issues of the 1992 volumes of *College Composition and Communication, English for Specific Purposes, and Research in the Teaching of English.* ❸ The sample amounted to about 230 running pages of text, comprising 12 articles (four from each journal). ❹ Each occurrence of a connector was identified, highlighted, and then coded for one of three positions in a clause. ❺ If the connector was the first or last word in the clause, it was designated "initial" or "final," respectively. ❻ If it occurred in any other position, it was classified as "medial." ❼ The following examples illustrate the coding system.

8 A paired *t*-test was performed;

however, the results were insignificant.	Initial
the results, however, were insignificant.	Medial
the results were, however, insignificant.	Medial
the results were insignificant, however.	Final

9 For the purposes of this study, the category of sentence connector was interpreted quite broadly. **10** We included items like *unfortunately* that are sometimes considered to be sentence adverbs. **11** We included items such as *as it were* and *in turn,* which have an uncertain grammatical status. **12** We also counted conjunctions like *but* as connectors when they occurred as first elements in sentences, because they seemed to be functioning as connectors in these contexts.

Comments

1. As is customary, the main tense in our Methods section is the past. In one sentence, however, the main verb is in the present: "The following examples illustrate . . ." The coding system remains (until we change it!).

2. Notice this pattern:

   1. we examined . . .
   5. Each occurrence was identified . . .
   6. it was designated . . .
   7. it was classified . . .
   9. the category was interpreted . . .
   10. We included . . .
   11. We included . . .
   12. We counted . . .

   These eight sentences describe what we did. As you can see, in four cases we used the past passive, and in four cases we used *we* and the past active. This switching might not be possible in all fields, but it is in ours. We have tended to use the passive when it was an obvious and straightforward part of the procedure but to use *we* when more personal judgment is involved (as in sentences 10–12).

3. We had some debate—and some class discussion—as to whether the third paragraph should come before the second. The general opinion seems to be that the last four sentences are fine where they are. It seems better to deal with the noncontroversial aspects of the methods first and leave "the tricky bits" until later. However, if any definitions or criteria are standard, it is probably better to introduce them earlier.

4. As it happens, our account of Methods is not quite accurate. In actual fact, we conducted a pilot study on one journal. When that experience appeared to work out, we extended the sample. We decided there was no good reason for mentioning this part of the (true) story. When you write up a Methods section, it is usually appropriate to simplify or straighten out the actual process to some degree. A Methods section is not simply a description of events as they happened. Obviously, though, there are limits to how far you should go (see *English in Today's Research World,* Unit Six).

We next turned to the Results section. Here is what we wrote.

Results

A total of 467 sentence connectors were found, averaging just over two per page. Eleven of the 12 articles used connectors with some frequency, with totals ranging from 24 to 58. The one exception was the only article in the sample that dealt with literary texts, which used only nine connectors. The scarcity of connectors in this paper may be due to its heavy use of commentary on literary passages.

Seventy different sentence connectors occurred in the sample. This large number is somewhat surprising, even taking into account our broad interpretation of "connector." Those that occurred eight times or more are listed in decreasing frequency of use in Table 23.

The heavy use of *however* and of enumerators such as *first* or *second* could have been predicted. However, there are also a number of surprises in the frequency data. Most people, for example, would not have anticipated that *thus* would be twice as common as *therefore.* There was unexpectedly heavy use of the "informal" connectors *but* (9 instances) and *yet* (8 instances). Although these are known to be frequent in newspapers and correspondence, we were somewhat surprised to find so many in refereed scholarly journals. In contrast, the minimal use of "conclusives," such as *in conclusion,* was less unexpected. In fact under 2% of all the connectors fell into this category.

We now turn to the positional data. Of the 467 connectors found, 352 occurred in initial position (75.4%), 109 in medial position, and only six in final position. Clearly, final position is very rare in this kind of writing, and we will not discuss it further. If we now examine the positional data in terms of individual connectors, we find that different connectors behave somewhat differently. In Table 34 all connectors occurring four times or more are categorized for percentage of occurrence in initial position. (Informal uses of *but* and *yet* have been excluded.)

Table 23   Frequency of Connectors

Rank	Item	Total Occurrence
1	however	62
2	first, second, etc.	52
3	thus	33
4	also	30
5	for example	29
6	in addition	20
7	finally	19
8	therefore	16
9	on the other hand	14
10	then	12
11	nevertheless for instance furthermore	11
14	moreover in particular but	9
17	in fact yet	8

It is clear from these results that individual connectors vary considerably as to their likelihood of occurring at the beginning of a sentence or somewhat later. Some common connectors (e.g., *first, nevertheless*) only occurred in the initial position in our small corpus, while others (e.g., *for example, therefore*) were more likely to be used in medial position. Further, position does not seem to depend on the *function* of the connector. As can be seen from Table 34, one common contrastive connector (*nevertheless*) fell into category A; on the other hand, another connector of the same function (*however*) fell into category C.

Table 34   Positional Categories of Connectors

Category	Connectors	Occurrence
A	first, second, etc.; in addition, nevertheless, finally, that is, as a result	100% in initial position
B	moreover, thus, in particular/in fact, in other words, of course	75–99% in initial position
C	however, for instance, on the other hand, furthermore	50–74% in initial position
D	also, for example, therefore, then	25–49% in initial position

Comments

1. We decided that two tables would carry the main body of data, but, in comparison to the first edition of *AWG*, we have shortened the first table by excluding connectors occurring between four and six times. We think this is OK.

2. Notice throughout that there are a lot of numbers, and here we have followed the "rule of Eleven"; that is, numbers eleven and below are written as words, while higher numbers (unless occurring at the beginning of the sentence) are written as digits. (However, as extracts in this book have shown, many science, social science, and engineering fields tend to use digits throughout.)

3. Also notice that we have not avoided commenting on and evaluating our results. Indeed, we have undertaken something of a selling job by referring several times to *surprising* findings. Doubtless, we are trying to compensate for the minor nature of our study!

The Introduction comes next.

Introduction

❶ Many commentators have noted that sentence connectors (e.g., *however*) are an important and useful element in expository and argumentative writing. ❷ Frequency studies of their occurrence in academic English extend at least as far back as Huddleston (1971). ❸ ESL writing textbooks have for many years regularly included chapters on sentence connectors (e.g., Herbert 1965). ❹ Most reference grammars deal only with their grammatical status, classification, meaning, and use.

❺ Nonetheless, some limited attention has also been given to the position of sentence connectors in clauses and sentences. ❻ Quirk and Greenbaum (1973) observed *(a)* that the normal position is initial; *(b)* that certain connectors, such as *hence* and *overall,* "are restricted, or virtually restricted, to initial position" (p. 248); and *(c)* that medial positions are rare for most connectors and that final positions are even rarer. ❼ The more recent large *Longman Grammar* (Biber et al. 1999) also notes that in academic prose, *thus, therefore,* and *however* quite commonly occur in medial position. ❽ The only attempt known to us to explain differences in position on semantic grounds is an unpublished paper by Salera (1978) discussed in Celce-Murcia and Larsen-Freeman 1999, but Celcia-Murcia and Larsen-Freeman conclude that "more usage studies dealing with the placement of logical connectors would be helpful" (p. 537). ❾ Particularly in light of the last comment, in the present paper we report on a study of sentence-connector position in a corpus of 12 published articles.

Comments

1. This is a very short nine-sentence introduction. It has been updated for this edition.

2. As the choice of words clearly shows, the first three sentences function as a centrality claim stressing the general salience of the phenomenon. Sentences 4–8 deal with previous studies of this phenomenon, closing in on the more specific research question. Because our paper is very much a short communication, and because of some more recent work, we in the end deleted the strong Move 2 we had in the 1994 version—"However, neither of these studies provides any descriptive evidence of the actual positions of sentence connectors in academic texts." Instead, we have now opted for the much "gentler" *Particularly in the light of the last comment. . . .*

3. In Unit Seven, we argued that RPs were not simple accounts of investigations. This is also very true of our own small project. If you look back at our Introduction, you will note that we never actually say what our motive or rationale for carrying out this small study was. Rather, the study seems to emerge as a natural and rational response to a discovered weakness in

the literature. In fact, this is not how the study started at all. In fall 1992, a student in John's Research Paper Writing class asked him if there were any rules for where to put the sentence connectors. Not having any immediate answer, John played for time and asked what the class did. Most said they always put them first, even though they had noticed that they did not always come first in the books and papers that they read. Then one student, Arthur Hsieng, said that he remembered a sociology professor telling the class never to put *however* in initial position. As English teachers, we were so struck by this piece of grammatical folklore that we decided to investigate.

4. As we have argued throughout, we can *position* ourselves better by a constructed Introduction with an intellectual focus, rather than by a narrative of how a practical question arose.

Now comes the Discussion. It may be helpful for you to look back at the Results before reading this closing section.

Discussion

❶ This investigation has revealed that sentence connectors are quite common in academic journals from the single disciplinary field that we examined, averaging about two per page. ❷ However, there were striking differences in the frequency with which individual connectors were used. ❸ As the first table shows, the commonest connector *(however)* was more than five times as frequent as its semantic equivalent, *nevertheless.* ❹ Another significant finding was that 25% of connectors did not occur in sentence-initial position. ❺ Although this percentage was higher than most grammar books would predict, it was lower than that predicted by Morrow (1999), who found 43% noninitial in an economics journal article. ❻ Morrow's data, however, is very small-scale, and he used a broader definition of connector than adopted here. ❼ Finally, sentence position varied from connector quite markedly; as the second table illustrates, four connectors (those in category D) were actually more commonly found in noninitial position.

❽ This study has examined 12 articles from a single field, and these limitations mean that the results need to be viewed with caution. ❾ Further, we are not yet in a position to offer explanations for choices of connector positions. ❿ With further research into other fields and into the rationale for placement decisions, it should be possible to produce materials of greater assistance to writers, especially to those who are not native speakers of English.

Comments

1. The first paragraph handles Move 1, the second paragraph Moves 2 and 3.

2. The overall level of the discussion is pitched at quite a high level of generality, although it does have a couple of examples too.

3. The "reporting accomplishments" aspect of Move 1 is enhanced by the use of "strong" adjectives and adverbs, such *striking, significant,* and *markedly.*

4. Sentences 5 and 6 introduce and then attempt to account for some findings that do not accord with ours.

5. Notice that in our Move 2 we refer only to the nature of the corpus, not to our methods of analysis. In other words, we only highlight the most obvious of the possible limitations. Note, too, that in the final sentence, we make mention of a possible future practical outcome.

References

Since this book is a guide to writing academic English, many of the illustrative texts contain citations. For obvious reasons, we have not included these illustrative citations in this reference list. Instead, we have two reference lists—the first to works that relate in some way to academic writing itself, the second to the authors of main extracts.

Every publisher requires its authors to use a particular style for references. The University of Michigan Press follows the *Chicago Manual of Style*. Other book and journal publishers may use other styles that may vary from the Chicago manual in minor or major ways.

References to Academic Writing

Bavelas, J. B. 1978. The social psychology of citations. *Canadian Psychological Review* 19:158–63.

Becher, T. 1987. Disciplinary discourse. *Studies in Higher Education* 12:261–74.

Belcher, D. 1995. Review of *Academic writing for graduate students*, by J. M. Swales and C. B. Feak. *English for Specific Purposes* 14:175–78.

Benfield, J. R., and K. M. Howard. 2000. The language of science. *European Journal of Cardio-thoracic Surgery* 18:642–48.

Björk, L., and C. Räisänen. 1997. *Academic writing: A university writing course.* Lund, Sweden: Studentlitteratur.

Brett, P. A. 1994. A genre analysis of the Results section of sociology articles. *English for Specific Purposes* 13:47–60.

Chang, Y.-Y., and J. M. Swales. 1999. Informal elements in English academic writing: Threats or opportunities for advanced non-native speakers? In *Writing: Texts, processes, and practices,* ed. C. Candlin and K. Hyland, 145–64. London: Longman.

Cooper, C. 1985. Aspects of article introductions in IEEE publications. Unpublished master's thesis, University of Aston, UK.

Dobson, B., and C. B. Feak. 2001. A cognitive modeling approach to teaching critique writing to nonnative speakers. In *Linking literacies: Perspectives on L2 reading-writing connections,* ed. D. Belcher and A. Hirvela, 186–99. Ann Arbor, MI: University of Michigan Press.

Giannoni, D. S. 2002. Worlds of gratitude: A contrastive study of acknowledgment texts in English and Italian research articles. *Applied Linguistics* 23:1–31.

Gilbert, N. G. 1977. Referencing as persuasion. *Social Studies of Science* 7:113–22.

Hartley, J. 1997. Is it appropriate to use structured abstracts in social science journals? *Learned Publishing* 10:313–17.

Hoey, M. 1983. *On the surface of discourse.* London: George Allen and Unwin.

Hyland, K. 1999. Academic attribution: Citation and the construction of disciplinary knowledge. *Applied Linguistics* 20:341–67.

Hyland, K. 2000. *Disciplinary discourses.* Harlow, UK: Longman.

Kanoksilapatham, B. 2003. A corpus-based investigation of scientific research articles: Linking move analysis and multidimensional analysis. Ph.D. diss., Georgetown University.

Knorr-Cetina, K. D. 1981. *The manufacture of knowledge.* Oxford: Pergamon.

Lewin, B. A., J. Fine, and L. Young. 2001. *Expository discourse: A genre-based approach to social science research texts.* London: Continuum.

Motta-Roth, D. 1998. Discourse analysis and academic book reviews: A study of text and disciplinary cultures. In *Genre studies in English for Academic Purposes,* ed. I. Fortanet, S. Posteguillo, J. C. Palmer, and J. F. Coll, 29–58. Castelló, Spain: Universitat Jaume I.

Noguchi, J. T. 2001. The science review article: An opportune genre in the construction of science. Ph.D. diss., University of Birmingham, UK.

Okamura, A. 2000. The roles of culture, sub-culture, and language in scientific research articles. Ph.D. diss., Newcastle University, UK.

Olsen, L. A., and T. N. Huckin. 1990. Point-driven understanding in engineering lecture comprehension. *English for Specific Purposes* 9:33–48.

Pearson, J. 1998. *Terms in context.* Amsterdam: Johns Benjamins Publishing Company.

Penrose, A. M., and S. B. Katz. 1998. *Writing in the sciences: Exploring conventions of scientific discourse.* New York: St. Martin's Press.

Ravetz, J. R. 1971. *Scientific knowledge and social problems.* Oxford: Oxford University Press.

Skelton, J. 1988. The care and maintenance of hedges. *English Language Teaching Journal* 42:37–44.

Swales, J. M., 1990. *Genre analysis.* Cambridge: Cambridge University Press.

Swales, J. M., and C. B. Feak. 1994. *Academic writing for graduate students: Essential tasks and skills.* 1st ed. Ann Arbor, MI: University of Michigan Press.

Swales, J. M. and C. B. Feak. 2000. *English in today's research world: A writing guide.* Ann Arbor, MI: University of Michigan Press.

Swales, J.M. and H. Najjar. 1987. The writing of research article introductions. *Written Communication* 4:175–92.

Tarone, E., S. Dwyer, S. Gillette, and V. Icke. 1998. On the use of the passive and active in astrophysics journal papers: with extensions to other languages and other fields. *English for Specific Purposes* 17:113–32.

Thompson, D. K. 1993. Arguing for experimental "facts" in science: A study of research article results sections in biochemistry. *Written Communication* 10:106–28.

Weissberg, R., and S. Buker. 1990. *Writing up research: Experimental research report writing for students of English.* Englewood Cliffs, NJ: Prentice Hall.

Williams, I. A. 1999. Results sections of medical research articles: Analysis of rhetorical categories for pedagogical purposes. *English for Specific Purposes* 18:347–66.

Wilson, D. 2002. *The Englishisation of academe: A Finnish perspective.* Jyväskylä: University Printing House.

Woodford, F. P. 1976. *Scientific writing for graduate students.* Washington, DC: Council of Biology Editors.

Sources of Main Extracts

Almosnino, D. 1985. High angle-of-attack calculations of the subsonic vortex flow in slender bodies. *AIAA Journal* 23:1150–56.

Baldry, A. C., and D. P. Farrington. 1999. Brief report: Types of bullying among Italian school children. *Journal of Adolescence* 22:423–26.

Bradley, A., T. Hall, and M. Harrison. 2002. Selling cities: Promoting new images for meetings tourism. *Cities* 19:61–70.

Cass, S. 2001. MEMS in space. *IEEE Spectrum,* July, 56–61.

Davis III, S. E. 2003. Review of *Wetland plants: Biology and ecology,* by Julie K. Cronk and M. Siobhan Fennessey. *Ecological Engineering* 19:351–52.

DePasquale, J. P., E. S. Geller, S. W. Clarke, and L. C. Littleton. 2001. Measuring road rage: Development of the Propensity for Angry Driving Scale. *Journal of Safety Research* 32:1–16.

DeWitte, S., and W. Lens. 2000. Procrastinators lack a broad action perspective. *European Journal of Personality* 14:121–40.

Dittmar, H., and J. Drury. 2000. Self image—is it in the bag? A qualitative comparison between "ordinary" and "excessive" consumers. *Journal of Economic Psychology* 21:109–42.

Goodman, S. M., and P. L. Meininger et al., eds. 1989. *The birds of Egypt.* Oxford: Oxford University Press.

Knorr-Cetina, K. D. 1981. *The manufacture of knowledge.* Oxford: Pergamon.

Martindale, D. 2001. Sweating the small stuff. *Scientific American,* February, 52–53.

Martinus, W. S., and A. Kurta. 2001. Eastern pipistrelle in Ottawa Co., MI. *Michigan Birds and Natural History* 8:133–35.

Maskan, F., D. E. Wiley, L. P. M. Johnston, and D. J. Clements. 2000. Optimal design of reverse osmosis module networks. *American Institute of Chemical Engineers Journal* 46:946–54.

Naczi, R. F. C., A. A. Reznicek, and B. A. Ford. 1998. Morphological, geographical, and ecological differentiation in the *Carex willdenowii* complex (cyperaceae). *American Journal of Botany* 85:434–47.

Noakes, T. D. 2000. Exercise and the cold. *Ergonomics* 43:1461–79.

Norrick, N. R. 1993. *Conversational joking.* Bloomington: Indiana University Press.

Pachucki, K., D. Leibfried, and T. W. Hänsch. 1993. Nuclear-structure correction to the lamb shift. *Physical Review A* 48:R1–R4.

Pölkki, T., A. M. Pietilä, and K. Vehviläinen-Julkunen. 2003. Hospitalized children's descriptions of their experiences with postsurgical pain relieving methods. *International Journal of Nursing Studies* 40:33–44.

Purvis, A. J., and N. T. Cable. 2000. The effects of phase control materials on hand skin temperature within gloves of soccer goalkeepers. *Ergonomics* 43:1480–88.

Rackham School of Graduate Studies, Horace H. 2002. *Years to doctorate for doctoral programs at the University of Michigan, Ann Arbor, for academic years 1996–2001.* Ann Arbor: University of Michigan.

Ranstam, J., et al. 2000. Fraud in medical research: An international survey of biostatisticians. *Controlled Clinical Trials* 21:415–27.

Schwer, R. K., and R. Daneshvary. 2000. Keeping up one's appearance: Its importance and the choice of type of hair-grooming establishment. *Journal of Economic Psychology* 21:207–22.

Sivam, A. 2003. Housing supply in Delhi. *Cities* 20:135–41.

Tiamiyu, M. F. 2000. University-community agency collaboration: Human service agency workers' views. *Journal of Multicultural Nursing and Health* 6:29–36.

Index

variation in, 224–28
Michigan Corpus of Academic Spoken
    English (MICASE), 17
Moves
    in discussion sections (*see* Research
        paper, discussion sections)
    in introduction sections (*see* Research
        paper, introduction sections)

Negative criticism, 206
Negative openings, 258
Nominal *that*-clauses, 165–66
Nouns
    countability, 289–92
    double, 291
    generic, 297–300
    specific, 298
Numbers, writing, 233

Organization, 12–16
    data commentary, 116
    problem-solution, 14, 85
    research paper, 215
Organizational patterns, 16

Paraphrasing, 158–59
Passive voice, 52, 91–94
Phrase linkers, 27
Plagiarism, 148, 158, 172–73
Positioning, 11, 42, 195, 221, 270
Prepositions
    in linking *as*-clauses, 123
    in restrictive relative clauses, 62
    of time, 145
Probability, 126–27
Problem, process, solution, 83–111
Problem-solution texts
    description of, 14, 41
    indirect questions in, 107–9
    introducing problems, 109
    parts of, 14, 85
    research paper and, 221
    verbs and agents in the solution, 91–94
Problem statements, 109
Problems with data, 11, 135, 137, 138–39
Procedures and processes, 88–104
Process descriptions, 68, 88–100
    active voice in, 98–100
    causes and effects in, 101–6
    change of state verbs in, 99
    -*ed* participles in, 96–97
    flow of ideas, 95–98
    passive voice in, 91–94
    similarity to methods sections, 106

Pronouns
    in abstracts, 263
    first person, 24
    second person, 22
Proofreading, 41
Publications, types of journal, 215–16
Punctuation, 28–30
Purpose statements, 263

Qualification, 125–30
Questions
    direct, 23
    indirect, 107–9

Reaction papers, 210–12
Reference styles, 167
Relative clauses
    prepositions and, 62
    reducing by change in word or word
        form, 58, 60–61
    reducing by deletion, 59
    restrictive, 56, 58–63
    word form, 60
Relative pronouns, 56
Research paper, 215–86
    abstracts, 282–84
        approaches to writing, 282
        importance of, 282
        indicative, 119, 282
        informative, 119, 282
        person, 284
        tense, 283–84
    acknowledgments, 221, 284–86
        common elements in, 285
    characteristics of, 220–23
    competition for research space, 243
    descriptive move, 262–63
    discussion sections, 221, 223, 268–77,
        321–22
        characteristics of, 268–70
        citation to literature in, 271
        cycles of moves in, 277
        levels of generalization in, 274–75
        limitations in, 272, 275–77
        moves in, 270, 277
        openings, 270–74
        overview, 268–70
        points in, 269
        positioning and, 270
        variation in, 268–69
        vs. conclusion, 268
        vs. results, 269
    IMRD, 215, 221, 222–23
    introduction sections, 242–68, 319–21
        abstracts and, 265